CLINICS IN DEVELOPMENTAL MEDICINE NO. 93

CRANIAL COMPUTED TOMOGRAPHY IN INFANTS AND CHILDREN

Clinics in Developmental Medicine No. 93

CRANIAL COMPUTED TOMOGRAPHY IN INFANTS AND CHILDREN

ERIC N. FAERBER, MBBCh, DMRD
Assistant Professor of Radiology, Temple
University; Clinical Associate Professor
of Radiology, Medical College of
Pennsylvania Hospital; Chief, Section
of Computed Tomography, Magnetic
Resonance and Neuroradiology,
St. Christopher's Hospital for
Children, Philadelphia

Spastics International Medical Publications
OXFORD: Blackwell Scientific Publications Ltd.
PHILADELPHIA: J. B. Lippincott Co.

First published 1986

British Library Cataloguing in Publication Data

Faerber, Eric N.
    Cranial computed tomography in infants and children—(Clinics
    in Developmental Medicine No. 93)
    1. Pediatric neurology—Diagnosis   2. Tomography—Data processing
    3. Skull—Radiography—Data processing
    I. Title   II. Series
    618.92′09751407572   RJ488.5.T65

ISBN (UK) 0-632-01296-X
      (USA) 0-397-48000-8

Printed in Great Britain at The Lavenham Press Ltd., Lavenham, Suffolk

To Esmé
Jennifer and Michael
and
Mary and Gerald Faerber
for their love, support and encouragement

'Children are the world's most valuable resource
and its best hope for the future'.

President John F. Kennedy
UNICEF appeal, July 25, 1963

CONTENTS

FOREWORD

A little more than a decade ago we entered the 'pioneer era' of computed radiology, and now we are in its 'golden age'. Hounsfield and Cormack, and Radon before them, lathed a key that opened the 'black box'—the brain. Although the images made by the early computed tomographic scanners were crude in comparison to today's standards, nonetheless the brain was visualized. The bony vault was no longer an obstacle. Children no longer needed to be subjected to high-risk procedures such as ventriculography or pneumo-encephalography. Such studies have since been relegated to the historic archives of our profession, and a decade of radiologists have little knowledge of them. Angiography, a high-risk invasive procedure, need only be done to answer specific questions.

Thoreau once said, 'Be not merely good; be good for something'. There is no doubt that computed radiography has been good for many things, but its greatest impact has been in the evaluation of the central nervous system. Since radiology's entry into the computer age, the technological advancements that have occurred have been of particular importance in the imaging of children in whom disturbances of the central nervous system are common and serious but often amenable to appropriate treatment if adequately diagnosed. The computed tomographic examination has revolutionized our understanding of the anatomy of the normal brain of infants and children, as well as our approach to the diagnosis and treatment of the numerous maladies affecting their central nervous system. Computed tomography of children differs in many ways from that of adults. It takes more time and care, and thus is often more difficult. In addition, the normal anatomy of the brain changes as the child grows, and the diseases affecting the central nervous system of children will often be unique to the specific age of the child. In this book, Dr. Faerber admirably presents the multifaceted aspects of computed tomography of the brain in children.

MARIE A. CAPITANIO, M.D., F.A.C.R.,
Professor of Radiology,
Temple University School of Medicine;
Clinical Professor of Radiology,
Medical College of Pennsylvania;
Director of Radiology,
St. Christopher's Hospital for Children,
Philadelphia.

PREFACE

The advent of computed tomography (CT) heralded a new era in diagnostic imaging. Not since Roentgen's epic discovery of x-rays in 1895 has such a diagnostic modality revolutionized diagnosis and patient management.

The initial applications of CT were directed toward neuroradiology, with a profound impact on the fields of neurology and neurosurgery. The ever-increasing use of this modality has led to a progressive decline in the use of more invasive techniques in patients of all ages. The simplicity and relative ease of this technique makes it eminently suitable for infants and children.

The aims of this monograph are to describe the basic physical principles and the essential CT features of the major disease processes encountered within the fields of neurology and neurosurgery.

I am deeply grateful to the many people who have willingly assisted me in this task.

Dr. Henry Baird has been the catalyst in his dual rôles as attending neurologist at St. Christopher's Hospital for Children, Philadelphia, and editorial member of Spastics International Medical Publications. He has always maintained a high personal interest, and has been a constant source of support and encouragement. Dr. Martin Bax, editor-in-chief of this series, has been a model editor, exhibiting a welcome blend of both patience and encouragement. The superb editorial assistance of Mr. Edward Fenton has been invaluable in the preparation of this manuscript.

Dr. Marie Capitanio, Director of Radiology at St. Christopher's Hospital for Children, Philadelphia, has been a great source of stimulation and encouragement, understanding the trials and tribulations of authors; she has played a major rôle in making this text readable. Dr. George Popky, Director of Radiology, Medical College of Pennsylvania, Philadelphia, has also been a constant source of support, and has readily made many resources available to my radiological associates and myself and for our patients. The very able assistance of my friend and neuroradiological colleague, Joel Swartz at the Medical College of Pennsylvania, is also very much appreciated.

Many friends and colleagues all made significant contributions to the preparation of this manuscript. I am very much indebted to Drs. Eileen Tyrala, David Rubenstein, Warren Grover, Anthony Pileggi, Raymond Truex, Jr., Catherine Foley, Caroline Eggerding, Sarah Long, and Margaret Fisher. I am very much indebted to Dr. Theodore Villafana for special assistance with CT physics, and also to Michael Stambaugh, MS, for his assistance.

My radiologic associates Marie Capitanio, Barbara Wolfson and Margaret Gainey continue to be a wonderful, warm group, always ensuring that this manuscript didn't replace my daily duties.

Carole Aspinall RN has played a key rôle in the development of our CT services, displaying a keen sense of efficiency enabling our scans to be performed smoothly. Sharon Schweitzer RT, Chief CT Technologist, has maintained a reputation for excellence and conscientiousness in her work. She and her colleagues Maureen Dugan and Robin Manning are a perfect team, particularly attentive to the infants and children at our hospital. Jack Dembow, assistant administrator at St. Christopher's Hospital for Children, continues to be of great assistance to us. The assistance of Barbara Basile RT in the preparation of illustrations, and Dr. Carson Schneck for review of these illustrations, is very much appreciated.

Mrs. Joan Colombaro has been a pillar of strength in the preparation of this manuscript. Her enthusiasm has been a source of great inspiration to me, as no task was too big for her. She was ably assisted by Mrs. Veronica Horn.

My wife Esmé and children Jennifer and Michael rightfully deserve my special gratitude. They made many sacrifices on my behalf. Their love and support guided me through my winters of discontent.

ERIC FAERBER

1
BASIC PHYSICAL PRINCIPLES OF COMPUTED TOMOGRAPHY

'As long as our brain is a mystery, the universe, the reflection of the structure of the brain, will also be a mystery'. Ramon y Cajal (1852-1934), Neuro-anatomist, Nobel Prizewinner 1906)

Computed tomography represents the cross-sectional image resulting from the combination of x-ray transmission and computer technology.

The term computed tomography (CT) is now generally accepted, although other terms used are computerized axial tomography (CAT) and computerized transverse axial tomography (CTAT). The abbreviation CT will be used throughout this text.

Historical background

Since the momentous discovery of x-rays in 1895 by William Roentgen in Wurzburg, Germany, the progress of radiology has pursued a relentless path forwards.

Simple planar images have been augmented by the introduction of conventional tomography, enabling the region of interest to be visualized clearly with blurring of surrounding areas. The advent of fluoroscopy, and procedures using positive contrast media, have further widened the diagnostic horizons.

Further innovative modalities have been ultrasonography, which has emerged as a major diagnostic modality for neonatal cranial imaging, and the introduction of radionuclide imaging.

The advent of CT has made a profound impact on the practice of medicine today. Initially the debut of cranial CT produced a revolutionary effect on neurology and neurosurgery. The unequivocal success of this modality then rapidly led to the development of body CT scanning.

The research leading up to the development of computed tomography suitable for clinical use is the result of the work of many eminent investigators, all working independently. Radon (1917) conducted mathematical experiments in the reconstruction of images. Oldendorf (1961) performed experiments on reconstruction and published the first attempt of a medical application of image reconstruction. He obtained United States patents in 1963 for his experimental data but was unable to commercially develop the results of his work, being rejected by manufacturers in the x-ray industry. One manufacturer stated that the device 'would result in nothing but a radiographic cross section of the brain' (Oldendorf 1978). Kuhl and Edwards (1963) developed tomographic radionuclide image scanners. Alan Cormack (Fig. 1.1), a physicist originally from South Africa, developed a

1

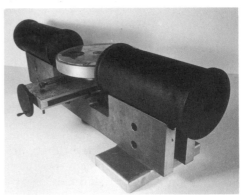

Fig. 1.1 *(left)*. Alan Cormack, Professor of Physics, Tufts University. He shared the Nobel Prize for Medicine and Physiology in 1979.

Fig. 1.2 *(above)*. Experimental apparatus for reconstruction tomography developed by Professor Cormack. The total cost of this equipment was under $100. (Illustration by courtesy of Professor Cormack and the Editor, *Journal of Computer Assisted Tomography.*)

mathematic theory for image reconstruction whilst on sabbatical at Harvard University. He subsequently joined the Physics Department of Tufts University, Medford, where he furthered his work which forms the basis of transmission computed tomography (Cormack 1963). His experimental apparatus used for reconstruction tomography cost less than one hundred dollars to assemble (Fig. 1.2).

Godfrey Hounsfield (Fig. 1.3), an electronic engineer working at the Central Research Laboratories of Electrical and Musical Industries (EMI) in England, commenced work on image reconstruction in 1968. His original apparatus consisted of a collimated isotope source mounted on a lathe bed (Fig. 1.4). The objects examined were phantoms contained within a 10-inch water box. The scan took nine days to complete, because of the low intensity of the x-radiation source, and a further 2½ hours to process the readings through a computer. The resulting image, though of poor quality, proved that the system worked (Bull 1981). To provide sufficient intensity the equipment was modified, by replacing the isotope with an industrial x-ray tube. A slice of brain, containing a suprasellar tumor, was mounted in a perspex box and examined by this method, and calcification within the mass was clearly defined.

A prototype scanner was then developed and installed in the Atkinson-Morley Hospital in Wimbledon, England on October 1, 1971. The first patient scanned was a 41-year-old female with a suspected left frontal lobe tumor. The subsequent data was put on tape and processed by a computer, taking two days. The tumor was clearly demonstrated on the scan. James Ambrose the neuro-radiologist remarked, 'this was the result that caused Hounsfield and I to jump up

Fig. 1.3 *(left)*. Sir Godfrey Hounsfield, Central Research Laboratories of Electrical and Musical Industries, London. He shared the Nobel Prize for Medicine and Physiology in 1979. (Illustration by courtesy of Sir Godfrey Hounsfield and Thorn EMI Central Research Laboratories.)

Fig. 1.4 *(above)*. Original lathe bed scanner used by Sir Godfrey Hounsfield. (Illustration by courtesy of Sir Godfrey Hounsfield and Thorn EMI Central Research Laboratories.)

and down like football players who had just scored the winning goal' (Ambrose 1977).

Hounsfield and Ambrose presented their paper on CT to the Annual Congress of the British Institute of Radiology on April 20, 1972, to great acclaim. The first CT papers, by these authors, appeared in the *British Journal of Radiology* in 1973 (Ambrose 1973, Ambrose and Hounsfield 1973, Hounsfield 1973).

Hounsfield and Cormack shared the Nobel Prize for Medicine and Physiology in 1979, in recognition of their momentous contributions.

Production of a CT scan

Three stages are involved in the evolution of a CT scan:
1. Data acquisition in order to obtain an image
2. Data processing by the computer system
3. Display of the image.

1. Data acquisition

The components necessary to obtain a CT image are the scanner gantry which contains the x-ray tube, detector array, and the data acquisition system, and the table which advances the patient into the scanning area (Fig. 1.5). The finely collimated x-ray beam passing through the region of interest is attenuated by the tissues of that area. The attenuation depends on the atomic number (z) of the tissue, effective atomic density and the photon energy (Seeram 1982). Photoelectric absorption occurs primarily in substances with a high z, such as positive contrast media and bone. The Compton effect occurs mainly in soft tissues. The

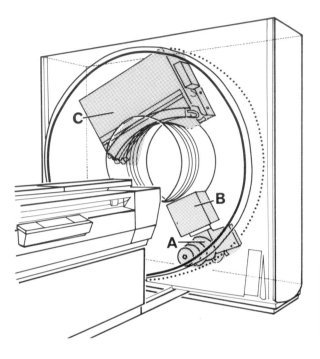

Fig. 1.5. The CT gantry. *A:* x-ray tube. *B:* filters and collimator housed beneath the x-ray tube. *C:* detector and data acquisition system. (Courtesy of General Electric Company, Milwaukee.)

data obtained by this attenuation process is collected by the detector array and data acquisition system housed within the gantry. The aperture size of the gantry varies with each system, with a range of 45 to 66cm (Seeram 1982).

X-RAY TUBE AND DETECTOR SYSTEM

Four generations of CT scanners have evolved up to the present time. Each generation has a specific x-ray beam shape, detector system, and scanning motion. There are advantages and disadvantages of each generation and the designation of a higher generation does not always imply superior image quality over other generations (Payne and McCullough 1982).

FIRST GENERATION (TRANSLATE-ROTATE TUBE AND DETECTOR)

First generation CT scanners employ an x-ray source with a tightly collimated x-ray beam, referred to as a pencil beam, and one or more detectors (Fig. 1.6). The detector system consists of scintillation crystals (sodium iodide as used in the EMI Mark I head scanner, or calcium fluoride as used in the ACTA 0100 whole body scanner).

The x-ray tube and detector are attached to each other and move or translate in linear fashion such that the x-ray beam traverses the area of interest. Multiple readings of the x-ray intensities are made throughout translational motion. The x-ray tube and detector(s) are then rotated further through 1° increments for 180° around the area of interest being scanned. This type of motion is referred to as translate/rotate.

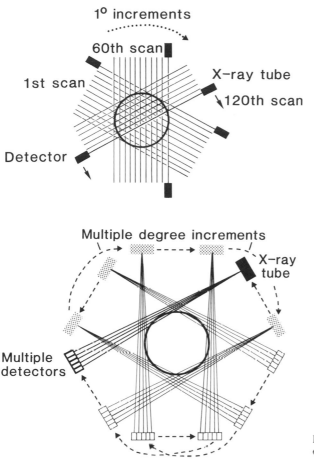

Fig. 1.6. Schematic representation of a first generation scanner.

Fig. 1.7. Schematic representation of a second generation scanner.

The first generation scanners are slow, taking up to five minutes per scan; this allows considerable patient motion, which in turn results in visible streak artifacts.

Examples of first generation scanners are the EMI Mark I head scanner, and the ACTA 0100 whole body scanner.

SECOND GENERATION (TRANSLATE-ROTATE TUBE AND DETECTOR)

Second generation scanners also have translate-rotate configuration, and can be designed to decrease scanning time up to within breath-holding scan times. The single detector and beam system of the first generation is replaced by a multiple pencil beam arrangement, with a corresponding system of multiple detectors (Fig. 1.7). The number and type of detectors vary with individual scanners. The Technicare Delta 50 and 100 series scanners employ three detectors; the Elscint Excel 905 scanner incorporates 52 bismuth germanate detectors.

Utilizing the multiple pencil/configuration fan beam, data over increments of 3° to 20° may be obtained simultaneously for each translational motion. The

5

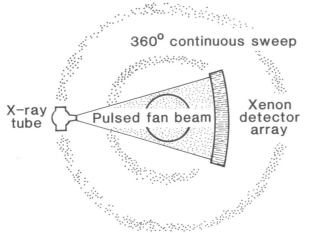

360° continuous sweep

X-ray tube

Pulsed fan beam

Xenon detector array

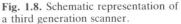

Fig. 1.8. Schematic representation of a third generation scanner.

increments of rotation may then be adjusted to yield the desired minimum of 180 different projections. For example, nine translations are required for a 20 detector beam, and 18 translations are required for a 10 detector beam. The decreased number of rotations and translations thus results in decreased scan times.

Scan times of 20 seconds are typical, but vary from 10 seconds to as long as 2½ minutes depending on the type of scanner. Examples of second generation scanners are the Technicare Delta 50 and Delta 100 series, the Elscint Excel 905, and EMI CT 5005.

THIRD GENERATION (ROTATING TUBE-ROTATING DETECTOR)
Third generation scanners employ a continuously pulsed rotating fan beam with an arc angle varying from 30 to 40°, and a curved array of detectors (Fig. 1.8).

The detectors most commonly used are ionization chambers containing Xenon gas. Scintillation solid state detectors such as cesium iodide crystals or cadmium tungstate are also available in some scanners.

Using this fan beam arrangement the x-ray source and detector array rotate simultaneously around the patient and usually through 360° for a single scan. The use of a fan beam instead of multiple pencil beams results in eliminating the translational motion altogether.

The third generation scanners have numerous advantages which include rapid scan times (two to 10 seconds), mechanical simplicity, and a rotating anode source with a small focal spot. The resulting images are thus improved, with decreased radiation to the patient. The disadvantages of this system are circular artifacts arising from detector and amplifier instabilities, detector drift, and high anode cooling periods between scans in some x-ray tube units (Payne and McCullough 1982). Examples of third generation CT scanners are the General Electric GE CT/T 7800, GE CT/T 8800 and 9800 (Fig. 1.9); Siemens Somatom DR1, 2 and 3; EMI CT 6000, Philip Tomoscan 300, Toshiba TCT-65A, CGR CE 10000, and Elscint Excel 1002.

6

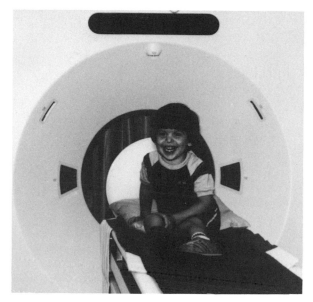

Fig. 1.9. GE 9800 CT scanner. (Courtesy of MEDIQ, New Jersey.)

FOURTH GENERATION (ROTATING TUBE-STATIONARY DETECTOR)
The fourth generation scanner unit consists of a stationary circular detector array within which the x-ray tube rotates through 360° (Fig. 1.10). The revolving continuous fan beam activates the detectors in its path.

A major advantage of the fan beam multiple detector system is rapid speed. The scan time varies from two to 10 seconds. There is no susceptibility to the ring artifacts which plague the third generation systems. Additionally the detector calibrations are easier. Disadvantages include increased amount of scattered radiation, since collimators cannot be used, and high cost of the additional detectors needed to go around the complete periphery of the gantry. Examples of fourth generation scanners are the Picker Synerview 6000, 1200; and Technicare 2020 HR, 2060 units.

In all generations, the x-ray photons are converted into electric signals by the data acquisition system. The information obtained from the detectors in analog form is amplified, converted into digital form, and then passed to the computer for processing.

2. Data processing
The scan data is composed of multiple readings from the detector array system. This data is transmitted to the computer and its array processor, where reconstruction of the data into a cross-sectional image occurs.

The final image is composed of a two-dimensional array or matrix of numbers. Each number of each picture position is dependent on the x-ray attenuation properties of the tissue at that position. Each individual number thus represents the x-ray attenuation of a small volume element (voxel) of tissue imaged (Fig. 1.11a),

7

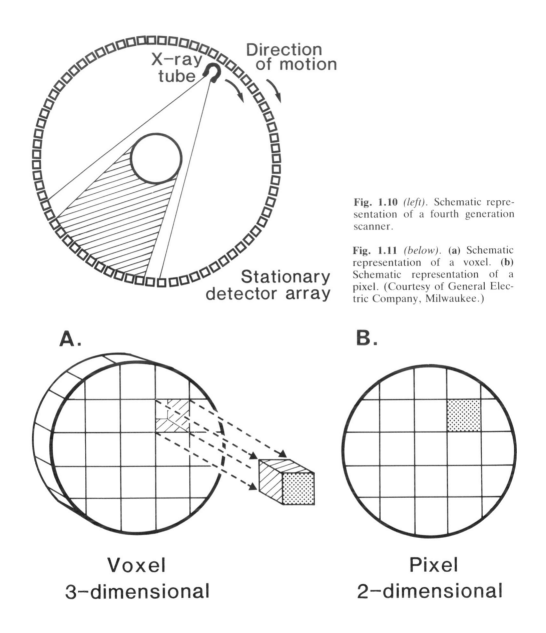

Fig. 1.10 *(left)*. Schematic representation of a fourth generation scanner.

Fig. 1.11 *(below)*. **(a)** Schematic representation of a voxel. **(b)** Schematic representation of a pixel. (Courtesy of General Electric Company, Milwaukee.)

A.

B.

Voxel
3-dimensional

Pixel
2-dimensional

and is termed a Hounsfield unit. Each voxel is represented in a two-dimensional display as a picture element or pixel. A large number of pixels are arranged in regular rows and columns called a matrix (Fig. 1.11b). An increased number of pixels improves image quality, since each pixel would then represent a smaller tissue volume.

An arbitrary scale of Hounsfield units has been created with water represented at 0 (Fig. 1.12). Bone, the densest body tissue, is assigned up to +1000 Hounsfield

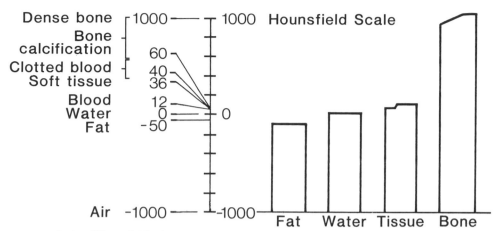

Fig. 1.12. Scale of Hounsfield units representing the various body tissues. The Hounsfield scale displays x-ray attenuation values as an arbitrary numerical scale with air represented as −1000 HU and water as 0 HU.

units, while air is represented at -1000 Hounsfield units. Fat is more dense than air and is represented in the range of -100 to 0 Hounsfield units. On the original EMI scanner the range of CT numbers was from -500 to +500.

3. Image display
After the image has been reconstructed by computer processing, it can be stored on the disc of the computer system, on a floppy disc or on magnetic tape. The stored images may be called from the disc or tape and viewed on a display monitor (cathode ray tube). The images may be photographed and recorded on x-ray film or as Polaroid prints. Other forms of recording the images are the line printer, for printing of CT numbers, or a hard copy imager which records information from the display screen onto a dry silver paper media.

Window level and window width
The CT numbers, representing the attenuation coefficients of structures within the region of interest, are converted to a gray scale for viewing. The higher CT numbers are represented as the lighter areas, and the lower CT numbers as darker areas. The window width is the range of CT numbers on the gray scale line between the lightest and darkest illumination on the cathode ray tube (CRT). The window level is the center of the gray scale, and indicates which CT number will appear on the display with mid-gray illumination. The window levels and widths can be manipulated at the console, to obtain maximal visualization of the region of interest, with adjustment for the type of tissue being examined. Wide windows are utilized for bone, and narrow windows for tissues of similar density such as brain (Fig. 1.13).

Artifacts
Artifacts represent distortions or errors in images which are unrelated to the area of

9

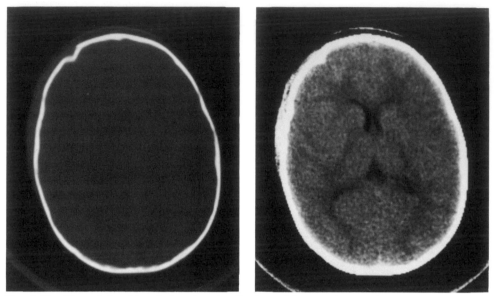

Fig. 1.13. *Above left:* wide window for visualization of bone. *Above right:* narrow window for visualization of brain.

interest being studied (Morgan 1983). The variety of causes leading to their relatively common occurrence has been classified by Villafana (1983) into four main groups, each related to the data obtained. These will be briefly described.

1. ARTIFACTS RELATED TO DATA FORMATION

(a) *Patient motion.* The long scan times of the original CT scanners resulted in considerable patient motion (Fig. 1.14). There is marked streaking, in addition to decreased spatial resolution (the ability to visualize fine spatial detail), and density resolution (the ability to visualize small differences in tissue densities). The advent of more rapid scan times has greatly reduced these artifacts. In young children sedation may be required, and in the older child the importance of remaining immobile during the examination must be stressed. Immobilization of the head with tape is recommended in most instances.

(b) *Beam hardening.* The x-ray beam consists of photons of varying energies. The lower-energy photons are more preferentially absorbed with passage of the beam through the patient, causing the effective energy of the remaining photons to become higher. The beam is thus more penetrating or 'harder'. There is more absorption of the x-ray beam along particular ray paths compared to other ray paths. There is thus an inconsistency in the resulting CT value at any pixel point where the two ray paths intersect, and this results in artifactual streaks. This effect is most pronounced where there are denser bony structures, such as the temporal bones (Fig. 1.15).

  A further feature of beam hardening is the phenomenon of cupping, due to

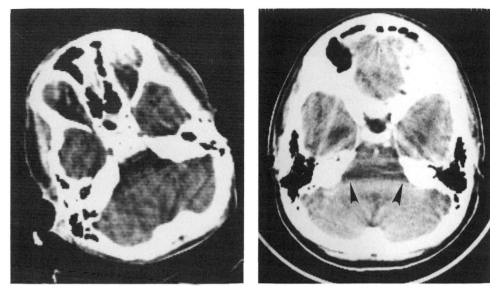

Fig. 1.14. Motion artifact leading to image degradation.

Fig. 1.15. Artifact due to beam hardening effect *(arrowheads)*.

less beam-hardening at the periphery than the center of a structure. This may be evident along the inner table of the skull, where initially the increased density due to cupping was thought to represent cerebral cortex (Ambrose 1973).

(c) *Misalignment of equipment.* Streaks may result from the misalignment of radiation detectors with the x-ray source.

(d) *Faulty x-ray source.* Fluctuations in the x-ray output during scans will result in faulty data formation. This potential source of artifact formation is obviated by the inclusion of reference detectors in CT units to detect such variations. Criss-crossing streaks with the formation of moire patterns results from x-ray output variations between angular views (Fig. 1.16). The cause is related to inconsistencies in the speed of anode rotation, referred to as anode wobble.

2. ARTIFACTS RELATED TO DATA ACQUISITION
(a) *Partial volume effect.* This effect is the consequence of the area of interest occupying only a part of the section thickness. The CT number of the voxel is a weighted average of the contents within that voxel. If the tissues within that voxel actually have CT numbers of 100 to 300 respectively, the average CT number is 200, which does not actually represent the correct CT number of the tissues within the voxel. This may be evident in regions near the calvarium and the lateral ventricles, especially in premature infants. When CT number differences within a voxel are very large, then visible streaks occur. The partial volume effect may be decreased by obtaining thinner sections or smaller pixels to form the image.

11

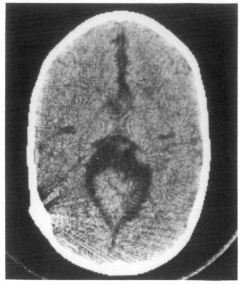
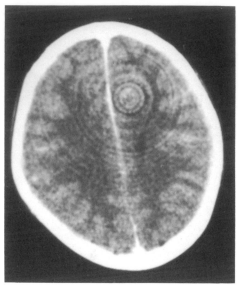

Fig. 1.16. Streak artifact produced by ventriculo-peritoneal shunt tube, and moire pattern.

Fig. 1.17. Ring artifact due to detector imbalance.

(b) *Aliasing streaks*. Aliasing streaks are due to undersampling the data. The resulting streaks overlap to form a moire pattern. The effect is particularly severe at sharp boundaries, such as liquid air interfaces or bone tissue interfaces. Aliasing streaks can also be minimized by using thinner slices or smaller pixels.

3. ARTIFACTS RELATED TO DATA MEASUREMENT

(a) *Detector imbalance*. Artifacts due to faulty detectors are especially prevalent with the third generation scanners. Ring or circular artifacts are due to detector imbalance (Fig. 1.17). This source of artifact is corrected by calibration.

(b) *Scatter*. Scatter radiation occurs more commonly with the fourth generation scanners where, due to the manner in which data is collected, collimation cannot be used. As a consequence, radiation from a wide area must pass through the detectors. Collimation is incorporated into first, second and third generation scanners, reducing scatter radiation significantly.

4. ARTIFACTS RELATED TO DATA PROCESSING

Artifacts may result from the algorithms used for the computer processing of data. The streaks which occur along high-contrast, bony or straight-edged structures, are reduced by employing narrower collimators for first and second generation scanners, smaller detectors for third and fourth generation scanners, and the use of filtered x-ray beams (Villafana 1983).

Technique for cerebral CT scans

The successful performance of cerebral CT scans is dependent on teamwork between the referring physician, nursing staff, radiologist and radiographic technologist.

Scheduling of patients

All CT scans should be scheduled by physicians in consultation with the appropriate members of the radiology department. Vital clinical data which will influence the method of scanning is thus conveyed to the radiologist, leading to optimal diagnosis and patient care.

At St. Christopher's Hospital for Children, Philadelphia, our policy is to schedule one patient per hour. This is so that both non-contrast and contrast CT studies can be performed if necessary, and also to allow for any problems which may arise relating to sedation, and for extra CT sections to be obtained if additional abnormalities are detected.

Preparations prior to the CT scan

Prior to performance of the scan, any previous x-rays and CT scans should be studied. A history of allergies and previous history of reactions to any drugs or previous contrast medium administration is ascertained.

The CT procedure is described to the parents and child, to allay their anxieties about the scan, and any questions relating to the scan (*e.g.* duration of the scan, amount of radiation) can be answered. At our hospital a photo album containing colored photographs of the entire procedure is shown to the parents, and child, if older. Some children prefer to see the actual CT scanner before the procedure is performed.

Food and fluid intake is generally restricted for four hours before the scan. Prior to the study, intravenous lines are inserted in all patients requiring a contrast enhanced scan.

Sedation

The purpose of sedation is to ensure a CT scan which will be of diagnostic quality. The approach is modified according to age-group. In neonates, sedation is generally not required provided the patient is securely immobilized. Certain clinical problems such as seizures may make sedation mandatory. For infants and children aged one month to six years, sedation is usually required. From six years onward the need for sedation is generally decreased, but the patient's clinical status will determine this. Emotional lability or mental retardation in some older children will lead to the use of sedation.

The sedative of choice ideally should have the following properties: ease of administration, consistency of action, safety, rapid action with complete immobilization, and controllable duration of action (Thompson *et al.* 1982).

A wide variety of regimens have been advocated for sedation in infants and children (Anderson and Osborn 1977, Byrd *et al.* 1977, White *et al.* 1979, Thompson *et al.* 1982).

Chloral hydrate administered orally is the sedative of choice at our institution. The dose is 100mg/kg (with a maximum of 2g) administered 30 minutes prior to the

13

study. The ease of administration, together with a wide safety margin, are two appealing factors in the pediatric age-group. Chloral hydrate (80mg/kg orally) has also been used by Thompson *et al.* (1982). In their series, a 15 per cent failure rate was recorded. When necessary, intravenous Secobarbital (2mg/kg maximum) was also used.

A *'cardiac cocktail'* (CM3) consists of a mixture of meperidine (25mg/ml), chlorpromazine (6.25mg/ml) and promethazine (6.25mg/ml). The dosage of 1.0ml/20lbs, up to a maximum of 2ml, is administered by intramuscular injection 30 to 60 minutes before the examination. The high meperidine content has the potential for respiratory depression, and thus may not be deemed suitable (Thompson *et al.* 1982).

Rectal thiopental administered by syringe has been found to be an effective alternative to intramuscular cardiac cocktail by White *et al.* (1979). They conclude from their series that this regimen, in a dose of 25mg/kg, has the ease of administration, control of timing of sedation (adequate sedation is achieved within 10 minutes), and a shorter duration of sedation. Although no complications were observed, careful observation for respiratory depression is suggested.

Intravenous *diazepam* (Valium) may often not be effective in bigger children and may not be safe in higher doses required for adequate mobilization (Thompson *et al.* 1982).

General anesthesia is usually indicated in those patients in whom other forms of sedation have failed, or in whom it is unsafe to use sedation.

Intravenous contrast medium
Renografin 60 (diatrizoate meglumine and diatrizoate sodium, E.R. Squibb) is administered as a bolus injection of 2 to 4ml/kg, (maximum 120ml) with immediate scanning.

The selection of patients for contrast medium administration will vary in different institutions.

No contrast	*Contrast*
Acute trauma	Suspected tumor
Hydrocephalus follow-up	Infection
Acute infarction	Vascular abnormalities
	Malformations (first examination)
	History of seizures
	Possible isodense subdural hematoma

Contrast enhancement in cranial computed tomography
The intravenous administration of iodinated contrast medium results in the subsequent accumulation in both the extravascular and intravascular spaces of the brain and meninges. The density of normal intracranial structures is markedly altered, thus permitting visualization of these structures. Structures not visualized on the pre-contrast scan may only become visible after contrast administration; structures poorly visualized may become more prominent on the post-contrast scan

14

(Ambrose 1973, New *et al.* 1974, Naidich *et al.* 1977).

Following intravenous injection of contrast medium, iodine is introduced into the systemic circulation and subsequently appears in the blood pool of lesions. The lack of detectable enhancement within normal brain tissue has been attributed by Gado *et al.* (1975*a*) to an absence of any significant iodine extravasation, the low attenuation value of normal cerebral blood volume, and a rapid drop of iodine concentration in the systemic circulation due to renal clearance and extravascular distribution in body tissues and fluids. These authors provide evidence of significant extravasation of contrast medium at the blood brain barrier in abnormal states (Gado *et al.* 1975*b*).

Metrizamide (Amipaque: Winthrop) may be administered *via* the intrathecal route (1.5 to 1.7ml of a 170mg I/ml concentration) or for intraventricular injection *via* a needle or shunt (1.5 to 2.0ml of a 210 to 220mg I/ml concentration).

The use of this agent is of value for sellar and suprasellar lesions, extra-axial masses, suspected posterior fossa cysts, and the demonstration of ventricular blocks, intraventricular loculations and cyst and porencephaly (Wolpert and Scott 1981, Fitz 1983).

Positioning of the patient

Adequate patient sedation and immobilization are key factors for a successful CT scan.

Standard head-rests available in all CT scanners are not practical for infants and small children. Special head-rests may be obtained for this age-group.

The patient is usually scanned in the axial plane (20° to the orbito-meatal line). Coronal plane scans are performed as the primary or secondary studies for the orbits, suprasellar area, temporal lobes, congenital anomalies, face, and surface masses (Fitz 1983). If coronal planes cannot be obtained (*e.g.* in neonates), a clival-perpendicular view can be obtained (Fitz *et al.* 1978) or thin section scans may be obtained with subsequent coronal and sagittal reformatted (reconstructed) images. Lesions around the fourth ventricle may also be assessed in the Towne projection (Byrd *et al.* 1978).

Radiation dosage

The considerable impact of computed tomography as a diagnostic imaging modality is accompanied by an associated radiation dosage to the patient, in contrast to ultrasonography and magnetic resonance imaging (MRI, NMR).

It is thus extremely important in infants and children to tailor the examination to the patient's needs, obviating the need for an excess number of CT slices. The appearance of newer generation scanners with rapid scan times and the ability for reformatted images to augment the conventional axial images has helped considerably to decrease the radiation dose.

The radiation dose delivered by cranial CT (surface, depth, thyroid, gonad and mean marrow dose) is higher than plain radiographs of the skull, but less than that obtained from typical cerebral angiography (Hilton 1984). The marrow dose following cranial CT is higher in children than adults because of the high fraction of active marrow in the cranium of children (Hilton 1984).

An updated comparison of the radiation dosage associated with newer high-resolution CT scanners by Brasch and Cann (1982) revealed central internal doses ranging from 0.4 rad to 3.64 rad for a series of eight to 10 slices.

REFERENCES

Ambrose, J. (1973) 'Computerized transverse axial scanning (tomography). Part 2: clinical application.' *British Journal of Radiology*, **46**, 1023–1047.
—— (1977) 'CT scanning: a backward look.' *Seminars in Roentgenology*, **12**, 7-11.
—— Hounsfield, G. (1973) 'Computerized transverse axial tomography.' *British Journal of Radiology*, **46**, 148. *(Abstract)*.
Anderson, R. E., Osborn, A. G. (1977) 'Efficacy of simple sedation for pediatric computed tomography.' *Radiology*, **124**, 739–740.
Brasch, R. C., Cann, C. E. (1982) 'Computed tomographic scanning in children: II. An updated comparison of radiation dose and resolving power of commercial scanners.' *American Journal of Roentgenology*, **138**, 127–133.
Bull, J. (1981) 'History of computed tomography.' *In:* Newton, T. H., Potts, D. G. (Eds.) *Radiology of the Skull and Brain. Vol. 5: Technical Aspects of Computed Tomography.* St. Louis: C. V. Mosby. pp. 3835–3849.
Byrd, S. E., Harwood-Nash, D. C. Barry, J. F., Fitz, C. R., Boldt, D. W. (1977) 'Coronal computed tomography of the skull and brain in infants and children. Part I: technique and results.' *Radiology*, **124**, 705–714.
—— —— Fitz, C. R., Barry, J. F., Rogovitz, D. M. (1978) 'Two projection computed tomography: the axial and Towne projection.' *Radiology*, **128**, 512–514.
Cormack, A. M. (1963) 'Representation of a function by its line integrals, with some radiological applications.' *Journal of Applied Physics*, **34**, 2722–2727.
Fitz, C. R. (1983) 'Practical techniques for pediatric computed tomography: 1. Cranio-cerebral computed tomography.' *Pediatric Radiology*, **13**, 148–155.
—— Harwood-Nash, D. C., Chuang, S. H., Resjo, I. M. (1978) 'The clival perpendicular or modified Water's view in computed tomography.' *Neuroradiology*, **16**, 15–16.
Gado, M. H., Phelps, M. E., Coleman, R. E. (1975a) 'An extra-vascular component of contrast enhancement in cranial computed tomography. Part 1: The tissue-blood ratio of contrast enhancement.' *Radiology*, **117**, 589–593.
—— —— —— (1975b) 'An extra–vascular component of contrast enhancement in cranial computed tomography. Part II: Contrast enhancement and the blood-tissue barrier.' *Radiology*, **117**, 595–597.
Hilton, J. W. (1984) 'Radiation effects and protection in children.' *In:* Hilton, S. von W., Edwards, D. K., Hilton, J. W. *Practical Pediatric Radiology.* Philadelphia: W. B. Saunders. pp. 575–602.
Hounsfield, G. N. (1973) 'Computerized transverse axial scanning (tomography) Part I: description of system.' *British Journal of Radiology*, **46**, 1016–1022.
Kuhl, D. E., Edwards, R. Q. (1963) 'Image separation radioisotope scanning.' *Radiology*, **80**, 653–661.
Morgan, C. L. (1983) *Basic Principles of Computed Tomography.* Baltimore: University Park Press. pp. 275–290.
Naidich, T. P., Pudlowski, R. M., Leeds, N. E., Naidich, J. B., Chisolm, A. J., Rifkin, M. D. (1977) 'The normal contrast-enhanced computed axial tomogram of the brain.' *Journal of Computer Assisted Tomography*, **1**, 16–29.
New, P. F. J., Scott, W. R., Schnur, J. A., Davis, K. R., Taveras, J. M. (1974) 'Computerized axial tomography with the EMI scanner.' *Radiology*, **110**, 109–123.
Oldendorf, W. H. (1961) 'Isolated flying spot detection of radiodensity discontinuities displacing the internal structure of a complex object.' *IRE Transactions in Biomedical Electronics*, **8**, 68–72.
—— (1978) 'The quest for an image of the brain: a brief historical and technical review of brain imaging techniques.' *Neurology*, **28**, 517–533.
Payne, J. P., McCullough, E. C. (1982) 'A CT primer in syllabus for the categorical course on computed body tomography.' *Presented at the Annual Meeting of the American Roentgen Ray Society, New Orleans, May 9–14, 1982.*

Radon, J. (1917) 'On the determination of functions from their integrals along certain manifolds.' *Berichte Sachische Akadamie der Wissenschaften Leipzig Mathematische-Physische Klasse*, **67**, 262–277.

Seeram, E. (1982) *Computed Tomography Technology*. Philadelphia: W. B. Saunders. pp. 1–211.

Thompson, J. R., Schneider, S., Aschwal, S., Holden, B. S., Hinshaw, D. B., Jr., Hasso, A. N. (1982) 'The choice of sedation for computed tomography in children: a prospective evaluation.' *Radiology*, **143**, 475–479.

Villafana, T. (1983) 'Physics and instrumentation.' *In:* Lee, H., Rao, K. C. V. G. (Eds.) *Cranial Computed Tomography*. New York: McGraw-Hill. pp. 1–46.

White, T. J., Siegle, R. E., Burckart, G. J., Ramey, D. R. (1979) 'Rectal thiopental for sedation of children for computed tomography.' *Journal of Computer Assisted Tomography*, **3**, 286–288.

Wolpert, S. M., Scott, R. M. (1981) 'Value of metrizamide CT cisternography in the management of cerebral arachnoid cysts.' *Americal Journal of Neuroradiology*, **2**, 29–35.

2
NORMAL ANATOMY

A cranial CT examination consists of a series of 10 or 11 slices, depending on the patient's age and head size. The CT scan is tailored to the patient's clinical diagnosis, and thus a series of slices may be obtained both prior to and following administration of intravenous contrast medium.

The thickness of each slice is usually 10mm (although in some scanners this may be 8mm). The initial scan is performed with the gantry angled at 20° to the orbito-meatal line starting at the skull base with nine or 10 successive slices above this extending up to the vertex (Fig. 2.1); the scans may also be obtained parallel to the orbito-meatal line.

A normal series of CT slices follows, accompanied by a brief description of anatomic structures at the level of the slice.

Section 1: 0 to 10mm above the orbito-meatal line (Fig. 2.2)
The posterior fossa is bordered by the clivus anteriorly, the occipital bone

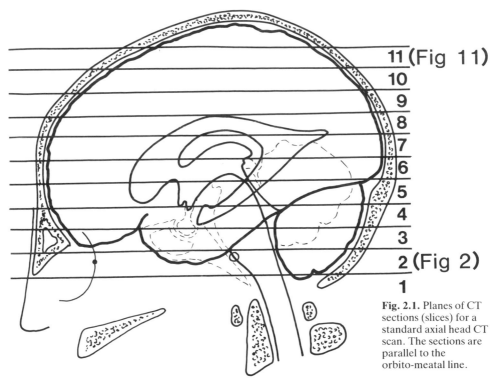

11 (Fig 11)
10
9
8
7
6
5
4
3
2 (Fig 2)
1

Fig. 2.1. Planes of CT sections (slices) for a standard axial head CT scan. The sections are parallel to the orbito-meatal line.

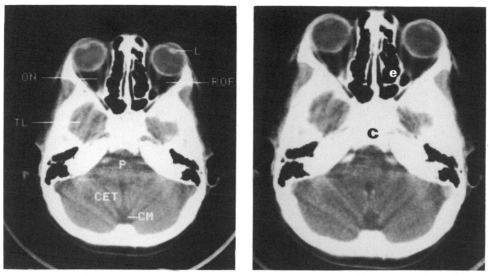

Fig. 2.2. 10mm above the orbito-meatal line. *Left:* non contrast scan; *right:* contrast-enhanced scan. Lens (L); optic nerve (ON); retro-orbital fossa (ROF); temporal lobe (TL); pons (P); cerebellar tonsil (CET); cisterna magna (CM); clivus (c); ethmoid sinus (e).

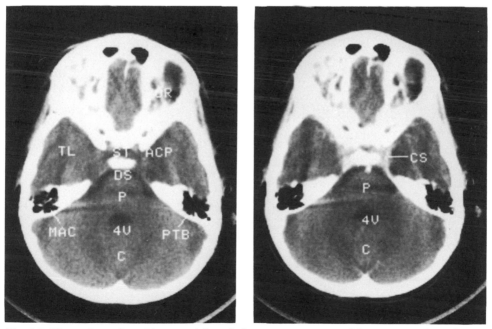

Fig. 2.3. 20mm above the orbito-meatal line. *Left:* non-contrast scan; *right:* contrast-enhanced scan. Orbital roof (OR); anterior clinoid process (ACP); sella turcica (ST); dorsum sellae (DS); temporal lobe (TL); pons (P); mastoid air cells (MAC); petrous temporal bone (PTB); fourth ventricle (4V); cerebellar vermis (C); cavernous sinus (CS).

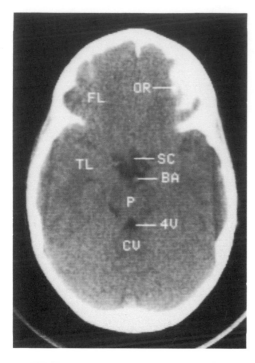

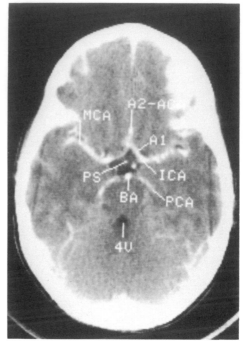

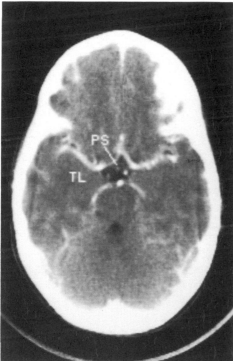

Fig. 2.4. 30mm above the orbito-meatal line. *Above left:* non-contrast scan; *left and above:* contrast-enhanced scans. Frontal lobe (FL); orbital roof (OR); suprasellar cistern (SC); pituitary stalk (PS); temporal lobe (TL); pons (P); fourth ventricle (4V); cerebellar vermis (CV); divisions of the anterior cerebral artery (A1, A2); anterior cerebral artery (ACA); internal carotid artery (ICA); middle cerebral artery (MCA); posterior cerebral artery (PCA); basilar artery (BA).

posteriorly and the posterior surface of the petrous temporal bones laterally.

The fourth ventricle separates the midbrain anteriorly and cerebellum posteriorly. The configuration of the ventricle at this level may merely be that of a transverse slit. The middle cranial fossa is defined by the sphenoid bone anteriorly, petrous temporal bones posteriorly, sella and cavernous sinuses medially, and temporal bones laterally. Portions of the temporal lobes are visualized at this level.

The orbital roof, frontal sinuses and sphenoid sinuses are demonstrated anteriorly. Visualization of the sinuses will depend on the age of the patient: pneumatization of the sphenoid sinuses commences from two years and the frontal sinuses in later childhood (Swischuk 1980).

The cisterna magna is the cistern located most posteriorly and inferiorly. It may appear asymmetric, with varying width, and may also have supratentorial extension (Weisberg *et al.* 1984). A markedly enlarged mega cisterna magna (Gonsette *et al.* 1968) may be encountered on CT without producing any specific symptoms (Adam and Greenberg 1978).

Section 2: 20mm above the orbito-meatal line (Fig. 2.3)

Section 3: 30mm above the orbito-meatal line (Fig. 2.4)
The fourth ventricle usually has an inverted v or triangular configuration. This may, however, vary with angulation of the gantry. Following contrast administration, there may be enlargement of the vermis which may simulate a tumor. This phenomenon has been termed the vermian pseudotumor (Kramer 1977).

The suprasellar cistern is bordered by the base of the frontal lobes, the planum sphenoidale and olfactory nerves anteriorly, the uncus of the temporal lobes laterally, and the pons cerebral peduncles and interpeduncular fossa posteriorly. The longitudinal fissure courses anteriorly in the midline, the sylvian fissures pass anterolaterally on each side and the crural cisterns pass posterolaterally. The interpeduncular cistern passes directly posteriorly. These extensions of the suprasellar cistern collectively form a five- or six-pointed 'star' or 'crown' (Naidich *et al.* 1976). The optic nerves and chiasm lie within the suprasellar cistern. The pituitary stalk may also be visualized within this cistern after contrast medium administration.

The circle of Willis outlines the borders of the suprasellar cistern. The two internal carotid arteries are situated anterolaterally, bifurcating into anterior and middle cerebral arteries. The basilar artery is posterior to the suprasellar cistern, within the prepontine cistern. The posterior cerebral arteries arise from the basilar artery.

Section 4: 40mm above the orbito-meatal line (Fig. 2.5)
The two frontal horns and anterior portions of the lateral ventricles are demonstrated at this level, diverging anteriorly. These structures are separated by the septum pellucidum. The third ventricle is an elongated structure situated inferiorly to the bodies of the lateral ventricles.

The lateral margins of the ventricular bodies are indented by the caudate

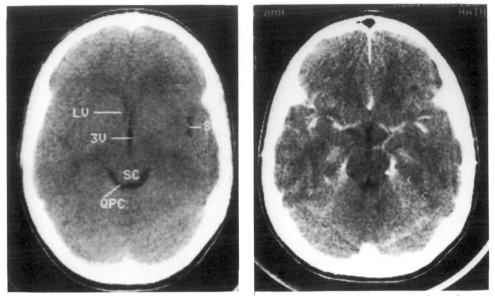

Fig. 2.5. 40mm above the orbito-meatal line. *Left:* non-contrast scan; *right:* contrast-enhanced scan. Frontal horn of the lateral ventricle (LV); third ventricle (3V); superior colliculi (SC); quadrigeminal plate cistern (QPC); Sylvian fissure (S); tentorium cerebelli *(arrowheads)*.

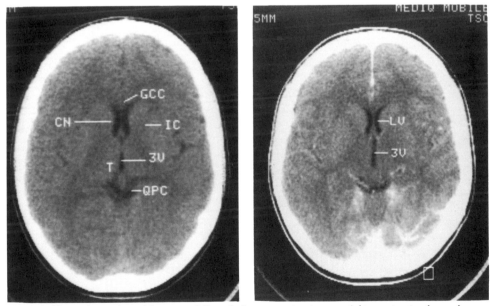

Fig. 2.6. 50mm above the orbito-meatal line. *Left:* non-contrast scan; *right:* contrast-enhanced scan. Internal capsule (IC); thalamus (T); quadrigeminal plate cistern (QPC); genu of corpus callosum (GCC); lateral ventricle (LV); third ventricle (3V).

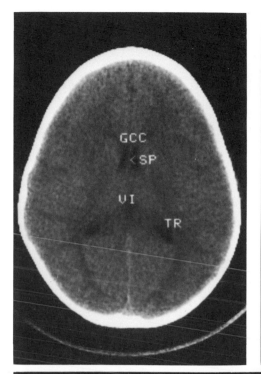

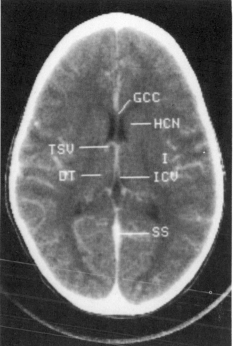

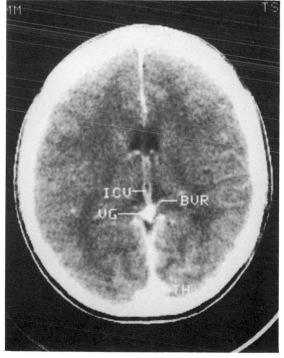

Fig. 2.7. 60mm above the orbito-meatal line. *Above left:* non-contrast CT scan; *left and above:* contrast-enhanced CT scans. Genu of corpus callosum (GCC); head of caudate nucleus (HCN); vein of Galen (VG); insula (I); dorsal thalamus (DT); thalamostriate vein (TSV); internal cerebral vein (ICV); basal vein of Rosenthal (BVR); torcula herophili (TH); septum pellucidum (SP); velum interpositum (VI); trigone of lateral ventricle (TR).

23

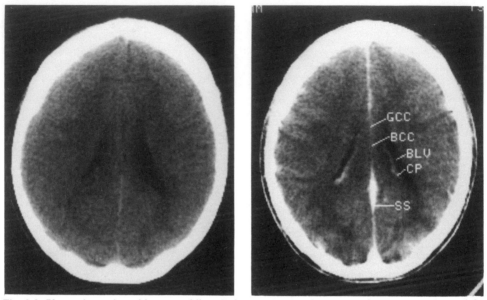

Fig. 2.8. 70mm above the orbito-meatal line. *Left:* non-contrast CT scan; *right:* contrast-enhanced CT scan. Genu of corpus callosum (GCC); body of corpus callosum (BCC); body of lateral ventricle (BLV); choroid plexus (CP); straight sinus (SS).

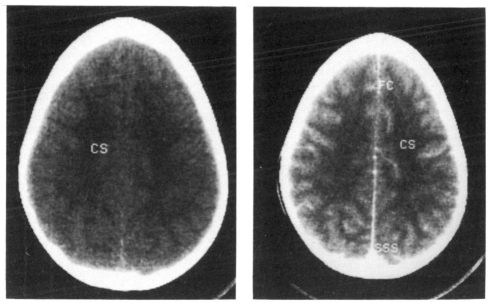

Fig. 2.9. 80mm above the orbito-meatal line. *Left:* non-contrast CT scan; *right:* contrast-enhanced CT scan. Falx cerebri (FC); centrum semiovale (CS); superior sagittal sinus (SSS).

nuclei bilaterally. The anterior limb of the internal capsule lies between the caudate nucleus and the lenticular nucleus (putamen and globus pallidus).

The quadrigeminal plate cistern is a curved structure, indented anteriorly by the superior colliculi. The wings of the ambient cisterns are lateral extensions of the quadrigeminal plate cistern.

Section 5: 50mm above the orbito-meatal line (Fig. 2.6)
At this level the genu of the corpus callosum is situated across the midline anterior to the frontal horns.

The foramen of Monro connects each lateral ventricle with the third ventricle.

The quadrigeminal cistern at this level has a rhomboid shape. The forward extension of this cistern is the velum interpositum which exhibits posterior flaring as it joins the quadrigeminal cistern. The posterior end of the third ventricle has a pointed end posteriorly (Gado and El Yousef 1982).

The trigone, or atrium, of each lateral ventricle is visualized at this level. The glomus of the chloroid plexus is contained within the trigone.

The pineal gland is located in the quadrigeminal cistern. This structure is not normally observed in infants and young children.

There are four main configurations of the tentorium seen on a contrast-enhanced CT scan, varying with the level and angle of the CT section (Naidich *et al.* 1977).
1. Gothic Arch. A section in the plane of the incisura may display the entire contour of the tentorial margin from the apex to the anterior clinoid processes.
2. V Configuration. Converging V-shaped bands are demonstrated on CT section above the torcula. The sides may either have laterally convex or straight sides.
3. Diverging bands. Thin or thick bands which are faintly or densely opacified after contrast administration, diverge laterally toward their calvarial attachments, below the plane of the torcula.
4. M Configuration. The M configuration of the tentorium is visualized on the CT section passing directly through the torcula.

Section 6: 60mm above the orbito-meatal line (Fig. 2.7)
The bodies of the lateral ventricles appear prominent at this level continuous with the occipital horns. The interhemispheric fissure separates the frontal lobes.

The parenchyma consists of the cortex of the lateral and medial surfaces of the cerebral hemispheres, and the white matter of the centrum semiovale.

The vein of Galen and straight sinus are prominent vascular structures (demonstrated on the enhanced scan at this level).

Section 7: 70mm above the orbito-meatal line (Fig. 2.8)
The two lateral ventricles are separated by the cingulate gyrus and body of the corpus callosum. The central sulcus dividing the frontal and lateral lobes is determined approximately by drawing a transverse line through the anterior ends of the two lateral ventricles (Gado and El Yousef 1983). The primary sensory and motor cortices lie on the sides of the central sulcus.

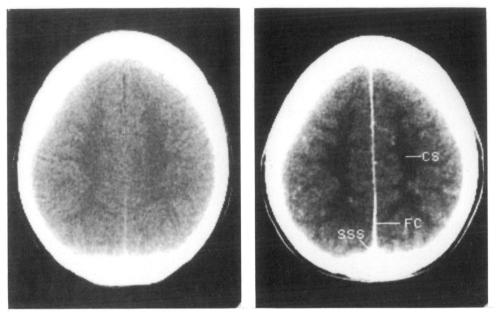

Fig. 2.10. 90mm above the orbito-meatal line. *Left:* non-contrast CT scan; *right:* contrast-enhanced CT scan. Falx cerebri (FC); centrum semiovale (CS); superior sagittal sinus (SSS).

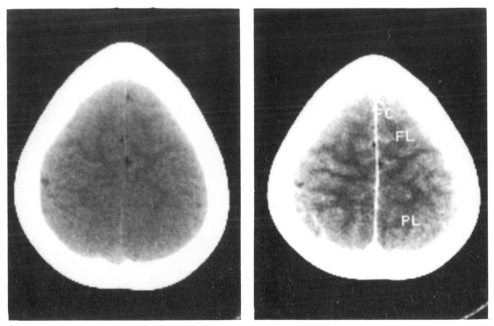

Fig. 2.11. 100mm above the orbito-meatal line. *Left:* non-contrast CT scan; *right:* contrast-enhanced CT scan. Falx cerebri (FC); frontal lobe (FL); parietal lobe (PL).

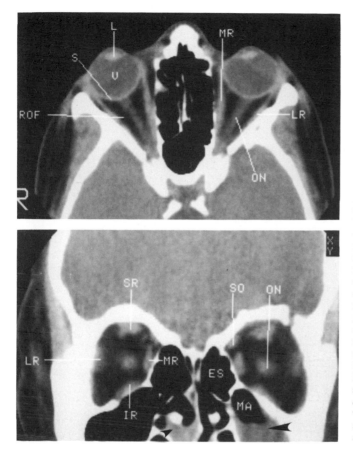

Fig. 2.12. Orbit. **(a)** axial non-contrast scan. Lens (L); vitreous humor (V); sclera (S); optic nerve (N); retro-orbital fat (ROF); medial rectus muscle (M); lateral rectus muscle (LR). **(b)** coronal non-contrast scan. Optic nerve sheath (ON); medial rectus muscle (MR); lateral rectus muscle (LR); superior oblique muscle (SO); superior rectus muscle (SR); inferior rectus muscle (IR); maxillary antrum (MA); ethmoid sinus (ES). Mucosal thickening around the superior turbinate *(small arrowhead)* and air fluid level within the left maxillary antrum *(large arrowhead)* are also demonstrated.

Section 8: 80mm above the orbito-meatal line (Fig. 2.9)

At this level the ventricular system is not recognized. The cerebral cortex and centrum semiovale are noted. The superior sagittal sinus is identified on the contrast enhanced scan.

Section 9: 90mm above the orbito-meatal line (Fig. 2.10)

Section 10: 100mm above the orbito-meatal line (Fig. 2.11)

The internal structure of the cerebral hemispheres is not recognized at these supraventricular levels. The centrum semiovale is discernible, surrounded by cerebral cortex. More rostrally the area formed by the cingulate gyrus is then represented by the paracentral lobule and precuneus.

Section 11: orbits (Fig. 2.12)

Axial plane CT scans are obtained parallel to Reid's baseline (infra-orbital point to the superior border of the external auditory meatus). This plane parallels the optic nerve. Contiguous thin sections not exceeding 5mm in thickness are obtained.

Coronal plane scans may be obtained with the patient lying either supine or prone. As with axial plane scans, thin sections should be obtained not exceeding 5mm in thickness. If direct coronal scans cannot be obtained, due to age or physical limitations, sagittal and coronal reformation images can be obtained, provided thin sections in the axial plane are initially obtained, and there is no patient movement during the examination.

The medial and lateral walls of the orbit are visualized. The thin medial wall is contiguous with the ethmoid and sphenoid sinus.

The globe has a spherical configuration. The lens appear hyperdense. The optic nerve has a uniformly dense appearance. It may have an undulating course, and may have variations in shape and size at certain positions where it is not parallel to the x-ray beam (Weisberg *et al.* 1984).

The lacrimal gland is an oval structure, which normally appears to be of increased density.

The medial rectus muscle is noted along the medial orbital wall, whereas the lateral rectus muscle is noted along the lateral orbital wall.

REFERENCES

Adam, R., Greenberg, J. D. (1978) 'The mega cisterna magna.' *Journal of Neurosurgery,* **48,** 190–192.
Gado, M., El Yousef, S. J. (1983) 'Normal functional anatomy of the brain.' *In:* Haaga, J. R., Alifidi, R. J. (Eds.) *Computed Tomography of the Whole Body.* St. Louis: C. V. Mosby. pp. 23–43.
Gonsette, R., Potvliège, G., André-Balisaux, G. (1968) 'La méga/grande citerne: étude clinique, radiologique et anatomopathologique.' *Acta Neurologica Belgica,* **68,** 559–570.
Kramer, R. A. (1977) 'Vermian pseudotumor: a potential pitfall of CT brain scanning with contrast enhancement.' *Neuroradiology,* **13,** 229–230.
Naidich, T. P., Pinto, R. S., Kushner, M. J., Lin, J. P., Kricheff, I. I., Leeds, N. E., Chase, N. E. (1976) 'Evaluation of sellar and parasellar masses by computed tomography.' *Radiology,* **120,** 91–99.
—— Leeds, N. E., Kricheff, I. I., Pudlowski, R. M., Naidich, J. B., Zimmerman, R. D. (1977) 'The tentorium in axial section. 1: Normal CT appearance and non-neoplastic pathology.' *Radiology,* **123,** 631–638.
Swischuk, L. E. (1980) 'Paranasal sinuses, mastoids and facial bones.' *In: Radiology of the Newborn and Young Infant.* Baltimore: Williams & Wilkins. pp. 830–831.
Weisberg, L. A., Nice, C., Katz, M. (1984) *Cerebral Computed Tomography. A Text Atlas. (2nd Edn.)* Philadelphia: W. B. Saunders. pp. 1–356.

3
THE NEONATE

Development of the brain

Toward the end of the fourth week of intra-uterine life, the neural tube expands to form three primary brain vesicles: the forebrain (prosencephalon), midbrain (mesencephalon) and hindbrain (rhombencephalon). During the fifth week there is further division of the forebrain and hindbrain. From the forebrain arise the telencephalon, with its primitive cerebral hemispheres, and the diencephalon, from which the optic vesicles are derived. The metencephalon (which is the anlage of the pons and cerebellum) and the myelencephalon (medulla oblongata) arise from the rhombencephalon (Snell 1983).

Progressive changes in the surface configuration of the brain throughout fetal life have been described by Larroche (1962, 1967). A brief description of her research follows. The surface of the brain hemispheres is generally smooth up to 18 weeks of fetal life. The first fissures to appear are the Sylvian, calcarine and cingular fissures which may be evident as early as 16 weeks. The parieto-occipital fissure develops at 18 weeks. The central (Rolandic) fissure is apparent at 20 to 21 weeks, reaching the interhemispheric fissure at 30 weeks. The olfactory sulci on the ventral surface of the brain are visible by 24 to 26 weeks. The superior temporal sulcus develops at 28 weeks. After this period the secondary sulci appear at a variable rate. From 28 to 40 weeks, fetal age can be accurately estimated from the sulcal pattern and brain size. Brain weight in both premature and term neonates accounts for $1/7$ to $1/10$ of total bodyweight compared with $1/50$ of bodyweight in adults (Larroche 1977).

The water content of the brain is approximately 88 per cent at birth, declining to 82 per cent at two years of age. This coincides with the rising lipid concentration (Dobbing and Sands 1973).

Myelination

The human brain grows most rapidly at the end of the gestational period; this is largely due to the deposition of a considerable amount of myelin (Gilles 1976).

The process of myelination consists of the deposition of a myelin membrane around axons. This begins in the second trimester of pregnancy and continues into adult life (Yakovlev and Lecours 1967, Gilles 1976). Myelination commences in the peripheral nervous system, with the motor roots being involved before the sensory roots. Myelination then appears within the central nervous system in parts of the major sensory and motor systems. Myelination of the cerebral hemisphere occurs after birth, especially in the regions involved with higher level associative functions and sensory discrimination. This process progresses over several decades (Larroche 1977, Volpe 1981*a*).

29

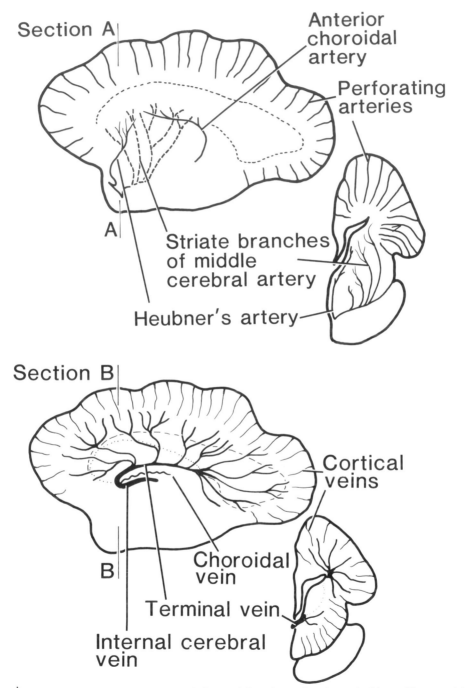

Fig. 3.1. Arterial supply and venous drainage of the subependymal germinal layer. *Top:* arterial supply to the basal ganglia at 29 weeks gestation. *Bottom:* veins related to the caudate nucleus at 30 weeks gestation. (From Hambleton and Wigglesworth 1976, reprinted with permission).

Vascular supply to the developing brain

The internal carotid artery is the sole artery supplying the brain of the early embryo (Pape and Wigglesworth 1979). At the 18mm embryo stage the anterior and middle cerebral arteries have developed from the cranial division, and the posterior cerebral and posterior communicating arteries have developed from the caudal division of the internal carotid artery. Remodeling of the longitudinal neural arteries results in formation of the basilar artery. The vertebral arteries are also derived from a remodeling process which involves the longitudinal anastomoses between the first six cervical intersegmental arteries.

The basal ganglia constitute a much larger portion of the cerebrum in the preterm fetus than the term infant or adult, and develop ahead of the cerebral cortex and white matter (Pape and Wigglesworth 1979). The subependymal germinal matrix tissue, located primarily over the head and body of the caudate nucleus, is supplied mainly by Heubner's artery with an additional blood supply from the terminal branches of the lateral striate arteries and branches of the choroidal arteries (Pape and Wigglesworth 1979). Heubner's artery and the choroidal arteries have been demonstrated to be particularly large in the preterm fetus (Potts *et al.* 1969, Kier 1974, Pape and Wigglesworth 1979).

The germinal matrix is the site of over 80 per cent of neonatal intraventricular hemorrhages. The subependymal matrix contains an immature vascular network which only remodels into a definite capillary bed when the germinal matrix involutes between 32 weeks gestation and term (Pape and Wigglesworth 1979). At this time the artery of Heubner becomes reduced to supplying a small area of the head of the caudate nucleus. The rate of growth of the cortex and white matter surpasses that of the basal ganglia in the last trimester.

Imaging of the neonatal brain

Imaging of the neonatal brain has reached new frontiers with the advent of newer imaging modalities. Neurologic diagnoses were previously established by angiography and ventriculography, which placed the neonate at risk, or by autopsy studies. Ultrasound (which does not involve ionizing radiation) and CT have made a major impact on neonatal neurologic disorders, especially intracranial hemorrhage. Positron Emission Tomography (PET) enables measurement of regional bloodflow in the neonate with high resolution and little risk (Volpe *et al.* 1983). Magnetic Resonance Imaging, or Nuclear Magnetic Resonance (NMR), which involves no ionizing radiation, has the potential to revolutionize diagnostic imaging of the neonatal brain.

CT appearances of the preterm and term neonates

There is a relatively high water content and low lipid content of the brain at birth, as described above. The CT attenuation numbers of infants of 23 to 29 weeks gestation are 7 to 19 Hounsfield units for white matter, 14 to 27 Hounsfield units for gray matter, and 8 to 11 Hounsfield units for ventricular cerebrospinal fluid (Fitz, cited by Harwood-Nash and Flodmark 1982).

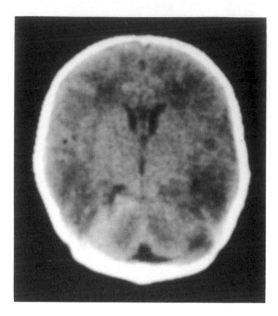

Fig. 3.2. Neonate. Non-contrast head CT scan. Areas of low density are present in the frontal and occipital regions. A cavum septi pellucidi is present between the frontal horns of the lateral ventricles.

The 'normal' CT appearances of preterm and term infants are variable. The findings of Picard *et al.* (1980) and Fitz (1981) will be described.

SKULL VAULT

The skull vault appears thin and of low density due to incomplete ossification. There may be an asymmetric appearance, which is attributed to the position in which the infant had been lying prior to the scan, and also to vault malleability and height of the CT section.

SUBARACHNOID SPACES, CISTERNS AND FISSURES

The subarachnoid space is large in the premature infant scanned at 24 to 27 weeks. The occipital subarachnoid space is particularly large at this age, with mild decrease occurring between 28 and 32 weeks. The subarachnoid space remains large until term and up to a year beyond this. A wide variability in the width of the subarachnoid space has been demonstrated by Kleinman *et al.* (1983).

The interhemispheric fissure is visible at 24 to 27 weeks gestational age, defining normal gray matter cortex on either side. Obliteration of the interhemispheric fissure is produced by subarachnoid hemorrhage. The central sulcus and Sylvian fissures are prominent at 26 to 27 weeks. The Sylvian fissure may remain prominent from 27 weeks on to term.

The superior cerebellar and quadrigeminal cisterns appear prominent at 24 to 27 weeks. The basal cisterns are large from 24 weeks to term, and continue to maintain this appearance for the first five to six years of life.

VENTRICULAR SYSTEM

The lateral and third ventricles are visualized at 24 weeks. The fourth ventricle is seen thereafter. Visualization of the ventricular system may be poor at 24 to 27 weeks because of the similar density of adjacent structures. At 28 to 32 weeks the ventricles may appear smaller than at 24 to 27 weeks, but are larger than the normal term infant. At this age the cavum septum pellucidum is well visualized. This structure is present in virtually all premature infants and in a large number of fullterm infants (see Chapter 4).

At 24 to 27 weeks most of the brain parenchyma is of a homogeneous low density, with a slightly mottled appearance. The cortical strips on either side of the interhemispheric fissure and in the region of the Sylvian fissures are of relatively increased density. The cerebellum at this age has a homogeneous appearance, slightly denser than the cerebrum.

At 28 weeks the cerebral peduncles and central periventricular substance appear denser than the insular cortex. The germinal matrix may be clearly defined. This normal appearance may have been previously ascribed to a subependymal hemorrhage (Fitz and Martin, cited by Harwood-Nash and Flodmark 1982). The germinal matrix typically has a symmetric distribution, unlike a hemorrhage which is commonly restricted to the head of the caudate nucleus with frequent extension asymmetrically into the periventricular white matter (Pape et al. 1983).

The cortical or gray matter strips are less well defined but are thicker at 28 to 32 weeks. The gray matter continues to become thicker with increasing gestational age.

At 34 weeks the central periventricular areas and brainstem are relatively denser than the insular cortex. At 39 weeks the brainstem and central areas appear denser than the insular cortex. The relatively low density of the posterolateral frontal cortex decreases considerably. The low-density areas in the anterior frontal periventricular areas and adjacent to the occipital horns persists. This 'normal' appearance of the preterm infant brain was previously often attributed to periventricular leukomalacia (Fitz and Martin, cited by Harwood-Nash and Flodmark 1982). Cortical gyri are present but the sulci are narrow in comparison to those of premature infants.

Periventricular leukomalacia
Periventricular leukomalacia or infarction is the major non-hemorrhagic lesion found in preterm infants dying within the neonatal period (Larroche 1977). There are discrete foci of necrosis which are situated in the white matter adjacent to the external angles of the lateral ventricles (Volpe 1981a). Areas which are particularly involved are the centrum semiovale, optic and acoustic radiations, which are related to the frontal, occipital and temporal horns respectively.

The condition was first described by Virchow (1867), who attributed the etiology of the periventricular white matter lesions to infection. Other theories proposed were circulatory changes during parturition (Rydberg 1932) and the driving force of parturition (Schwartz 1961). Banker and Larroche (1962) first considered this entity as a form of neonatal anoxic encephalopathy. The areas involved were correlated with areas of poor vascularization in the watershed territory of blood supply (the 'border zone' theory). DeReuck *et al.* (1972) also demonstrated the occurrence of periventricular leukomalacia in arterial border zones between ventriculo-petal and ventriculo-fugal arterial branches. Hypotension or decreased cerebral perfusion producing damage at the arterial end zones of perfusion is believed to be the main cause.

Congestion and infarction of veins within the germinal matrix was postulated by Towbin (1968, 1969) to be the underlying cause of hypoxia in the fetus and newborn. The rôle of an endotoxin has also been incriminated by Larroche (1977) and Gilles *et al.* (1977).

This lesion occurs especially in premature infants, with postnatal survival of more than a few days, and in infants with cardiorespiratory disturbance (Volpe 1981*a*).

Coagulation necrosis is the earliest feature histologically. Reactive astrocytosis ensues over the next few weeks with liquefaction of the central areas of large lesions resulting in cavity formation. These cavities seldom communicate with the ventricular system in contrast to posthemorrhagic porencephalic cysts (Pape 1981).

CT appearances
The diagnosis of periventricular leukomalacia previously made only on a pathologic basis has been readily facilitated by the advent of CT and real-time ultrasound. Although the criteria for the diagnosis by ultrasound are well established, CT is considered preferable in this instance (Volpe 1982, Rumack and Johnson 1983).

Di Chiro *et al.* (1978) demonstrated symmetric periventricular areas of decreased attenuation, especially in the frontal region. This decreased attenuation is attributed to increased water content of that part of the brain, representing an area of reversible hypoxic brain damage, or infarction. This appearance is very similar to the undermyelination in a premature infant (Harwood-Nash and Flodmark 1982), so the findings must be correlated with the clinical history of perinatal or neonatal hypoxia, or respiratory distress syndrome, and clinical confirmation of frank signs of brain dysfunction (Estrada *et al.* 1980). After four to six weeks, a follow-up scan is recommended for the accurate evaluation of these patients (Goldberg 1983).

Intracranial hemorrhage
Intracranial hemorrhage is the most significant neurologic problem of the neonate. The four types of intracranial hemorrhage encountered are periventricular, subdural, subarachnoid and intracerebellar (Volpe 1979).

Periventricular hemorrhage
Periventricular hemorrhage comprises the commonest and most serious form of intracranial hemorrhage in the neonate (Volpe 1981*a*). The advent of the newer imaging modalities, real-time ultrasound and computed tomography, have revealed the extremely high incidence of intracranial hemorrhage in this age-group (Pevsner *et al.* 1976, Krishnamoorthy *et al.* 1977, Papile *et al.* 1978).

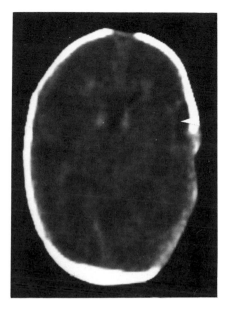

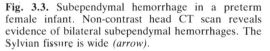

Fig. 3.3. Subependymal hemorrhage in a preterm female infant. Non-contrast head CT scan reveals evidence of bilateral subependymal hemorrhages. The Sylvian fissure is wide *(arrow)*.

Pathogenesis

The vast majority of periventricular hemorrhages occur within the subependymal germinal matrix at the head of the caudate nucleus and at the level of the foramen of Monro. Hemorrhages in infants of 28 weeks gestational age or less have been found over the body of the caudate nucleus (Hambleton and Wigglesworth 1976) and in the choroid plexus in mature infants (Donat *et al.* 1978). This variation in site with gestational age suggests that maturity of the germinal layer capillary bed may be the determining factor in the location of bleeding (Hambleton and Wigglesworth 1976). Hemorrhages are occasionally also noted in the matrix lateral to the temporal and occipital horns (Volpe 1981*a*).

The subependymal germinal matrix which persists in the preterm infant provides poor support for the numerous small vessels. The pathogenesis has been attributed by Volpe (1981*b*) to intravascular, vascular, and extravascular factors.

(a) INTRAVASCULAR FACTORS

1. *Cerebral bloodflow distribution.* Because of the prominence of the vascular supply to the subependymal germinal matrix, any factors which produce increased cerebral bloodflow will result in over-perfusion of the periventricular region.

2. *Cerebral bloodflow regulation.* Regional bloodflow within the periventricular region is extremely sensitive to changes in arterial blood pressure. Vascular autoregulation, immature to begin with, may be further impaired in the neonatal brain by slight asphyxia (Lou *et al.* 1979).

3. *Venous pressure.* Increased venous pressure (obstruction to venous return) may result from pneumothorax, stasis and thrombosis (more rarely) induced by the abrupt change in direction ('U-turn') of draining veins uniting to form the internal cerebral veins.

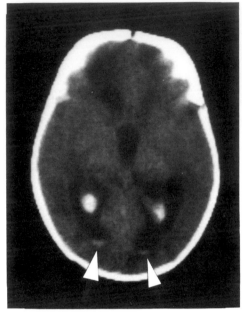 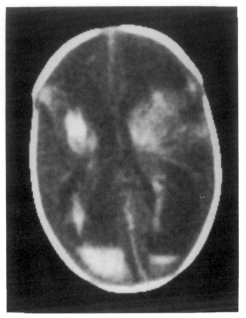

Fig. 3.4. Choroid plexus hemorrhage and intraventricular hemorrhage. Term male infant with seizures. Non-contrast head CT scan. Hemorrhages are present within choroid plexi bilaterally. CSF blood fluid levels *(arrows)* are present within occipital horns of lateral ventricles.

Fig. 3.5. Subependymal, intraventricular and parenchymal hemorrhage. 29 week preterm male infant. Non-contrast head CT scan. Bilateral subependymal hemorrhages in association with parenchymal and intraventricular hemorrhages are present.

(b) VASCULAR FACTORS

The capillary bed within the germinal matrix is immature (Pape and Wigglesworth 1979) and may thus be more prone to rupture. The endothelium of small blood vessels may be directly impaired by hypoxia or its associated metabolic consequences. Hypoxia may also precipitate circulatory failure, resulting in venous congestion (Volpe 1978).

(c) EXTRAVASCULAR FACTORS

Increased fibrinolytic activity has been found in the periventricular region of the preterm infant by Gilles *et al.* (1971). This may account for extension of the hemorrhage into the surrounding cerebral parenchyma or ventricular system (Volpe 1981*b*). Additional contributing factors are hypercapnea, hyperosmolarity, and coagulation defects.

Grading of periventricular-intraventricular hemorrhage
Papile *et al.* (1978) defined four grades:
  I: subependymal hemorrhage
 II: intraventricular hemorrhage without ventricular dilatation
 III: intraventricular hemorrhage with ventricular dilatation
 IV: intraventricular hemorrhage with parenchymal hemorrhage.

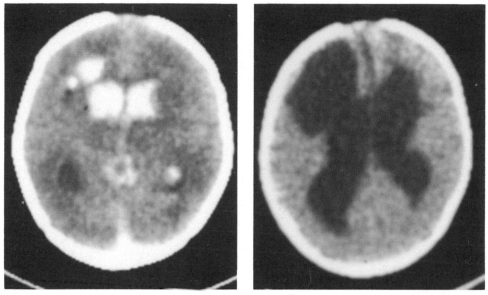

Fig. 3.6. Intraventricular and parenchymal hemorrhage with progression to encephaloclastic porencephaly. Preterm infant. Non-contrast scans. *Top:* intraventricular hemorrhage within both lateral ventricles and third ventricle. *Bottom:* hydrocephalus is demonstrated on follow-up CT scan. Area of right hemorrhage is now replaced by low-density area of encephaloclastic porencephaly.

CT *appearances*

The rôle of CT scanning in the demonstration of periventricular-intraventricular hemorrhages is well established (Pevsner *et al.* 1976, Papile *et al.* 1978, Harwood-Nash and Flodmark 1982). CT demonstrates the location and extent of the hemorrhage (Figs. 3.3, 3.4, 3.5, 3.6). In some instances the underlying cause of hemorrhage (*e.g.* arteriovenous malformation) may be detected. Ventricular size is readily demonstrated. Sequential scans may reveal progression to porencephaly.

(a) HEMORRHAGE

Hemorrhage is readily identified by the areas of increased absorption values. The appearances can be correlated with the grading system of Papile, as described above. As there is a change in the character and composition of blood clots with time, the ventricular size will vary and thus grading may not be dependable (Flodmark *et al.* 1980).

(b) VENTRICULAR SIZE

Ventricular dilatation begins within two weeks of the onset of hemorrhage, pre-dating the increase in head growth by days to weeks (Volpe *et al.* 1977). The incidence of progressive increase in ventricular size following intraventricular hemorrhage in different series varies from 18 to 32 per cent (Harwood-Nash and Flodmark 1982).

Hydrocephalus is related directly to the size of hemorrhage, occurring in 25

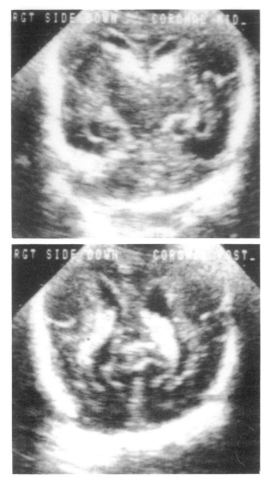

Fig. 3.7. Periventricular-intraventricular hemorrhages demonstrated by real-time ultrasonography. *Left:* coronal ultrasound scan. Subependymal hemorrhages demonstrated bilaterally. These are detected as highly echogenic lesions adjacent to and inferior to the lateral ventricles. *Right:* coronal ultrasound scan. Hydrocephalus with intraventricular hemorrhages bilaterally.

per cent of survivors of mild to moderate hemorrhage and 50 to 75 per cent of survivors of moderate to severe hemorrhage (Volpe 1979). This appears days or weeks after the development of ventricular dilatation (Korobkin 1975).

(c) PORENCEPHALY

Porencephaly may develop at the site of intraventricular hemorrhage, developing weeks later. This is attributed to focal cerebral destruction rather than periventricular encephalomalacia (Pasternak *et al.* 1980). The CT appearance of porencephaly is that of a low-density lesion, corresponding to the previous site of hemorrhage (Fig. 3.6).

Accuracy of CT in detection of neonatal hemorrhage

Germinal matrix hemorrhage occurring in very immature neonates (less than 32 weeks) is easily detected by CT if greater than 5mm in size (Pape *et al.* 1983). The normal vascular germinal matrix is readily demonstrated due to the improved resolution of modern CT scanners (Harwood-Nash and Flodmark 1982) and may simulate a germinal layer hemorrhage. The normal germinal layer has a symmetric distribution, in contrast with the localized area of hemorrhage usually confined to the head of the caudate nucleus and extending asymmetrically into the periventricular white matter (Pape *et al.* 1983).

These authors found that coexisting germinal matrix hemorrhage or intracerebral hemorrhages were not accurately distinguished from massive intraventricular hemorrhage due to averaging effect.

Protocol for neonatal brain imaging
Although protocols for imaging of the neonatal brain will vary between institutions, the choice of modality will ultimately be decided by the clinical problem at hand, and the optimal time at which the study is considered appropriate.

The rôle of both CT and real-time ultrasonography in neonatal brain imaging is well established, with a plethora of reports on their respective merits in the medical literature. Real-time ultrasonography has made a major impact on the imaging of the neonatal brain (Johnson and Rumack 1980, Babcock and Han 1981) (Fig. 3.7).

Advantages of real-time ultrasonography over CT include the non-ionizing form of imaging, the ease of performing the procedure, and ability to obtain the study within the isolette obviating the need to disrupt vital life-support systems. Ventricular size is easily documented and quantitated by this modality (Pape *et al.* 1979).

Preterm infants
There is a high incidence of germinal matrix and intraventricular hemorrhages on the first postnatal day, varying from 40 to 50 per cent (Perlman and Volpe 1982) to 90 per cent (Bejar *et al.* 1980). Progression of the hemorrhages will occur in 10 to 20 per cent of cases (Perlman and Volpe 1982, Shankaran *et al.* 1982). In view of this high incidence of hemorrhage, ultrasonography is performed within the first week. Harwood-Nash and Flodmark (1982) recommend real-time ultrasonography within 48 hours of birth and up to seven to 10 days after birth. CT is also indicated after the ultrasound examination if the hemorrhage is very extensive or if the clinical findings are worse than the initial findings on ultrasound examination (Harwood-Nash and Flodmark 1982). Additional indications for CT include suspected hemorrhage within the posterior fossa (Harwood-Nash and Flodmark 1982), if a peripheral lesion appears most likely, and if neurologic signs are present (Rumack and Johnson 1983).

Term infants
Ultrasonography is the initial modality in infants with increasing head size, infection acquired *in utero,* possible arteriovenous malformation, or clinical signs of central nervous system malformation (Rumack and Johnson 1983).

CT is indicated for infants with both asphyxia and trauma, neonatal seizure, infection and tumor (Rumack and Johnson 1983).

REFERENCES

Babcock, D. S., Han, B. K. (1981) 'The accuracy of high resolution, real time ultrasonography of the head in infancy.' *Radiology,* **139,** 665–676.

Banker, B. Q., Larroche, J.-C. L. (1962) 'Periventricular leukomalacia of infancy.' *Archives of Neurology,* **7,** 386-410.

Bejar, R., Curbelo, V., Coen, R., Leopold, G., James, H., Gluck, L. (1980) 'Diagnosis and follow up of intraventricular and intracerebral hemorrhages by ultrasound studies of infant's brains through the fontanelles and sutures.' *Pediatrics,* **66,** 661–673.

DeReuck, J., Chattha, A. S., Richardson, E. P., (1972) 'Pathogenesis and evolution of periventricular leukomalacia in infancy.' *Archives of Neurology,* **27,** 229–236.

DiChiro, G., Arimitsu, T., Pellock, J. M., Landes, R. D. (1978) 'Periventricular leukomalacia related to neonatal anoxia: recognition by computed tomography.' *Journal of Computer Assisted Tomography,* **2,** 352–356.

Dobbing, J., Sands, J. (1973) 'Quantitative growth and development of human brain.' *Archives of Disease in Childhood,* **48,** 757–767.

Donat, J. F., Okazaki, H., Kleinberg, F., Reagan, T. J. (1978) 'Intraventricular hemorrhages in fullterm and premature infants.' *Mayo Clinic Proceedings,* **53,** 437–441.

Estrada, M., El-Gammal, T., Dyken, P. R. (1980) 'Periventricular low attenuations. A normal finding in computerized scans of neonates?' *Archives of Neurology,* **37,** 754–756.

Fitz, C. (1981) 'Computed tomography in the newborn.' *In:* Korobkin, R., Guilleminault, C. (Eds.) *Progress in Perinatal Neurology.* Baltimore: Williams & Wilkins. pp. 85–120.

Flodmark, O., Fitz, C. R., Harwood-Nash, D. C. (1980) 'CT diagnosis and short term prognosis of intracranial hemorrhage and hypoxic/ischemic brain damage in neonates.' *Journal of Computer Assisted Tomography,* **4,** 775–787.

Gilles, F. H. (1976) 'Myelination in the neonatal brain.' *Human Pathology,* **7,** 244–248.

—— Averill, D. R., Kerr, C. S. (1977) 'Neonatal endotoxin encephalopathy.' *Annals of Neurology,* **2,** 49–56.

—— Price, R. A., Kevy, S. V., Berenberg, W. (1971) 'Fibrinolytic activity in the ganglionic eminence of the premature human brain.' *Biology of the Neonate,* **18,** 426–432.

Goldberg, H. I. (1983) 'Stroke.' *In:* Lee, S. H., Rao, K. C. V. G. (Eds.) *Cranial Computer Tomography.* New York: McGraw Hill. pp. 583–657.

Hambleton, G., Wigglesworth, J. S. (1976) 'Origin of intraventricular hemorrhage in the preterm infant.' *Archives of Disease in Childhood,* **5,** 651–659.

Harwood-Nash, D. C., Flodmark, O. (1982) 'Diagnostic imaging of the neonatal brain: review and protocol.' *American Journal of Neuroradiology,* **3,** 103–115.

Johnson, M. L., Rumack, C. M. (1980) 'Ultrasonic evaluation of the neonatal brain.' *Radiologic Clinics of North America,* **18,** 117–131.

Kier, E. L. (1974) 'Fetal cerebral arteries: a phylogenetic and autogenetic study.' *In:* Newton, T. H., Potts, D. G. (Eds.) *Radiology of the Skull and Brain, Volume 2, Book 1.* St. Louis: C. V. Mosby. pp. 1089–1130.

Kleinman, P. K., Zito, J. L., Davidson, R. I., Raptopoulos, V. (1983) 'The subarachnoid spaces in children: normal variations in size.' *Radiology,* **147,** 455–457.

Korobkin, R. (1975) 'The relationship between head circumference and the development of communicating hydrocephalus following intraventricular hemorrhage.' *Pediatrics,* **56,** 74–77.

Krishnamoorthy, K. S., Fernandez, R. A., Momose, K. J., DeLong, G. R., Moylan, F. M. B., Todres, I. D., Shannon, D. C. (1977) 'Evaluation of neonatal intracranial hemorrhage by computerized tomography.' *Pediatrics,* **59,** 165–172.

Larroche, J.-C. L. (1962) 'Quelques aspects anatomiques du développement cérébral.' *Biologia Neonatorum,* **4,** 126–153.

—— (1967) 'Maturation morphologique du système nerveux central: ses rapports avec le développement ponderal du foetus et son âge gestationnel.' *In:* Minkowski, A. (Ed.) *Regional Development of the Brain in Early Life.* Oxford: Blackwell. pp. 247–256.

—— (1977) *Developmental Pathology of the Neonate.* Amsterdam: Excerpta Medica. pp. 320–353.

Lou, H. C., Lassen, N. H., Friis-Nansen, B. (1979) 'Impaired autoregulation of cerebral blood flow in the distressed newborn.' *Journal of Pediatrics,* **94,** 118–121.

Pape, K. E. (1981) 'Intraventricular hemorrhage: diagnosis and outcome.' *Birth Defects,* **17,** 143–151.

—— Blackwell, R. J., Cusick, G., Sherwood, A., Houang, M. T., Thorburn, R., Reynolds, E. O. R. (1979) 'Ultrasound detection of brain damage in preterm infants.' *Lancet,* **1,** 1261–1264.

40

—— Wigglesworth, J. S. (1979) *Haemorrhage, Ischemia and the Perinatal Brain. Clinics in Developmental Medicine, Nos. 69/70.* London: S.I.M.P. with Heinemann; Philadelphia: J. B. Lippincott. pp. 11–38.

—— Bennett-Britton, S., Szymonowicz, W., Martin, D. J., Fitz, C. R., Becker, L. (1983) 'Diagnostic accuracy of neonatal brain imaging: a postmortem correlation of computed tomography and ultrasound scans.' *Journal of Pediatrics,* **102,** 275–280.

Papile, L., Burstein, J., Burstein, R., Koffler, H. (1978) 'Incidence and evolution of subependymal and intraventricular hemorrhage: a study of infants with birth weights less than 1,500 gm.' *Journal of Pediatrics,* **92,** 529–534.

Pasternak, J. F., Mantovani, J. F., Volpe, J. J. (1980) 'Porencephaly from periventricular intracerebral hemorrhage in a premature infant.' *American Journal of Diseases of Children,* **134,** 673–675.

Perlman, J. M., Volpe, J. J. (1982) 'Cerebral blood flow velocity in relation to intraventricular hemorrhage in the premature newborn infant.' *Journal of Pediatrics,* **100,** 956–959.

Pevsner, P. H., Garcia-Bunuel, R., Leeds, N., Finkelstein, M. (1976) 'Subependymal and intra-ventricular hemorrhage in neonates.' *Radiology,* **119,** 111–114.

Picard, L., Claudon, M., Roland, J., JeanJean, E., Andre, M., Plenat, P., Vert, P. (1980) 'Cerebral computed tomography in premature infants, with an attempt at staging developmental features.' *Journal of Computer Assisted Tomography,* **4,** 435–444.

Potts, D. G., Suave, G. T., Bergeron, R. T. (1969) 'The developing brain: correlations between radiologic and anatomical findings.' *Acta Radiologica [Diagnosis],* **9,** 430–439.

Rumack, C. M., Johnson, M. L. (1983) 'Role of computed tomography and ultrasound in neonatal brain imaging.' *CT: The Journal of Computed Tomography,* **7,** 17–29.

Rydberg, E. (1932) 'Cerebral injury in newborn children consequent on birth trauma: with an inquiry into the normal and pathological anatomy of the neuroglia.' *Acta Pathologica et Microbiologica Scandinavica (Suppl.),* **10,** 1–247.

Schwartz, P. (1961) *Birth Injuries of the Newborn: Morphology, Pathogenesis, Clinical Pathology and Prevention.* New York: Hafner. p. 384.

Shankaran, S., Slovis, T. L., Bedard, M. P., Poland, R. L. (1982) 'Sonographic classification of intracranial hemorrhage. A prognostic indicator of mortality, morbidity and short-term neurologic outcome.' *Journal of Pediatrics,* **100,** 469–475.

Snell, R. S. (1983) *Clinical Embryology for Medical Students. 3rd edn.* Boston: Little Brown. pp. 273–299.

Towbin, A. (1968) 'Cerebral intraventricular hemorrhage and subependymal matrix infarction in the fetus and premature newborn.' *American Journal of Pathology,* **52,** 121–140.

—— (1969) 'Cerebral hypoxic damage in fetus and newborn: basic patterns and their clinical significance.' *Archives of Neurology,* **20,** 35–43.

Virchow, R. (1867) 'Zur pathologischen Anatomie des Gehirns. 1. Congenitale encephalitis und myelitis.' *Virchow Archiv für pathologische Anatomie,* **38,** 129–138.

Volpe, J. J. (1978) 'Neonatal periventricular hemorrhage: past, present, and future.' *Journal of Pediatrics,* **92,** 693–696.

—— (1979) 'Intracranial hemorrhage in the newborn: current understanding and dilemmas.' *Neurology,* **29,** 632–635.

—— (1981a) *Neurology of the Newborn.* Philadelphia: W. B. Saunders. pp. 28–59.

—— (1981b) 'Current concepts in neonatal medicine: neonatal intraventricular hemorrhage.' *New England Journal of Medicine,* **304,** 886–891.

—— (1982) 'Anterior fontanel: window to the neonatal brain.' *Journal of Pediatrics,* **100,** 395-398.

—— Pasternak, J. F., Allan, W. C. (1977) 'Ventricular dilation preceding rapid head growth following neonatal intracranial hemorrhage.' *American Journal of Diseases in Children,* **131,** 1212–1215.

—— Jerscovitch, P., Perlman, J. M., Raichle, M. E. (1983) 'Positron emission tomography in the newborn: extensive impairment of regional cerebral blood flow with intraventricular hemorrhage and hemorrhagic intracerebral involvement.' *Pediatrics,* **72,** 589–601.

Yakovlev, P. I., Lecours, A. R. (1967) 'The myelogenetic cycles of regional maturation of the brain.' *In:* Minkowski, A. (Ed.) *Regional Development of the Brain in Early Life.* Oxford: Blackwell. pp. 3–70.

41

4
CONGENITAL ABNORMALITIES

The nervous system is frequently affected by congenital defects. The initiation of most congenital malformations occurs between the second and sixth weeks of gestation. Folding of the neural plate of the embryo occurs between the middle and end of the third week. Two processes basic to the causation of congenital malformations are genetic abnormalities and early intra-uterine environmental influences.

Chromosomal abnormalities are believed to account for 10 per cent of congenital defects, inheritance (dominant or recessive) for 20 per cent, and environmental factors for 10 per cent. In 60 per cent of cases the underlying cause is unknown (Holt 1963). A World Health Organization study revealed an incidence of 2.66 central nervous system anomalies per 1000 births, with anencephaly, hydrocephalus, and spina bifida (with or without meningocele) being commonest (Stevenson *et al.* 1966). CT is an excellent modality for the demonstration of congenital defects. A wide spectrum of both common and uncommon disorders (Fig. 4.1) are detected by this modality.

Cerebral malformations have been classified by DeMyer (1971) into disorders of cytogenesis, organogenesis and histogenesis (Fig. 4.2).

Disorders of organogenesis
Closure disorders
ENCEPHALOCELE
An encephalocele is a protrusion of cranial contents beyond the normal confines of the skull. The cranial defect is termed cranium bifidum, analogous to spina bifida. Types of encephalocele include:
1. Cranial meningocele (meninges and cerebrospinal fluid)
2. Encephalomeningocele (brain tissue and meninges)
3. Hydroencephalomeningocele (brain tissue, a portion of ventricle and meninges) (French 1982)

Encephaloceles may occur within the occipital area (Fig. 4.3), cranial vault, cranial base and fronto-ethmoidal areas. Occipital location is commonest in the Western hemisphere, with marked female preponderance (French 1982). Most occipital encephaloceles are associated with Chiari II malformation. They are located above, below or through the torcular herophili (Byrd *et al.* 1978*b*).

Frontal and ethmoidal encephaloceles are associated with a forehead or nasal mass. Basal encephaloceles may present with nasopharyngeal masses (Fitz 1983). The amount of brain within the encephalocele can usually be visualized on CT, but angiography may be required in some instances to demonstrate what part of the brain is involved (Fitz 1983).

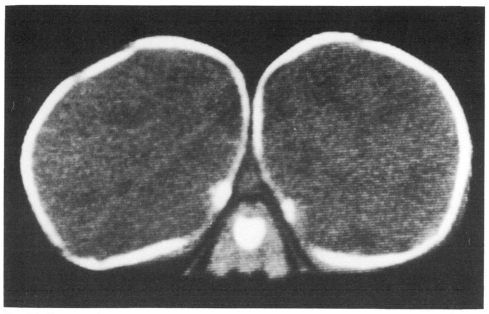

Fig. 4.1. Siamese twins. Non-contrast CT scan demonstrates complete duplication of the central nervous system. (Courtesy of Ehsan Afshani MD, Buffalo.)

Cavum septi pellucidi and cavum vergae

The cavum septi pellucidi (CSP) and cavum vergae (CV) are two cavities which are essentially the same structure, being located anteriorly and posteriorly to an arbitrary vertical plane which is formed by the column of the fornix. The two cavities usually have free communication, but may occasionally be separated by columns of the fornix (Shaw and Alvord 1969).

The main cavity has been shown by Rakic and Yakovlev (1968) to develop from secondary cleavage with necrobiosis in the site of fusion of the cerebral hemispheres (banks of the sulcus medianus telencephali medii).

The cavum vergae begins to disappear at six months of gestation, and the cavum septi pellucidi begins to close just before term and is finally closed at two months after birth. The incidence of cavum septi pellucidi in premature infants is 100 per cent (Larroche and Baudey 1961).

Although cavities within the septum pellucidum are considered to be clinically significant, symptomatic congenital cysts have been described with varying congenital presentations (Dandy 1931, Craig *et al.* 1953).

The CT appearance of a cavum septi pellucidi is that of a midline CSF-containing space, situated anteriorly between the frontal horns of the lateral ventricles (Byrd *et al.* 1978*b*) (Figs. 4.4, 4.5). The third ventricle is in normal position.

The cavum vergae is demonstrated on CT as a midline CSF-containing space situated posteriorly beyond the interventricular foramina of Monro (Fig. 4.5).

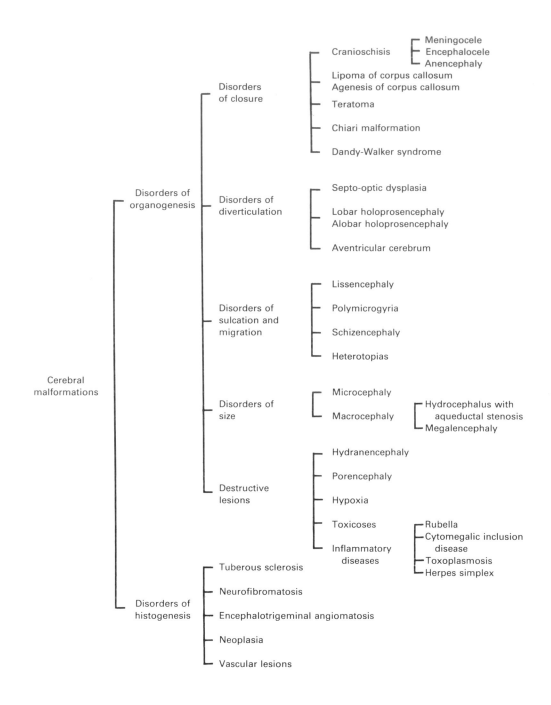

Fig. 4.2. DeMyer classification of cerebral malformations (1971), modified by Harwood-Nash and Fitz (1976*a*) (Reprinted by permission.)

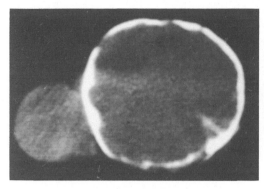

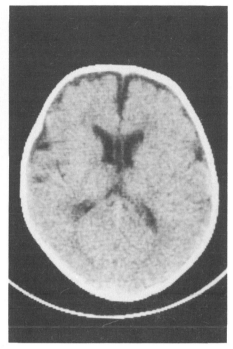

Fig. 4.3 *(above)*. Occipital encephalocele. Non-contrast CT scan demonstrates a large posterior occipital encephalocele-containing brain and CSF. There is also associated Luckenschadel (craniolacunia). The scan was obtained with the infant lying on his side because of the large size of the encephalocele.

Fig. 4.4 *(right)*. Cavum septi pellucidi: preterm male infant non-contrast CT scan demonstrates the cavum septi pellucidi as a CSF-containing space between the two frontal horns of the lateral ventricles.

Cavum veli interpositi

The cavum veli interpositi is a triangular CSF-containing space which represents dilatation of the cistern of the velum interpositum.

It is a normal finding, commonly seen in young children on CT; it is shaped like a bishop's mitre, and situated between the posterior roof of the third ventricle and the floor of each lateral ventricle (Byrd *et al.* 1978*b*) (Fig. 4.5).

Lipoma

Intracranial lipomas are rare tumors of maldevelopmental origin. They are usually found at or near the mid-sagittal plane. The corpus callosum is the commonest site, although the tuber cinereum, quadrigeminal plate and cerebellopontine angle cisterns may also be involved less frequently (Fukui *et al.* 1977).

Many patients are asymptomatic and thus the lesions are only noted incidentally. The advent of CT has greatly increased the detection rate. Prior to the introduction of CT, lipoma of the corpus callosum was diagnosed on plain skull radiographs by the presence of symmetric U-shaped midline calcification, or less commonly midline amorphous calcification (Larsen and Stiris 1970), often with radiolucency representing fat.

The diagnosis on CT is made by the typical appearance of a low-density area consistent with fat (−100 Hounsfield units, −1000 scale) (Fig 4.6). There is no change in density following contrast administration (Faerber and Wolpert 1978, Zimmerman *et al.* 1979*a*). As lipomas of the corpus callosum are frequently

45

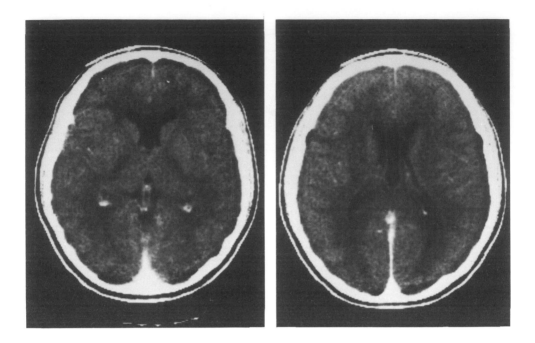

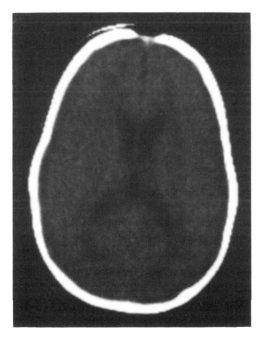

Fig. 4.5. Cava septi pellucidi et vergae. 15-year-old girl. Contrast-enhanced CT scans. *Above left:* cavum septi pellucidi is demonstrated between the frontal horns. *Above right:* cavum vergae is demonstrated as a larger CSF-containing space which extends beyond the foramina of Monro. *Left:* cavum veli interpositi. Eight-month-old boy. Non-contrast head CT scan demonstrates a midline triangular CSF-containing space situated between the two lateral ventricles, above the third ventricle.

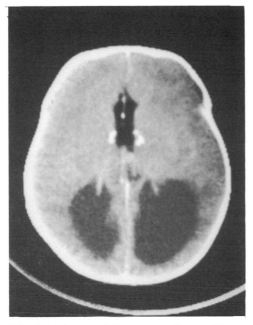 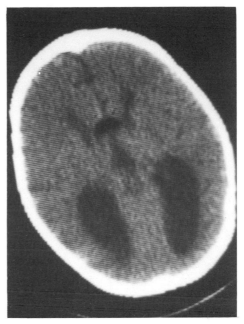

Fig. 4.6. Lipoma of the corpus callosum. Three-year-old girl, non-contrast CT scan shows a tumor of fat density anteriorly within the corpus callosum, with peripheral calcification.

Fig. 4.7. Agenesis of corpus callosum. 2½-year-old boy presenting with hyponatremia and inappropriate antidiuretic hormone secretion. Non-contrast CT scan demonstrates separation of frontal horns of lateral ventricles. Associated lipoma of corpus callosum is also present. (Reproduced by permission of the editor, *Journal of Computer Assisted Tomography*.)

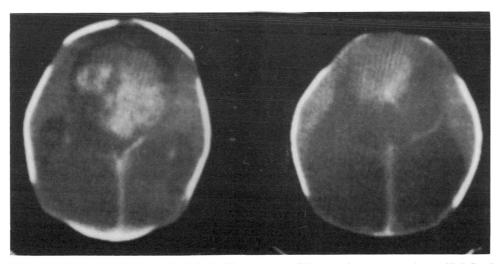

Fig. 4.8. Teratoma. Term male infant. Non-contrast CT scan demonstrates large ill-defined supratentorial mass with distortion of ventricular system.

associated with agenesis of the corpus callosum , the typical CT features of agenesis will be found (see below).

Agenesis of the corpus callosum

The three telencephalic commissures (anterior, callosal, hippocampal) originate from the commissural plate, a thickening in the lamina terminalis. The first fibers of the corpus callosum appear in the third month of intra-uterine life, after which there is rapid growth and expansion (mainly backwards), attaining the adult position by the fifth month (Urich 1976).

There are three forms of agenesis of the corpus callosum (Loeser and Alvord 1968):

1. Total absence of the telecephalic commissures. The onset of complete agenesis occurs before the 11th and 12th weeks of gestation, at which time there is formation of the earliest crossing fibers (Rakic and Yakovlev 1968).

2. Absence of the corpus callosum with preserved anterior and hippocampal commissures.

3. Partial absence of the posterior part of the corpus callosum.

Absence of the corpus callosum may be congenital or acquired. Acquired causes may be vascular or inflammatory in origin, resulting in encephalomalacia and callosal hypoplasia or destruction (Harwood-Nash and Fitz 1976a).

The abnormality may occur as an isolated lesion or may be associated with numerous other congenital malformations, including septo-optic dysplasia, holoprosencephaly, Chiari malformation, Dandy-Walker cyst, microcephaly, arachnoid cyst, encephalocele, midline lipoma, polymicrogyria, and white matter heterotopias (Byrd et al. 1978b). Although most cases occur sporadically, familial examples have been reported (Menkes et al. 1964).

Agenesis of the corpus callosum is also a constituent of the Aicardi syndrome (Aicardi et al. 1965, de Jong et al. 1976). This syndrome occurs only in females and is characterized by infantile spasms, mental retardation, agenesis of the corpus callosum, chorioretinopathy and vertebral abnormalities.

The CT appearances of agenesis of the corpus callosum are characteristic in both axial and coronal planes (Byrd et al. 1978b, Lynn et al. 1980).

1. There is a wide separation of the frontal horns in the axial plane (Fig. 4.7). The frontal horns appear narrow in the absence of hydrocephalus.

2. The frontal horns and bodies of the lateral ventricles have lateral beaks.

3. The occipital horns may appear dilated in comparison to the bodies of the lateral ventricles.

4. The elevated third ventricle is interposed between the bodies of the lateral ventricles, and is usually enlarged.

5. Rarely, an interhemispheric arachnoid cyst may be associated with agenesis of the corpus callosum (Solt et al. 1980).

6. Abnormal proximity of the interhemispheric fissure to the third ventricle on contiguous CT slices. This is considered to be a highly reliable feature and has been called the interhemispheric fissure sign of dysgenesis of the corpus callosum (Sarwar et al. 1984).

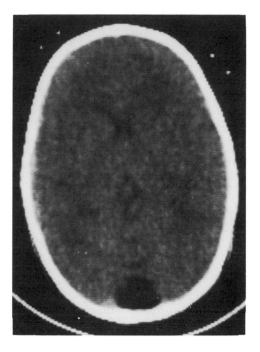

Fig. 4.9. Dermoid. 2¾-year-old girl. Non-contrast CT scan demonstrates a midline low-density mass lesion (−1 Hounsfield units). There is no demonstrable calcification within the mass.

Teratoma, epidermoid, dermoid

Teratoma, epidermoid and dermoid are rare congenital disorders with similar development and clinical course. Epidermoids account for 2 per cent of intracranial neoplasms, teratomas for 0.2 to 0.9 per cent and dermoids for 0.1 to 0.7 per cent (McCormack *et al.* 1978).

Teratomas are primarily located within the pineal region, followed by the suprasellar and posterior fossa regions. These three locations account for approximately two-thirds of intracranial teratomas with the remaining third widely distributed (Russell and Rubinstein 1971, Harwood-Nash and Fitz 1976*b*).

The CT appearances are of masses of mixed density (Fig. 4.8). Fat, soft tissue and osseous components may be recognized. The tumor may rupture into the ventricles, resulting in fat-CSF interfaces (Lee and Rao 1983).

Epidermoids and dermoids develop as displaced embryonic rests. The displacement occurs between the third and fifth weeks *in utero* (Harwood-Nash and Fitz 1976*b*).

Dermoids are cystic lesions usually situated close to the midline, with a predilection for the skull base or posterior fossa. Lesions within the posterior fossa may be intra- or extracerebellar, intra- or extradural, but all are usually associated with a dermal sinus (Harwood-Nash and Fitz 1976*b*).

The age-range is that of the first three decades of life with a slight female preponderance (Lee and Rao 1983).

The CT appearance is that of a cyst wall isodense with surrounding brain (Fig. 4.9). The contents are well marginated with fat density (Zimmerman *et al.* 1979*a*).

49

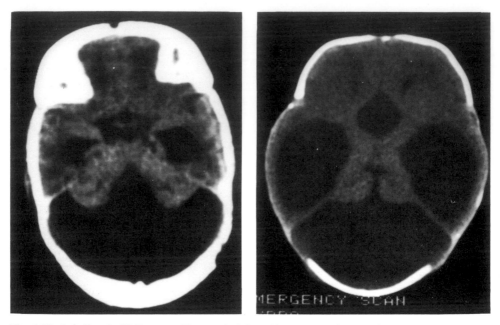

Fig. 4.10. *Left:* Dandy-Walker cyst. Term male infant. Non-contrast CT scan demonstrates a large cyst occupying the entire posterior fossa. There is evidence of obstructive hydrocephalus. (Courtesy of Samuel Wolpert MD, Boston.) *Right:* Dandy-Walker variant. Term male infant. Contrast-enhanced CT scan demonstrates a dilated fourth ventricle with posterior extension through the widened vallecula.

Incomplete calcification may be noted within the cyst wall. Contrast enhancement of the capsule is rare (Lee and Rao 1983).

As with epidermoid and teratoma, a dermoid cyst may rupture into the ventricular and subarachnoid spaces (Laster and Moody 1977, Amendola *et al.* 1978, Zimmerman *et al.* 1979*a*).

Epidermoids are soft tissue masses most commonly located within the cerebellopontine angle. Other sites include the parasellar region and midposterior cranial fossa. The lesions are mainly intradural, but may also be extradural or intraventricular. Epidermoids are usually encountered in adulthood, with an age-range of 25 to 60 years (Lee and Rao 1983). The CT appearance is of low density, closer to CSF than fat because of the keratinized debris and cholesterin (Davis and Taveras 1976, Zimmerman 1979*a*). Calcification may occasionally be present within the tumor. Contrast enhancement has not been observed with these tumors (Kieffer and Lee 1983).

Dandy-Walker syndrome
The Dandy-Walker syndrome is characterized by cystic dilatation of the fourth ventricle, hypoplastic cerebellar hemispheres and absent vermis.

Hydrocephalus in association with these features was described by Sutton (1887), and Dandy and Blackfan (1914) who attributed the underlying cause to be

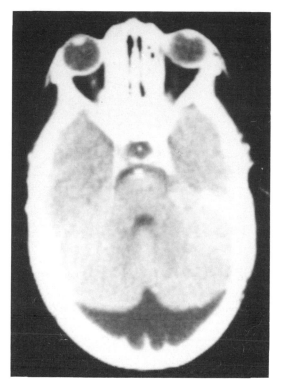

Fig. 4.11. Mega cisterna magna. Two-year-old male. Non-contrast CT scan demonstrates the large retrocerebellar CSF-containing structure. The fourth ventricle is in normal position.

atresia of the foramina of Luschka and Magendie. Benda (1954) concluded that this is a complex developmental anomaly not due to foraminal atresia but to failure of regression of the posterior medullary velum, and absence of the vermis, with resultant cyst formation at the caudal end of the fourth ventricle. Patent foramina were demonstrated in some of these cases. The presence of cerebellar tissue in the cyst wall, demonstrated by Bonnevie and Brodal (1946) and Hart *et al.* (1972), suggests that the cyst is a remnant of the anterior membranous area of the roof of the fourth ventricle. Gardner (1959) has postulated that the entity may be due to a disorder of closure of the neural tube, citing similarities with the Arnold-Chiari malformation.

Associated malformations which may be present include agenesis of the corpus callosum (Benda 1954, Scarcella 1960), gyral anomalies and heterotopias, cleft palate, holoprosencephaly, polydactylism-syndactylism (Hart *et al.* 1972), and encephaloceles (McLaurin 1964).

The syndrome has been reported in siblings, suggesting an inherited malformation (Benda 1954, D'Agostino *et al.* 1963).

The CT appearance of a Dandy-Walker cyst is a large low-density cystic lesion which occupies most of the posterior fossa (Fig. 4.10). The fourth ventricle is not visualized. Tentorial malposition is present, recognized by the inverted malpositioned tentorial bands which bulge outwards and straightening of the normally

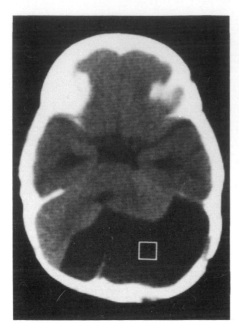

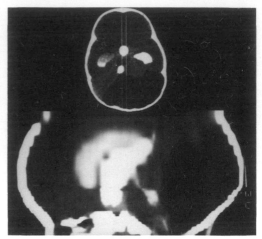

Fig. 4.12. Retrocerebellar arachnoid cyst. Nine-month-old female. *Left:* non-contrast CT scan demonstrates large retrocerebellar cystic mass. *Above:* metrizamide CT. Axial CT scan and sagittal reconstructed images demonstrate large retrocerebellar mass which does not fill with metrizamide.

concave tentorial border. This appearance suggests the presence of the Dandy-Walker syndrome even when there is no ventricular dilatation (Naidich *et al.* 1977).

Dandy-Walker variant
Evagination of the roof of the fourth ventricle posterosuperiorly into the retrocerebellar space was described by Blake in 1900. Evagination accompanying hypoplasia of the inferior vermis with a pouchlike extension of the fourth ventricle containing cerebrospinal fluid (Harwood-Nash and Fitz 1976 *a*) has been referred to as Dandy-Walker variant (Fig. 4.10).

Several entities which must be differentiated from the Dandy-Walker syndrome and Dandy-Walker variant:
1. *The mega cisterna magna.* The cisterna magna lies posterolateral to the fourth ventricle, communicating with it through the vallecula. A very large cisterna magna (mega cisterna magna) may be encountered (Fig. 4.11). Adam and Greenberg (1978) reported an incidence of 0.4 per cent. This is considered to be an anatomic variant usually without clinical significance. Most enlarged cisternae magnae are moderate in size, but a few are large enough to serve as space-occupying lesions and make differentiation difficult from the Dandy-Walker syndrome (Archer *et al.* 1978).
2. *Trapped fourth ventricle (isolated fourth ventricle).* Occlusion of the aqueduct of Sylvius and the foramina of Luschka and Magendie results in dilatation of the fourth ventricle, which becomes isolated from the ventricular system and circulation of cerebrospinal fluid. This phenomenon is most often secondary to previous subarachnoid hemorrhage or meningitis (Zimmerman *et al.* 1978, Scotti *et*

al. 1980). The vermian hypoplasia and abnormality of the tentorium, as described in the Dandy-Walker syndrome, are absent (Fig. 5.12).

3. *Retrocerebellar arachnoid cyst.* Non-visualization of the fourth ventricle may result from invagination of the cyst between the two cerebellar hemispheres (Rao and Harwood-Nash 1983). Metrizamide CT cisternography will be useful in differention of this condition (Drayer *et al.* 1977). The non-communicating posterior fossa extra-axial cyst is visualized as an area of decreased absorption surrounded by metrizamide in surrounding subarachnoid spaces (Fig. 4.12).

The Chiari malformations

In 1891, Chiari classified the cerebellar malformations frequently associated with hydrocephalus into three types. He enlarged his series in 1895. Description of this malformation was actually described previously in 1883 by Cleland. In 1894 Arnold described a case with associated meningomyelocele without hydrocephalus.

CHIARI I MALFORMATION

The type I malformation consists of inferior displacement of the tonsils and cerebellum without displacement of the fourth ventricle or medulla.

Syringomyelia is an associated finding and there may be associated bony malformations, including platybasia, achondroplasia or the Klippel-Feil anomaly (Urich 1976).

Type I changes are encountered occasionally in older children and adults. (Wilkins and Brody 1971).

There are few reports of the CT appearance of the type I malformation (Forbes and Isherwood 1978, Weisberg *et al.* 1981). High-resolution scanners and the use of water soluble contrast medium (Metrizamide) enable the diagnosis of this disorder to be made (Rao and Harwood-Nash 1983). The low position of the cerebellar tonsils separated from the cord may be demonstrated. The widened cord due to syringomyelia may also be readily visualized, although Metrizamide within the central cavity may only be seen on delayed scans (Rao and Harwood-Nash 1983).

CHIARI II MALFORMATION (ARNOLD-CHIARI MALFORMATION)

This is the most common type seen in neonates and infants. As described by Chiari the protrusion of the lower parts of the cerebellum is accompanied by elongation of the fourth ventricle, extending into the spinal canal. There is an associated meningomyelocele. Five types of this malformation have been described by Schwalbe and Gredig (1907):

1. The cerebellar protrusion covers the upper part of the elongated ventricle only.
2. The elongated fourth ventricle contains choroid plexus which is displaced.
3. A substantial portion of the inferior vermis is contained within the cavity of the elongated fourth ventricle.
4. A protrusion of the vermis is situated dorsal to the roof of the fourth ventricle.
5. A thick glial membrane forms the roof of the fourth ventricle. This frequently obliterates the foramen of Magendie, and thus may produce cystic dilatation of the

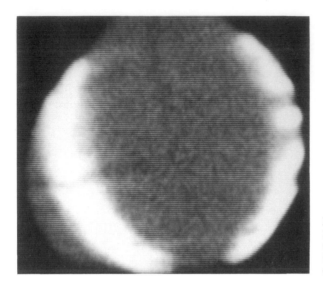

Fig. 4.13. Luckenschadel (cranio-lacunia). Term male infant with Chiari II malformation. Non-contrast CT demonstrates a pitted appearance on the inner table of the skull.

ventricle at this site (Peach 1964).

CT appearances of this malformation, as described extensively by Naidich *et al.* (1980*a, b, c,* 1981), may be divided into three groups:

1. *Abnormalities of the bone and dura*

(a) *Luckenschadel* (craniolacunia, lacunar skull). This is due to dysplasia of the membranous skull bones and is present in the vast majority of patients with the Arnold-Chiari malformation. Luckenschadel usually indicates the presence of an encephalocele, meningocele or myelocele. The lacunae usually disappear by six months of age. Luckenschadel appears as pits or areas of thinning, especially in the upper half of the calvaria and vertex. The appearance on CT is improved by utilizing bone-window images (Fig. 4.13).

(b) *Scalloping of the petrous bone and clivus.* Scalloping of the posteromedial aspects of the petrous bones in patients with the Arnold-Chiari malformation was first described by Kruyff and Jeffs (1966) on plain skull radiographs. On CT the normal posterior convexity of the posterior surface of the petrous pyramid is replaced by concave scalloping or flattening (Fig. 4.14). There is shortening of the internal auditory canals. The petrous ridges and jugular tubercles are usually spared. Naidich *et al.* (1980*a*) believe that the petrous erosion increases with cerebellar growth, enabling greater CT detection of the scalloping with age. It is thus mild in neonates but marked in older children. Scalloping of the clivus is best appreciated on sagittal reconstruction images (Rao and Harwood-Nash 1983).

(c) *Enlargement of the foramen magnum* occurs in approximately 75 per cent of patients with the Arnold-Chiari malformation (Kruyff and Jeffs 1966) (Fig. 4.14). This is best visualized in coronal and sagittal images (Naidich 1981).

54

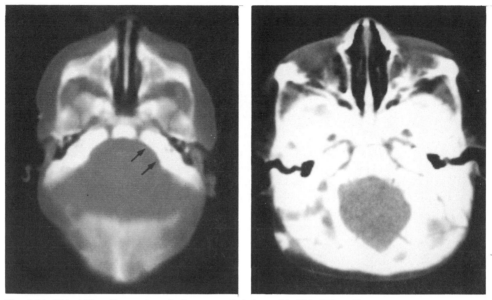

Fig. 4.14. Chiari II malformation. *Left:* term male infant with Chiari II malformation. Non-contrast CT scan demonstrates the typical petrous scalloping with concave posterior surface of the petrous pyramids *(arrows)*. The fourth ventricle is not visible. *Right:* 10-year-old boy with Chiari II malformation and myelomeningocele. Non-contrast CT scan demonstrates a large foramen magnum.

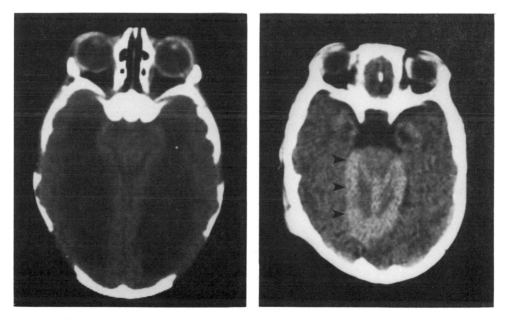

Fig. 4.15. Chiari II malformation. *Left:* three-year-old girl with myelomeningocele. Non-contrast CT scan shows marked beaking of the midbrain. Luckenschadel is also demonstrated on this scan. *Right:* 10-month-old boy with myelomeningocele and hydrocephalus. There is a wide tentorial incisura *(arrowheads)*, through which there has been elevation of the cerebellum.

(d) *Falx.* The falx is always abnormal. There is either partial absence, hypoplasia, and/or fenestration. In most cases the anterior third of the falx is markedly hypoplastic (Peach 1965). On contrast-enhanced axial CT scans falx hypoplasia becomes evident due to failure of visualization of the usual falx blush. Fenestration of the falx is appreciated as an interruption in the linear falx blush.

(e) *Tentorium.* The tentorium has been noted to be hypoplastic in almost all patients with the Chiari II malformation (Peach 1965). Poor development of the tentorial leaves results in an incisura, which is extremely wide from side to side and also elongated in the sagittal plane (Daniel and Strich 1958, Peach 1965). The wide separation of the left and right tentorial blushes is demonstrated on contrast-enhanced axial CT images. Coronal images obtained after contrast administration demonstrate the low insertion of the tentorial leaves and small posterior fossa.

2. *Midbrain and cerebellum*
(a) *Mesencephalic beaking.* Abnormalities of the midbrain are found in all patients with Chiari II malformation (Adeloye 1976, Naidich *et al.* 1980b). The midbrain is beaked with caudal elongation (Fig. 4.15). The magnitude of beaking will be influenced by the angle and level of the CT section. The beaking will be best visualized at lower levels where the midbrain invaginates into the cerebellum.

(b) *Cerebellum.* Numerous abnormalities of the cerebellum have been described. The midline cerebellar portion invaginates to receive the beaked midbrain. Elevation of the cerebellum superiorly through the wide incisura results in the formation of a heart-shaped mass which simulates a neoplasm (Peach 1965, Zimmerman *et al.* 1979b, Naidich *et al.* 1980b). this 'towering' cerebellum is seen on CT as a midline supratentorial mass which often has a prominent lucent pericerebellar cistern. Cerebellar upgrowth was noted in 35 per cent of cases by Peach (1965). The cerebellum may grow forward between the free tentorial edge and brainstem to wrap around the lateral borders of the brainstem. There is eventual separation of midbrain from the hippocampus. With lateral growth to the pons the cerebellopontine angle cisterns are filled partially presenting as cerebellopontine angle masses. The margins of the cerebellum may cover the basilar artery anteriorly (Daniel and Strich 1958). An undulating cerebellar surface with paramedian depressions resembling sulci may be created by the deep invagination of the midline cerebellum by the beaked midbrain and infolding of the anterior cerebellar margins at or above the tentorium.

3. *Ventricles and cisterns*
(a) *Fourth ventricle.* In patients with Chiari II malformation the fourth ventricle is usually an elongated cavity, sagittally flattened and extending into the cervical canal. In the series of Naidich *et al.* (1980c), the fourth ventricle was not visualized within the posterior fossa in the majority of cases (Fig. 4.16). In 5 per cent of cases in this series the fourth ventricle appeared dilated, presumed due to secondary entrapment of adhesions.

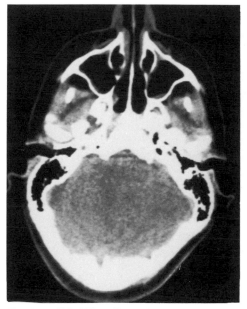

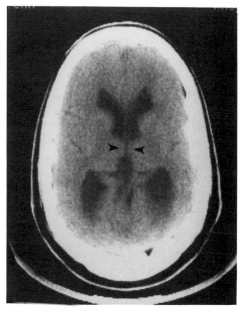

Fig. 4.16. Chiari II malformation. 12-year-old girl with hydrocephalus. The non-contrast CT scan shows absence of the fourth ventricle. Petrous scalloping is present.

Fig. 4.17. Chiari II malformation. *Above:* term female infant. Non-contrast CT scan demonstrates large massa intermedia *(arrowheads)* close to foramen of Monro. *Below left:* 16-year-old boy. Non-contrast CT scan shows prominence of caudate nuclei *(arrowheads). Below right·* serrations of interhemispheric fissure are demonstrated.

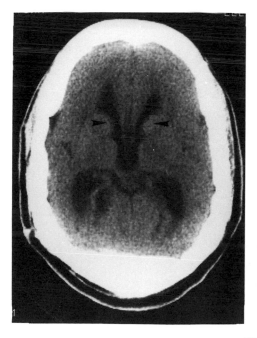

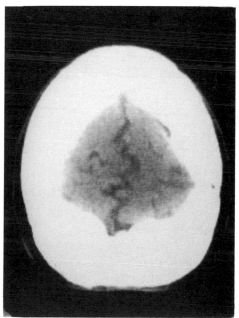

(b) *Third ventricle*. The third ventricle is usually mildly dilated in patients with Chiari II malformation. The massa intermedia is unusually large, lying very close to the foramen of Monro (Gooding *et al.* 1967) (Fig. 4.17). The size of the third ventricle is small in comparison with the dilated lateral ventricles. The walls are nearly parallel or biconcave, with maximal concavity at the insertion of the massa. These features are seen on CT scans in most patients.

(c) *Lateral ventricles*. The lateral ventricles are dilated in almost all patients with Chiari II malformation. The dilatation is bilaterally asymmetric, with greater dilatation of the atria, and occipital horns. The cortical mantle is thinnest over the occipital lobes and vertex. This will be readily visualized on CT. The frontal horns are indented by the prominent heads of the caudate nuclei (Gooding *et al.* 1967). This produces sharp laterally directed pointing of the inferior margins of the ventricles (Fig. 4.17). This is well visualized on coronal CT sections. In 40 per cent of cases the septum pellucidum was noted to be absent (Peach *et al.* 1965). This was found to be absent on axial CT in 12 per cent of cases by Naidich *et al.* (1980*c*).

(d) *Subarachnoid cisterns*. The basal cisterns are poorly visualized in contrast to the suprasellar, prepontine and lateral pontine cisterns which are well visualized and may be prominent in patients with Chiari II malformation. A midline diamond-shaped cistern is present at the apex of the incisura in 26 per cent of patients, formed by the confluence of the cistern of the velum interpositum, superior vermian cistern, and either enlarged wings of the ambient cisterns or infolded cortex at the medial aspect of the atria. The concave lateral borders are characteristic.

(e) *Interhemispheric fissure*. This has a variable appearance in patients with Chiari II malformation. Dilated lateral ventricles may entirely obliterate the fissure or it may be widely patent and increased in width in patients with large head size and raised intracranial pressure. Serrations of the interhemispheric fissure corresponding to interdigitations of the apposing gyri were found in over 20 per cent of patients with Chiari II malformation (Naidich *et al.* 1980 *c*) (Fig. 4.17).

CHIARI III
There is an occipital encephalocele or high cervical encephalocele.

CHIARI IV
Cerebellar hypoplasia is present, without inferior displacement.

Disorders of diverticulation
Septo-optic dysplasia
Septo-optic dysplasia is a rare congenital malformation of anterior midline structures of the brain, first described by de Morsier in 1956. The abnormalities include agenesis of the septum pellucidum, hypoplasia of the optic chiasm, nerves and infundibulum, and a primitive optic ventricle.

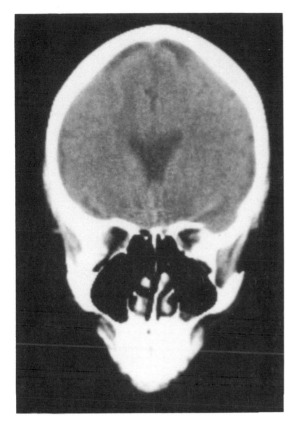

Fig. 4.18. Septo-optic dysplasia. Two-month-old girl. Non-contrast CT shows a single monoventricle.

The malformation is thought to commence as early as two weeks gestational age, when there is mesodermal induction of overlying ectoderm to form the neural plate (Huseman *et al.* 1978). Septo-optic dysplasia is considered to be a form of holoprosencephaly as it is the result of abnormal induction of forebrain tissue (Harwood-Nash and Fitz 1976*a*). An association with hypopituitarism was first described by Hoyt *et al.* (1970), and attributed to extension of the midline abnormality into the hypothalamus (Brook *et al.* 1972).

A review of cases in literature reveals that most patients are female, usually firstborn children of healthy mothers. Seizures and hypotonia are frequently encountered within the first days of life. Hypoplasia of one or both optic discs are detected on funduscopic examination. Diabetes insipidus has been found in nearly half of the cases reported. Hypothalamic-hypopituitary disorders are frequently present (Manelfe and Rochiccioli 1979).

CT is the best modality for the evaluation of this disorder, replacing axial tomography of the optic canals and pneumo-encephalography. CT features have been described by Harwood-Nash and Fitz (1976*b*), Byrd *et al.* (1977) and Manelfe and Rochiccioli (1979):

1. The septum pellucidum is demonstrated to be absent (Fig. 4.18).

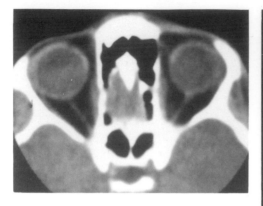

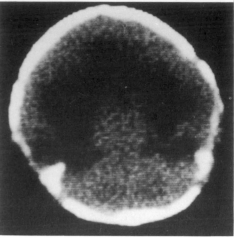

Fig. 4.19 *(above)*. Septo-optic dysplasia. 16-year-old girl. Axial non-contrast CT reveals slender optic nerves bilaterally.

Fig. 4.20. *Above right:* alobar holoprosencephaly. Axial non-contrast head CT scan demonstrates single lateral ventricle surrounding fused thalami. (Courtesy of Ehsan Afshani MD, Buffalo.) *Below:* semilobar holoprosencephaly. Non-contrast head CT scans demonstrate single lateral ventricle, with attempt at formation of frontal and occipital horns. (Courtesy of Joel D. Swartz MD, Philadelphia.)

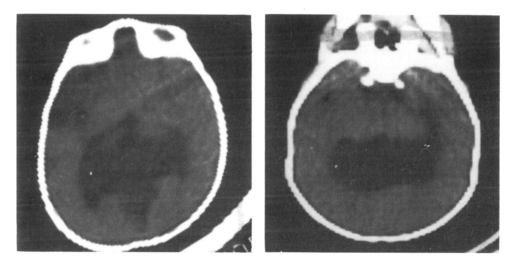

2. Dilatation of the lateral ventricles is present. The roof of the frontal horns is flattened, with inferior pointing of the floor of the lateral ventricles.

3. The optic nerves are small (Fig. 4.19). Coronal CT scans are preferable to axial scans in order to assess the size of the optic nerves.

4. There is dilatation of the chiasmatic and suprasellar cisterns, indicating dysgenesis of the hypothalamus.

5. Enlargement of the pituitary stalk and infundibulum may be seen when there is associated diabetes insipidus. This feature is noted after administration of contrast

media.

6. There is cortical atrophy with dilated sulci.

7. Diverticular expansion of the optic recess of the anterior third ventricle, a feature described by de Morsier (1956), has not yet been demonstrated on CT although sagittal reconstruction images could probably demonstrate this (Manelfe and Rochiccioli 1979).

Holoprosencephaly

The prechordal mesoderm induces the overlying neural ectoderm to form the prosencephalon (DeMyer *et al.* 1964). Cleavage of the prosencephalon into cerebral hemispheres occurs in the sagittal plane, horizontally into the olfactory and optic bulbs, and transversely into the telencephalon and diencephalon.

Holoprosencephaly represents failure of cleavage of the prosencephalon. This term is preferable to arrhinencephaly, because although there is failure of evagination of the olfactory bulbs in holoprosencephaly, this defect is only a minor feature (Yakovlev 1959, DeMyer and Zeman 1963).

A spectrum of abnormalities is classified according to the degree of failure of cleavage.

1. ALOBAR HOLOPROSENCEPHALY

This is the most extreme form of complete failure of cleavage of the prosencephalon. There is a small cerebrum with a single large ventricle and fused thalamic nuclei. Associated facial abnormalities include cyclopia, ethomocephaly, cebocephaly, median cleft lip and philtrum-premaxilla anlage (DeMyer *et al.* 1964). In the vast majority of cases the etiology is unknown. There is some association with chromosomal aberrations; trisomy 13 is the commonest chromosomal cause of holoprosencephaly, and the 18p- and 13q- karyotypes with this disorder are well known but less common (Cohen 1982). Maternal diabetes, viral infections, toxoplasmosis, and drugs (phenytoin and salicylates) have been postulated to have teratogenic effect in humans (Benawra *et al.* 1980, Cohen 1981). The CT appearance is that of a large low-density area with a thin surrounding area of brain tissue. The interhemispheric fissure and septum pellucidum are absent (Fig. 4.20).

2. SEMILOBAR HOLOPROSENCEPHALY

There is increased cerebral tissue present although there is a single lateral ventricle. The septum pellucidum and interhemispheric fissure are absent (Fig. 4.20).

3. LOBAR HOLOPROSENCEPHALY

The cerebral hemispheres and lateral ventricles are well formed. Ventricular dilatation is present due to deficient brain substance rather than hydrocephalus (Harwood-Nash and Fitz 1976*a*).

Disorders of sulcation and migration

Lissencephaly (agyria, pachygyria)

Lissencephaly (smooth brain) is the term used to describe the flat smooth surface of

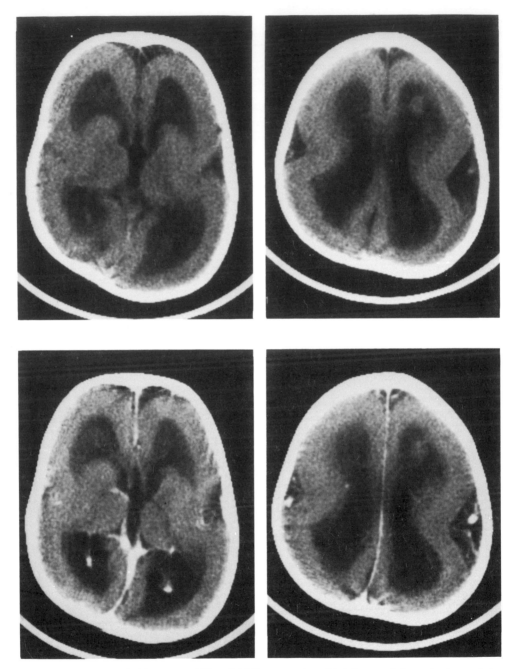

Fig. 4.21. Lissencephaly. Four-year-old boy, initially presenting with failure to thrive and microcephaly. *Top:* non-contrast head CT scans, and *bottom:* contrast-enhanced head CT scans. The cortical gray mantle is markedly thickened, with a small amount of white matter present around the ventricles. Small islands of heterotopic gray matter are present within the white matter. The Sylvian fissures are shallow, containing superficially located arteries and veins.

the malformed human brain, to differentiate it from the normal smooth surface of lower mammals (Walker 1942). The malformation arises from abnormal maturation of the fetal brain, due to impaired migration of neurons from periventricular neural centers to the cortical plate before the eighth week of gestation (Hanaway *et al.* 1968).

The two essential features of this malformation are a reduction in the number of secondary gyri and increased depth of the gray matter underlying the smooth part of the cortex. In severe cases the only visible indentations externally over the brain are the Sylvian fissures which have shorter and more oblique courses than normal. The insula is exposed and operculation is defective (Urich 1976). The abnormality of the cerebral convolutions may only involve the posterior portions of the cerebral hemispheres (Stewart *et al.* 1975).

Association with the Dandy-Walker syndrome has been described (Chemke *et al.* 1975) as well as ocular abnormalities such as cataracts and retinal dysplasia (Walker 1942). Numerous other associated congenital anomalies have been described, including congenital heart disease, renal agenesis, duodenal atresia, cryptorchidism, polydactyly and syndactyly (Wright 1982). Most cases are sporadic, although familial cases have been reported (Dieker *et al.* 1969, Garcia *et al.* 1978).

The CT appearances are of large subarachnoid spaces without demonstrable sulci, producing a smooth brain surface, and dilated ventricles (Garcia *et al.* 1978) (Fig. 4.21). The Sylvian fissures are widened, appearing as deep grooves, with a lack of insular operculization (Ohno *et al.* 1979).

Heterotopic gray matter
Heterotopic gray matter occurs as a consequence of migratory arrest of primitive neuroblasts in the developing fetal cerebrum. The heterotopic areas may be subependymal in location, and involve the frontal horns and bodies and occipital horns more commonly than the temporal horns. There may be associated congenital abnormalities of the central nervous system (Bergeron 1967).

The CT appearance is that of nodules, usually of the same density as normal gray matter, protruding into the ventricular cavity (Rumack and Johnson 1984).

Destructive lesions
Hydranencephaly
Hydranencephaly is a congenital disorder in which the cerebral hemispheres are replaced by thin sacs which contain cerebrospinal fluid. The cranial vault and meninges are intact. Although the term appears to be a combination of hydrocephalus and anencephaly, it is unrelated to anencephaly and thus 'hydrencephaly' is more appropriate (Crome and Sylvester 1958).

The pathogenesis is believed to be that of cerebral infection following internal carotid artery occlusion in utero (Urich 1976). Walsh and Lindenberg (1961) suggested that it results from compression of the internal carotid arteries against the sphenoid bones following swelling of the fetal brain from anoxia. Thrombosis of the internal carotid arteries and branches leading to hydranencephaly has been proven experimentally in dogs by Becker (1949).

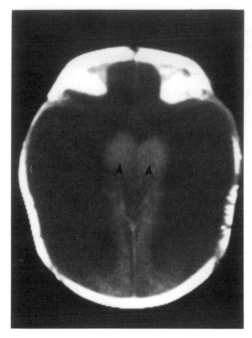 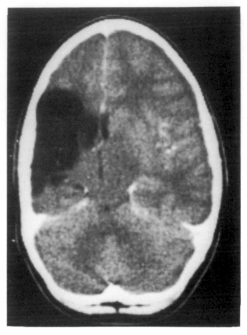

Fig. 4.22. Hydranencephaly. Nine-month-old girl. Non-contrast CT scan demonstrates the cranial cavity mostly filled with cerebrospinal fluid. The ventricular system is not identifiable. There is sparing of the thalami *(arrowheads)* and portions of the occipital lobe.

Fig. 4.23. Porencephaly. Five-year-old girl. Non-contrast head CT scans demonstrate right-sided hemiatrophy. A large area of porencephaly is noted, communicating with the right lateral ventricle.

Specific etiologic agents implicated include maternal syphilis, toxoplasmosis, infective hepatitis, listeriosis, herpes virus, equine virus, ionizing radiation and trauma (Crome 1972, Altshuler 1973, Wenger 1977, Von Herzen and Benirschke 1977).

CT has proven to be an excellent modality for the evaluation of infants with hydranencephaly. The CT appearances (Fig. 4.22), described by Dublin and French (1980), include:

1. A fluid-filled cranium with demonstration of the falx cerebri and tentorium. The falx may be midline or deviated but is usually not thickened.
2. Remnants of the temporal, occipital or subfrontal cortex are present.
3. Rounded thalamic masses are characteristic. The CT appearance may be simulated by other disorders such as infarction, hydrocephalus, subdural effusions, and alobar holoprosencephaly.

Porencephaly
Porencephaly is an area of cavitation within the cerebral hemisphere. The term was introduced by Heschl (1859), who described a defect extending from the surface of

the cerebral hemisphere to underlying ventricle. He attributed this to germ plasm injury or genetic abnormality.

Schizencephaly is a form of porencephaly which is due to arrested growth of the cerebral mantle. This condition is characterized by clefts within the cerebral cortex (Yakovlev and Wadsworth 1946a,b). The clefts are of two distinct types. The first type has fused lips, in contrast to the second type which has a hole or defect, the porus, which separates the lips. Absence of the septum pellucidum and corpus callosum may be associated with the second type (Yakovlev and Wadsworth 1946a,b).

Porencephaly follows an injury from a variety of causes, most commonly vascular occlusion due to hypoxic-ischemic insult (Marburg and Casamajor 1944, Freeman and Gold 1964). Other causes include infection, trauma and surgery (Ramsey and Huckman 1977). Periventricular intracerebral hemorrhage, a very frequent lesion in premature infants, is considered by Pasternak *et al.* (1980) to be a frequent cause.

Encephalomalacia is the earliest change, followed by necrosis. Cystic degeneration is the end result. CT is superior to other radiologic modalities in the detection and delineation of porencephalic lesions (Ramsey and Huckman 1977). The CT appearances described by these authors are:
1. Well-defined areas of decreased density (Fig. 4.23). The absorption coefficient values are usually in the range of cerebrospinal fluid. There may or may not be demonstrable communication with the ventricle. Metrizamide, following intrathecal and intraventricular introduction, may be employed to establish if there is communication with the ventricular system.
2. The absence of a vascular capsule following administration of iodinated contrast medium is useful in differentiation from malignancy or an abscess.
3. The ventricular system and midline structures may be shifted toward or away from the side of the lesion.
4. Hemiatrophy of the ipsilateral ventricle and/or cortical sulci on the affected side may be present.
5. Thinning or asymmetry of the cranial vault may also be demonstrated.

Inflammatory lesions
Rubella, cytomegalic inclusion disease, toxoplasmosis and herpes simplex have all been incriminated in the pathogenesis of congenital disorders. These infective agents are described in Chapter 8.

Disorders of histogenesis
Phakomatoses
The phakomatoses are neuro-ectodermal dysplasias with a tendency to tumor formation in the skin, viscera and central nervous system. Van der Hoeve (1932) described the similarities between neurofibromatosis and tuberous sclerosis, introducing the term 'phakomatosis' (from the Greek *phakos,* 'birthmark, or round motherspot'). CT scanning is the most useful single investigative modality for confirmation of the clinical diagnosis and follow-up of phakomatoses (Kingsley 1977).

TUBEROUS SCLEROSIS (BOURNEVILLE'S DISEASE, EPILOIA)

Tuberous sclerosis is a hereditary disorder characterized by seizures, mental retardation, and adenoma sebaceum. The patchy sclerotic areas of the cerebral cortex were first described by von Recklinghausen in 1862. Bourneville described a series of patients in 1880 and applied the name tuberous sclerosis to the cortical changes.

Hamartomatous involvement of virtually every organ has been described. The disease is inherited as an autosomal dominant trait (Gunther and Penrose 1935). Approximately 70 per cent of occurrences of this disorder are sporadic, believed to represent spontaneous mutation. Many geneticists are currently recommending that parents of apparently sporadic patients have a head CT scan and excretory urogram to search for hamartomatous lesions in order to increase the detection rate of this disorder (Carey 1982).

The hamartomatous foci are mostly situated within the cerebrum although the cerebellum, medulla, and spinal cord may also be affected (Critchley and Earl 1932). The lesions are of two types, cortical nodules (tubers) and subependymal nodules (Fig. 4.24).

The cortical nodules are of varying size, situated at the summit of gyri. Neuronal lamination is disturbed. An increased number of astrocytes is present.

The subependymal nodules are well circumscribed. They are situated along the ventricular system especially in proximity to the foramen of Monro. The nodules may project into the ventricular system producing the 'candle guttering' appearance, demonstrated by pneumo-encephalography (Lind 1924). Increase in size of nodules near the foramen of Monro or aqueduct of Sylvius will result in obstructive hydrocephalus.

Brain tumors occur infrequently in tuberous sclerosis (Kapp et al. 1967) with transformation of a nodule into a giant cell astrocytoma (Fig. 4.25), or less commonly glioblastoma (Kufs 1949, Kapp et al. 1967, Cooper 1971). They tend to be slow growing, without invasive tendency, and do not appear to be highly sensitive to radiation (Kapp et al. 1967, Cooper 1971, Russell and Rubenstein 1971).

The typical CT appearances of this disorder have been described by Gomez et al. 1975, Martin et al. 1976 and Lee and Gawler 1978.

1. Subependymal nodules are usually calcified, often to a marked extent. There is no enhancement of the nodule after contrast administration (Fig. 4.24). In addition to being situated close to the foramina of Monro they are also sited along the lateral aspect of the lateral ventricles, in contrast to choroid plexus which is situated medially or in the center of the trigone and exhibits marked contrast enhancement. Hydrocephalus may be present due to occlusion of cerebrospinal fluid pathways.

2. Parenchymal tubers have the same characteristics as subependymal nodules. They may be simulated by calcified arteriovenous malformations, which will however have contrast enhancement, and the gyral calcification of the Sturge-Weber syndrome. Adjacent cerebral atrophy will however be present in this condition.

3. Intraventricular tumors have a slightly higher density than surrounding brain and will demonstrate contrast enhancement.

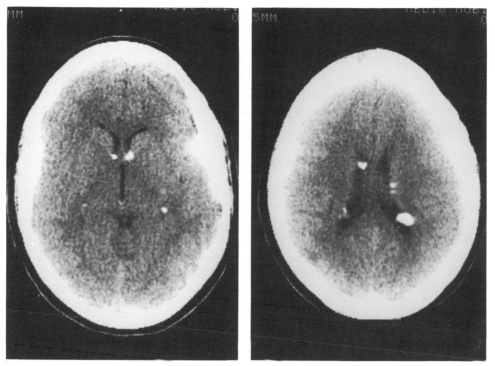

Fig. 4.24. Tuberous sclerosis. Nine-year-old girl presenting with mental retardation. Non-contrast CT scans demonstrate numerous calcified hamartomas located along the ependymal surfaces. The close proximity of the lesions to the foramina of Monro is demonstrated *(left)* although there is no hydrocephalus.

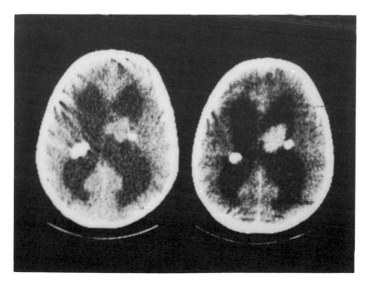

Fig. 4.25. Tuberous sclerosis with malignant change in a hamartoma. Nine-year-old boy with symptoms and signs of raised intracranial pressure. Non-contrast *(left)* and contrast-enhanced *(right)* CT scans. Typical subependymal hamartomatous nodule is demonstrated with associated soft tissue mass. Contrast enhancement is noted within mass. This was histologically proven to be a giant cell astrocytoma. (Courtesy of Samuel Wolpert MD, Boston.)

NEUROFIBROMATOSIS (VON RECKLINGHAUSEN DISEASE)

Neurofibromatosis is a hereditary hamartomatous disorder, probably of neural crest origin, which involves neuro-ectoderm, mesoderm and endoderm, and has the potential to appear in any organ system of the body (Holt 1978).

The disease is an autosomal dominant condition, characterized by multiple neurofibromas, cutaneous pigmentary changes, bone abnormalities, a predilection for certain tumors, especially within the central nervous system, vascular and endocrine abnormalities.

The condition was first described in detail by von Recklinghausen in 1882, although the cutaneous and subcutaneous tumors were originally described by Tilesius von Tilenau in 1793.

The incidence is one in 3000 liveborn infants (Crowe *et al.* 1956). This is the most common serious autosomal dominant condition in childhood. About half of the individuals are thought to represent spontaneous mutations (Carey 1982). There are two age peaks at which severe problems arise, occurring under 10 years of age and in the 30 to 50 year-group (Riccardi and Kleiner 1977).

Only the CNS abnormalities will be described in this section. Mental retardation occurs in 8 per cent of patients. Epilepsy is a common neurologic symptom (Etheridge 1982). Precocious puberty is observed in patients with neurofibromatosis in whom hamartomas of the posterior hypothalamus are found.

A wide spectrum of abnormalities involves the central nervous system, including macrocranium, macrencephaly, dysplastic defects involving the calvaria, facial bones, petrous and sphenoid bones, orbits, and association with tumors (Holt 1978).

Macrocranium and macrencephaly

Macrocranium is a common feature of neurofibromatosis, as evidenced by measurements of head circumference and skull diameters on plain radiographs (Norman 1972, Weichert *et al.* 1973). Holt and Kuhns (1976) attributed macrocranium to increased brain size after finding that 44 per cent of their patients had cranial capacities above the 95th percentile and 70 per cent above the 50th percentile, using the volumetric method of Gordon (1966).

Ventricular dilatation is a common feature of this disorder. It was demonstrated in 32 to 45 per cent of cases by CT depending on the level where the ventricular size was measured. The possible mechanisms include partial intraventricular obstruction or altered absorption of cerebrospinal fluid, or atrophy secondary to cerebrovascular disease (Patronas *et al.* 1982).

Craniofacial dysplasia

Children with neurofibromatosis usually have underlying defects of the skull (Fig. 4.26), facial bones or brain (Holt 1978). The orbito-facial disfigurement and proptosis may be due to disease processes which include orbital osseous dysplasia, buphthalmos, plexiform neurofibromatosis and orbital tumors, all readily differentiated by CT (Zimmerman *et al.* 1983).

Calvarial defects may involve bone encompassing or adjacent to the lambdoid

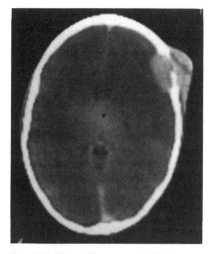

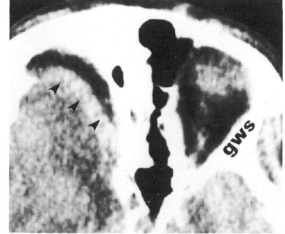

Fig. 4.26. Neurofibromatosis. Eight-year-old girl with left frontal lytic defect and an associated soft tissue mass, proven to be a neurofibroma.

Fig. 4.27. Neurofibromatosis. 10-year-old girl with orbital osseous dysplasia. Non-contrast CT scan demonstrates absence of greater wing of sphenoid on right side, compared with normal left-sided greater wing of sphenoid (gws). Middle cranial fossa is expanded with temporal lobe herniation into upper orbit *(arrowheads)*. (Courtesy of Joel Swartz MD, Philadelphia.)

suture, with lack of normal mastoid pneumatization and no adjacent soft tissue neurofibroma (Joffe 1965). Although the original four children reported by Joffe had left lambdoid suture defects, both sides may be involved with a left-sided predominance (Holt 1978). This defect has been demonstrated on CT by Mann *et al.* (1983).

Orbital osseous dysplasia was originally documented by LeWald (1933), who described congenital absence of a portion of the orbital wall. CT demonstrates hypoplasia of greater and lesser wings of the sphenoid (Fig. 4.27), deformity of the sella, lateral aspect of the posterior ethmoid cells and extension of the temporal lobe into the posterior portion of the orbit which may be enlarged (Zimmerman *et al.* 1983).

Buphthalmos (congenital glaucoma) results from the obstruction of outflow of aqueous humor. The elastic outer coats of the eye become distended resulting in over-all globe enlargement. CT will demonstrate enlargement of the globe in all directions, compared with the normal opposite globe (Zimmerman *et al.* 1983).

1. *Optic nerve tumors* in association with neurofibromatosis are slow-growing in childhood (Davis 1940). The tumors involving the optic nerve or chiasm are pilocytic astrocytomas and are the commonest brain tumors encountered in neurofibromatosis (Gardeur *et al.* 1983). The tumor may focally involve the intra-orbital segment of the nerve or the intracranial compartment, or may diffusely involve both the intra-orbital and intracranial portions of the optic nerve (Fitz and Rao 1983). CT is the modality of choice for demonstration of the entire

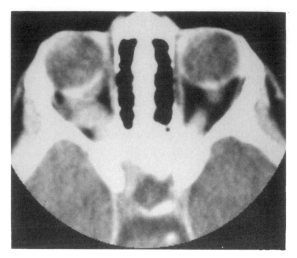

Fig. 4.28. Neurofibromatosis. Eight-year-old girl with decreased visual acuity. Non-contrast orbital CT scan demonstrates bilateral optic nerve gliomas.

optic nerve (Byrd *et al.* 1978*a*).

The gliomas may appear on CT as irregular enlargements of the optic nerve, or less commonly as fusiform enlargements, usually with contrast enhancement (Zimmerman and Bilaniuk 1982) (Fig. 4.28). Intracranial involvement will result in asymmetry of the anterior aspect of the suprasellar cistern (Naidich *et al.* 1976). Dilatation of the basal and Sylvian cisterns has been observed by Savoiardo *et al.* (1981).

2. *Acoustic neuromas* are Schwannomas surrounding the auditory nerve. Over two-thirds arise from the vestibular division, with the remaining third arising from the cochlear division (Levine *et al.* 1982). Unilateral acoustic neuromas arise at any age; the youngest reported was seven years of age (Krause and McCabe 1971). Bilateral lesions are rare in childhood (Holt 1978). Most acoustic neuromas in childhood and adolescence are associated with neurofibromatosis (Jacoby *et al.* 1980).

The tumors tend to be relatively large compared with those in adults. The CT appearances are of an enlarged internal auditory canal, with mild contrast enhancement of the rim of the mass (Fitz and Rao 1983) (Fig. 4.29). If there is a positive clinical history, and a scan shows bony changes without evidence of a mass, the introduction of metrizamide intrathecally in combination with CT is required (Levine *et al.* 1982). Intrathecal air as an alternative to metrizamide is also used (Kricheff *et al.* 1980). The marked contrast between air and soft tissue enables detection of small lesions.

3. *Meningiomas, supratentorial and midbrain gliomas.* Intracranial meningiomas in patients with neurofibromatosis may frequently coexist with other types of tumor. Abnormal choroid plexus calcification occurring in the temporal horn of the lateral ventricle is pathognomonic of neurofibromatosis (Fig. 4.30), and is usually related to an intraventricular meningioma (Zatz 1968).

The CT appearances of meningiomas, supratentorial and midbrain gliomas are

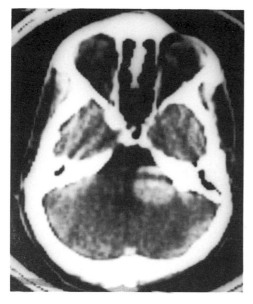

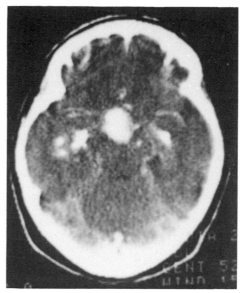

Fig. 4.29. Neurofibromatosis. 19-year-old male with left-sided hearing loss. Contrast-enhanced CT scan demonstrates large soft tissue mass with homogeneous contrast enhancement adjacent to left internal auditory canal. (Courtesy of Joel Swartz MD, Philadelphia.)

Fig. 4.30. Neurofibromatosis. 13-year-old girl with neurofibromatosis, presenting with decreased visual acuity. Contrast-enhanced head CT scan demonstrates homogeneous contrast-enhancing glioma of the optic chiasm. Temporal horn calcification is also present.

described in Chapter 8.

4. *Tumors occurring less frequently with neurofibromatosis* are hypothalamic hamartomas, ependymomas and pituitary adenomas (Gardeur *et al.* 1983).

STURGE-WEBER SYNDROME (ENCEPHALOTRIGEMINAL ANGIOMATOSIS)

The Sturge-Weber syndrome, as described by Sturge (1879), consists of facial nevus flammeus in the distribution of the first division of the trigeminal nerve and leptomeningeal angiomatosis, usually within the posterior parietal, temporal or occipital lobes. Calcification is present within the cortex below the area of angiomatosis. The characteristic intracranial calcification was first demonstrated radiographically by Weber in 1922.

Additional manifestations include mental retardation, seizures, hemiatrophy and hemiparesis contralateral to the facial nevus, and glaucoma (Coulam *et al.* 1976). An enlarged hemicranium on the affected side has been described by Enzmann *et al.* (1977).

The CT appearances are characteristic.

1. The gyriform pattern of calcification is well demonstrated (Fig. 4.31). This calcification may not be detected by conventional skull radiography, especially under the age of two years (Enzmann 1977, Welsh *et al.* 1980). The distribution of

71

calcification may occasionally be bilateral (Boltshauser *et al.* 1976). Enhancement in the involved area, following administration of contrast medium, has been reported by Enzmann (1977) and Welsh *et al.* (1980) (Fig. 4.32). This may represent the actual malformation, or merely a permeability defect of the abnormal vessels.
2. Cortical atrophy is invariably present, either with an enlarged or diminished hemicranium.

Vascular abnormalities
Congenital vascular lesions are described in Chapter 7.

Neoplasia
Congenital intracranial tumors are described in Chapter 8.

Arachnoid cysts
Intracranial arachnoid cysts are generally considered to be congenital in origin, although trauma (Taveras and Ransohoff 1953) and infection (Horrax 1924) have also been suggested as possible causes. The pathogenesis of arachnoid cysts was first described by Starkman *et al.* in 1958. Arachnoid cysts were noted to lie between two membranes contiguous at the cyst margin with normal arachnoid mater. This cyst may or may not communicate with the subarachnoid space (Rengachary 1981).

Location of the cysts may be supratentorial or infratentorial. The commonest site is the Sylvian fissure (Brackett and Rengachary 1982) followed by the posterior fossa (Fitz 1983). Supratentorial cysts have been classified into interhemispheric, convexity and Sylvian types (Anderson *et al.* 1979) but may also occur in other sites including sellar and suprasellar regions, quadrigeminal and ambient cisterns. A cyst arising from the choroid plexus of the lateral ventricle has also been described (Yeates and Enzmann 1979).

The cysts act as space-occupying lesions which compress and distort the adjacent cerebrum and also produce bulging of the calvaria (Anderson and Landing 1966).

The advent of CT has led to an increased incidence of reported cases of arachnoid cysts (Hoffman *et al.* 1982). The unusual locations of the cysts as described above have also been revealed by this modality.

The CT appearance of an arachnoid cyst is that of a well-defined lesion which has the same density as cerebrospinal fluid and does not exhibit contrast enhancement (Fig. 4.33). The cyst may have a straight inner margin which is considered to represent the cyst attachment with the arachnoid membrane (Banna 1976). Lesions over the cerebral convexity usually have a biconvex or semicircular configuration.

Suprasellar arachnoid cysts may enlarge and obstruct the foramina of Monro and also extend into the lateral ventricles. The obstructive hydrocephalus will be readily demonstrated on CT although this appearance may simulate aqueduct stenosis (Leo *et al.* 1979). Positive contrast ventriculography has been advocated in

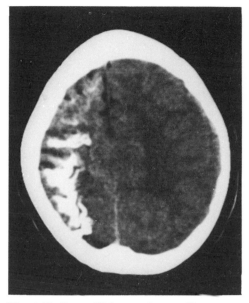

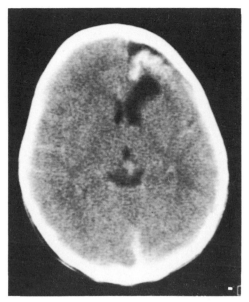

Fig. 4.31. Sturge-Weber syndrome. Three-year-old girl. Non-contrast CT demonstrates the typical peripheral calcification which has a gyral configuration. There is hemiatrophy of the affected side.

Fig. 4.32. Sturge-Weber syndrome. 18-month-old girl. Contrast-enhanced head CT scan. There is a frontal area of calcification which displays slight contrast enhancement, and ipsilateral dilatation of the left frontal horn.

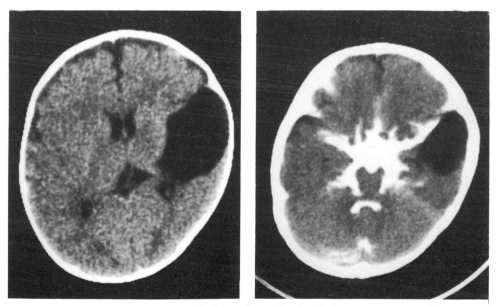

Fig. 4.33. Arachnoid cyst. 14-year-old girl with a seizure disorder. *Left:* non-contrast scan demonstrates a low-density area within the region of the Sylvian cistern. Contrast enhancement was not demonstrated. *Right:* metrizamide CT reveals no evidence of communication between the cyst and basal cisterns.

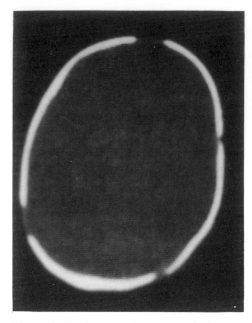 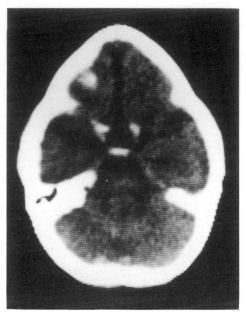

Fig. 4.34. Craniosynostosis. Six-month-old male infant. Non-contrast CT scan demonstrates premature fusion of the right coronal suture.

Fig. 4.35. Trigonocephaly. Term male infant. Non-contrast CT scan demonstrates typical keel-shaped head following premature fusion of metopic suture. (Courtesy of Ehsan Afshani MD, Buffalo.)

those cases by Leo *et al.* (1979), as the contrast medium will not enter the cyst but will enter a dilated third ventricle in a patient with aqueduct stenosis.

Infratentorial cysts are usually retrocerebellar (Little *et al.* 1973, Mori *et al.* 1977). The CT appearance is that of a well-defined low-density retrocerebellar lesion which does not exhibit contrast enhancement (Leo *et al.* 1979). A Dandy-Walker cyst variant may have a similar appearance which may require sagittal reformatted images, air encephalography (Archer *et al.* 1978), or angiography (Wolpert *et al.* 1970) for differentiation.

The CT appearance following post-operative connection of the cyst with the subarachnoid space is that of very slow collapse, as described by Fitz (1983) who suggests that there is underlying permanent brain atrophy or growth anomaly.

Craniosynostosis
Craniosynostosis refers to the absence of one or more sutures separating the membranous bones of the skull. This term usually refers to primary synostosis, always present before birth. Secondary craniosynostosis represents premature obliteration of one or more cranial sutures, due to causes other than primary sutural abnormalities (Shillito 1982).

74

Expansion of the skull cannot occur in a direction perpendicular to an involved suture, and thus the shape of the head in untreated cases will account for the sutures involved.

Sagittal synostosis (scaphocephaly) results in an increased anteroposterior diameter. Unilateral coronal synostosis (Fig. 4.34) produces flattening of the affected side, with exaggeration of frontal bossing on the unaffected side. Bilateral coronal synostosis results in flattening of the forehead, with an absence of frontal bossing. Metopic synostosis (trigonocephaly) presents as a ridge with a keel-like contour of the forehead (Fig. 4.35).

The sutures involving the skull base and calvaria are most accurately identified by high-resolution CT scans in both axial and coronal planes (Furuya *et al.* 1984*a*). The axial plane is used for all sutures involving the cranial vault except the sagittal suture, for which the coronal scan is superior (Furuya *et al.* 1984*a*). The developmental changes in sutures and synchondroses occurring with age and alterations in skull tables and diploic space are best demonstrated by CT (Furuya *et al.* 1984*a*).

The evaluation of patients with syndromes in which the radiographic features are similar, such as acrocephalosyndactyly (Apert's syndrome), craniofacial dysostosis (Crouzon's syndrome) and Pfeiffer's syndrome, is best achieved by CT which can demonstrate changes in brain, bone and facial soft tissues (Fitz 1984).

CT enables accurate imaging of the deformities involving the calvaria and skull base secondary to craniosynostosis prior to surgical correction (Furuya *et al.* 1984*b*).

REFERENCES

Adam, R., Greenberg, J. D. (1978) 'The mega cisterna magna.' *Journal of Neurosurgery*, **48**, 190–192.

Adeloye, A. (1976) 'Mesencephalic spur (beaking deformity of the tectum) in Arnold–Chiari malformation.' *Journal of Neurosurgery*, **45**, 315–320.

Aicardi, J., Lefebvre, J., Lerique-Koechlin, A. (1965) 'A new syndrome: spasm in flexion, callosal agenesis, ocular abnormalities.' *Electroencephalography and Clinical Neurophysiology*, **19**, 609.

Altshuler, G. (1973) 'Toxoplasmosis as a cause of hydranencephaly.' *American Journal of Diseases in Children*, **125**, 251–252.

Amendola, M. A., Garfinkle, W. B., Ostrum, B. J., Katz, M. R., Katz, R. I. (1978) 'Preoperative diagnosis of a ruptured intracranial dermoid cyst by computerized tomography: case report.' *Journal of Neurosurgery*, **48**, 1035–1037.

Anderson, F. M., Landing, B. H. (1966) 'Cerebral arachnoid cysts in infants.' *Journal of Pediatrics*, **69**, 88–96.

—— Segall, H. D., Caton, W. L. (1979) 'Use of computerized tomography scanning in supratentorial arachnoid cysts.' *Journal of Neurosurgery*, **50**, 333–338.

Archer, C. A., Darwish, H., Smith, K. (1978) 'Enlarged cisternae magnae and posterior fossa cysts simulating Dandy-Walker syndrome on computed tomography.' *Radiology*, **127**, 681–686.

Arnold, J. (1894) 'Myelocyste, transposition von gewebskeimen und sympodie.' *Bieträge zur pathologischen Anatomie und allgemeinen Pathologie*, **16**, 1–28.

Banna, M. (1976) 'Arachnoid cysts on computed tomography.' *American Journal of Roentgenology*, **127**, 979–982.

Becker, H. (1949) 'Uber Hirngefassausschaltungen. II.' *Deutsche Zeitschrift für Nervenheilkunde*, **161**, 446–505.

Benawra, R., Mangurten, H. H., Duffell, D. R. (1980) 'Cyclopia and other anomalies following maternal ingestion of salicylates.' *Journal of Pediatrics*, **96**, 1069–1071.

Benda, C. E. (1954) 'The Dandy-Walker syndrome or the so-called atresia of the foramen of Magendie.'

Journal of Neuropathology and Experimental Neurology, **13,** 14–29.

Bergeron, R. T. (1967) 'Pneumographic demonstration of subependymal heterotopic cortical gray matter in children.' *American Journal of Roentgenology,* **101,** 168–177.

Blake, J. A. (1900) 'The roof and lateral recess of the fourth ventricle, considered morphologically and embryologically.' *Journal of Comparative Neurology,* **10,** 79–108.

Boltshauser, E., Wilson, J., Hoare, R. D. (1976) 'Sturge–Weber syndrome with bilateral intracranial calcification.' *Journal of Neurology, Neurosurgery and Psychiatry,* **39,** 429–435.

Bonnevie, K., Brodal, A. (1946) 'Hereditary hydrocephalus in the house mouse. IV: The development of the cerebellar anomalies during fetal life with notes on the normal development of the mouse cerebellum.' *Skr. Norske Vidensk Akad 1 Mat Nat Kl* No. 4, 1–60.

Bourneville, D. M. (1880–81) 'Sclérose tubéreuse des circonvolutions cérébrales: idiotie et épilepsie hémiplégique.' *Archives de Neurologie (Paris),* **1,** 81–91.

Brackett, C. E., Rengachary, S. S. (1982) 'Arachnoid cysts.' *In:* Youmans, J. R. (Ed.) *Neurological Surgery, Vol. 6.* Philadelphia: W. B. Saunders. pp. 1436–1446.

Brook, C. G. D., Sanders, M. D., Hoare, R. D. (1972) 'Septo-optic dysplasia.' *British Medical Journal,* **3,** 811–813.

Byrd, S. E., Harwood-Nash, D. C., Fitz, C. R., Rogovitz, D. M. (1977) 'Computed tomography evaluation of holoprosencephaly in infants and children.' *Journal of Computer Assisted Tomography,* **1,** 456–463.

—— —— —— Barry, J. F., Rogovitz, D. M. (1978*a*) 'Computed tomography of intraorbital optic nerve gliomas in children.' *Radiology,* **129,** 73–78.

—— —— —— (1978*b*) 'Absence of the corpus callosum: computed tomographic evaluation in infants and children.' *Journal of the Canadian Association of Radiologists,* **20,** 108–112.

Carey, J. C. (1982) 'Tuberous sclerosis.' *In:* Rudolph, A. M., Hoffman, J. I. E. (Eds.) *Pediatrics, 17th edn.* Connecticut: Appleton–Century–Crofts. pp. 404–405.

Chemke, J., Czernobilsky, B., Mundel, G., Barishak, Y. R. (1975) 'A familial syndrome of central nervous system and ocular malformations.' *Clinical Genetics,* **7,** 1–7.

Chiari, H. (1891) 'Ueber Veränderungen des kleinhirns infolge von hydrocephalie des grosshirns.' *Deutsche Medizinische Wochenschrift,* **17,** 1172–1175.

—— (1895) 'Uber die veränderungen des kleinhirns, des pons, und der medulla oblongata infolge von congenitaler hydrocephalie des grosshirns.' *Denkschriften der Akademie der Wissenschaften, Wien,* **63,** 71–116.

Cleland, J. (1883) 'Contribution to the study of spina bifida, encephalocele and anencephalus.' *Journal of Anatomy and Physiology,* **17,** 257–292.

Cohen, M. M. (1981) 'Holoprosencephaly: cyclopia series.' *In:* Warkany, J., Lemire, R. T., Cohen, M. M., Jr. *Mental Retardation and Congenital Malformations of the Central Nervous System.* Chicago: Year Book Medical Publishers. pp. 176–190.

—— (1982) 'An update on the holoprosencephalic disorders.' *Journal of Pediatrics,* **101,** 865–869.

Cooper, J. R. (1971) 'Brain tumors in hereditary multiple system hamartomas (tuberous sclerosis).' *Journal of Neurosurgery,* **34,** 194–202.

Coulam, C. M., Brown, L. R., Reese, D. F. (1976) 'Sturge-Weber syndrome.' *Seminars in Roentgenology,* **11,** 55–60.

Craig, W. M., Miller, R. H., Holman, C. B. (1953) 'Cysts of the septum pellucidum: interesting case reports.' *Proceedings of Staff Meetings of the Mayo Clinic,* **28,** 330–355.

Critchley, M., Earl, C. J. C. (1932) 'Tuberous sclerosis and allied conditions.' *Brain,* **55,** 311–346.

Crome, L. (1972) 'Hydrencephaly.' *Developmental Medicine and Child Neurology,* **14,** 224–234.

—— Sylvester, P. E. (1958) 'Hydranencephaly (hydrencephaly).' *Archives of Disease in Childhood,* **33,** 235–245.

Crowe, F. W., Schull, W. S., Neel, J. V. (1956) *Clinical, Pathological and Genetic Study of Multiple Neurofibromatosis.* Springfield, Illinois: C. C. Thomas.

D'Agostino, A. N., Kernohan, J. W., Brown, J. R. (1963) 'The Dandy–Walker syndrome.' *Journal of Neuropathology and Experimental Neurology,* **22,** 450–470.

Dandy, W. E. (1931) 'Congenital cerebral cysts of the cavum septum pellucidi (fifth ventricle) and cavum vergae (sixth ventricle).' *Archives of Neurology and Psychiatry,* **25,** 44–66.

—— Blackfan, K. D. (1914) 'Internal hydrocephalus, an experimental clinical and pathological study.' *American Journal of Diseases in Childhood,* **8,** 406–482.

Daniel, P. M., Strich, S. J. (1958) 'Some observations on the congenital deformity of the central nervous system known as the Arnold–Chiari malformation.' *Journal of Neuropathology and Experimental Neurology,* **17,** 255–266.

Davis, F. A. (1940) 'Primary tumors of the optic nerve (a phenomenon of Recklinghausen's disease).'

Archives of Ophthalmology, **23**, 957–1022.
Davis, K. R., Taveras, J. M. (1976) 'Diagnosis of epidermoid tumor by computed tomography.' *Radiology*, **119**, 347–353.
de Jong, J. G. Y., Delleman, J. W., Manschot, W. A., de Minjer, A., Mol, J., Sloof, J. L. (1976) 'Agenesis of the corpus callosum, infantile spasms, ocular anomalies (Aicardi's syndrome): clinical and pathologic findings.' *Neurology*, **26**, 1152–1158.
de Morsier, G. (1956) 'Etudes sur les dysraphies cranio-encéphaliques. Part 3 (agénésie de septum lucidum avec malformation du trachus optique. La dysplasie septo-optique).' *Schweizer Archiv für Neurologie, Neurochirurgie und Psychiatrie*, **77**, 267–292.
DeMyer, W. (1971) 'Classification of cerebral malformations.' *Birth Defects*, **7**, 78–93.
—— Zeman, W. (1963) 'Alobar holoprosencephaly (arhinencephaly) with median cleft lip and palate; clinical, electroencephalographic and nosologic considerations.' *Confinia Neurologica*, **23**, 1–36.
—— —— Palmer, C. G. (1964) 'The face predicts the brain: diagnostic significance of median facial anomalies for holoprosencephaly (arhinencephaly).' *Pediatrics*, **34**, 257–263.
Dieker, H., Edwards, R. H., ZuRhein, G., Chou, S. M., Hartman, H. A., Opitz, J. M. (1969) 'The lissencephaly syndrome.' *Birth Defects*, **5** (2), 53–64.
Drayer, B. P., Rosenbaum, A. E., Maroon, J. C., Bank, W. O., Woodford, J. E. (1977) 'Posterior fossa extra-axial cyst. Diagnosis by metrizamide CT cisternography.' *American Journal of Roentgenology*, **128**, 431–436.
Dublin, A. B., French, B. N. (1980) 'Diagnostic image evaluation of hydranencephaly and pictorially similar entities with emphasis on computed tomography.' *Radiology*, **137**, 81–91.
Enzmann, D. R., Hayward, R. W., Norman, D., Dunn, R. P. (1977) 'Cranial computed tomographic scan appearance of Sturge–Weber disease: unusual presentation.' *Radiology*, **122**, 721–724.
Etheridge, J. E., Jr. (1982) 'Birth defects and developmental disorders.' *In:* Farmer, T. W. (Ed.) *Pediatric Neurology. 3rd edn.* Philadelphia: Harper & Row. pp. 61–115.
Faerber, F. N., Wolpert, S. M. (1978) 'The value of computed tomography in the diagnosis of intracranial lipomata.' *Journal of Computer Assisted Tomography*, **2**, 297–299.
Fitz, C. R. (1983) 'Congenital anomalies of the brain.' *In:* Haaga, J. R., Alfidi, R. J. (Eds.) *Computed Tomography of the Whole Body.* St. Louis: C. V. Mosby Company. pp. 44–63.
—— (1984) 'Developmental abnormalities of the brain.' *In:* Rosenberg, R. N. (Ed.) *The Clinical Neurosciences.* New York: Churchill Livingstone. pp. 215–246.
—— Rao, K. C. V. G. (1983) 'Primary tumors in children.' *In:* Lee, S. H., Rao, K. C. V. G. (Eds.) *Cranial Computed Tomography.* New York: McGraw-Hill. pp. 295–343.
Forbes, W., Isherwood, I. (1978) 'Computed tomography in syringomyelia and the associated Arnold–Chiari Type I malformation.' *Neuroradiology*, **15**, 73–78.
Freeman, J. M., Gold, A. P. (1964) 'Porencephaly simulating subdural hematoma in childhood.' *American Journal of Diseases of Children*, **107**, 327–335.
French, B. N. (1982) 'Midline fission defects and defects of formation.' *In:* Youmans, J. R. (Ed.) *Neurological Surgery.* Philadelphia: W. B. Saunders. pp. 1236–1380.
Fukui, M., Tanaka, A., Kitamura, K., Okudera, T. (1977) 'Lipoma of the cerebellopontine angle. Case report.' *Journal of Neurosurgery*, **46**, 544–547.
Furuya, Y., Edwards, M. S. B., Alpers, C. E., Tress, B. M., Ousterhout, D. K., Norman, D. (1984a) 'Computerized tomography of cranial sutures. Part 1: Comparison of suture anatomy in children and adults.' *Journal of Neurosurgery*, **61**, 53–58.
—— —— —— —— Norman, D., Ousterhout, D. K. (1984b) 'Computerized tomography of cranial sutures. Part 2: Abnormalities of sutures and skull deformity in craniosynostosis.' *Journal of Neurosurgery*, **61**, 59–70.
Garcia, C. A., Dunn, D., Trevor, R. (1978) 'The lissencephaly (agyria) syndrome in siblings.' *Archives of Neurology*, **35**, 608–611.
Gardeur, D., Palmieri, A., Mashazy, R. (1983) 'Cranial computed tomography in the phakomatoses.' *Neuroradiology*, **25**, 293–304.
Gardner, W. J. (1959) 'Anatomic features common to the Arnold–Chiari and Dandy–Walker malformations suggest a common origin.' *Cleveland Clinical Quarterly*, **26**, 206–222.
Gomez, M. R., Mellinger, J. F., Reese, D. F. (1975) 'The use of computerized transaxial tomography in the diagnosis of tuberous sclerosis.' *Mayo Clinic Proceedings*, **50**, 553–556.
Gooding, C. A., Carter, A., Hoare, R. D. (1967) 'New ventriculographic aspects of the Arnold–Chiari malformation.' *Radiology*, **89**, 626–632.
Gordon, I. R. S. (1966) 'Measurement of cranial capacity in children.' *British Journal of Radiology*, **39**, 377–381.
Gunther, M., Penrose, L. S. (1935) 'The genetics of epiloia.' *Journal of Genetics*, **31**, 413–430.

Hanaway, J., Lee, S. I., Netzky, M. G. (1968) 'Pachygyria: relation to findings to modern embryologic concepts.' *Neurology,* **18,** 791–799.

Hart, M. N., Malamud, N., Ellis, W. G. (1972) 'The Dandy–Walker syndrome. A clininco-pathological study based on 28 cases.' *Neurology,* **22,** 771–780.

Harwood-Nash, D., Fitz, C. (1976*a*) 'Congenital malformations of the brain.' *In: Neuroradiology in Infants and Children.* St. Louis: C. V. Mosby. pp. 998–1053.

—— —— (1976*b*) 'Brain neoplasms.' *In: Neuroradiology in Infants and Children.* St. Louis: C. V. Mosby. pp. 668–788.

Heschl, R. (1859) 'Gehirndefect und hydrocephalus.' *Vierteljährschrift für praktikale Heilkunde,* **61,** 59–74.

Hoffman, H. J., Hendrick, E. B., Humphreys, R. P., Armstrong, E. A. (1982) 'Investigation and management of suprasellar arachnoid cysts.' *Journal of Neurosurgery,* **57,** 597–602.

Holt, G. W. (1963) 'Congenital malformations of the nervous system.' *American Journal of the Medical Sciences,* **246,** 104–113.

Holt, J. F. (1978) 'Neurofibromatosis in children.' *American Journal of Roentgenology,* **130,** 615–639.

—— Kuhns, L. R. (1976) 'Macrocranium and macrocephaly in neurofibromatosis.' *Skeletal Radiology,* **1,** 25–28.

Horrax, G. (1924) 'Generalized cisternal arachnoiditis simulating cerebellar tumor: its surgical treatment and end-results.' *Archives of Surgery,* **9,** 95–112.

Hoyt, W. F., Kaplan, S. L., Grumbach, M. M., Glaser, J. S. (1970) 'Septo-optic dysplasia and pituitary dwarfism.' *Lancet,* **1,** 893–894.

Huseman, C. A., Kelch, R. P., Hopwood, N. J., Zipf, W. B. (1978) 'Sexual precocity in association with septo-optic dysplasia and hypothalamic hypopituitarism.' *Journal of Pediatrics,* **92,** 748–753.

Jacoby, C. G., Go, R. T., Beren, R. A. (1980) 'Cranial CT of neurofibromatosis.' *American Journal of Neuroradiology,* **1,** 311–315.

Joffe, N. (1965) 'Calvarial bone defects involving the lamboid suture in neurofibromatosis.' *British Journal of Radiology,* **38,** 23–27.

Kapp, J. P., Paulson, G. W., Odom, G. L. (1967) 'Brain tumors with tuberous sclerosis.' *Journal of Neurosurgery,* **26,** 191–202.

Kieffer, S. A., Lee, S. H. (1983) 'Intracranial neoplasms'. *In:* Haaga, J. R., Alfidi, R. J. *Computed Tomography of the Whole Body.* St. Louis: C. V. Mosby. pp. 64–109.

Kingsley, D. P. E. (1977) 'C.A.T. in phakomatoses.' *In:* du Bonlay, G. H., Mosely, I. F. (Eds.) *The First European Seminar on Computerized Axial Tomography in Clinical Practice.* Berlin: Springer–Verlag. pp. 174–181.

Krause, C. J., McCabe, B. F. (1971) 'Acoustic neuroma in a 7 year old girl. Report of a case.' *Archives of Otolaryngology,* **94,** 359–363.

Kricheff, I. I., Pinto, R. S., Bergeron, R. T., Cohen, N. (1980) 'Air CT cisternography and canalography for small acoustic neuromas.' *American Journal of Neuroradiology,* **1,** 57–63.

Kruyff, E., Jeffs, R. (1966) 'Skull abnormalities associated with the Arnold Chiari malformation.' *Acta Radiologica [Diagnosis],* **5,** 9–24.

Kufs, H. (1949) 'Uber eine Spätform der Tuberösen. Hirnsklerose unter dem Bild des Hirntumors und andere abnorme Befunde bei dieser Krankheit.' *Archiv für Psychiatrie und Nervenkrankheiten,* **182,** 177–186.

Larroche, J. C., Baudey, J. (1961) 'Cavum septi lucidi, cavum vergae, cavum veli interpositi: cavities de la ligne médiane. Etude anatomique et pneumoencéphalographique dans la période néonatale.' *Biologia Neonatorum,* **3,** 193–236.

Larsen, J. L., Stiris, G. (1970) 'Lipoma of the corpus callosum with atypical calcification.' *British Journal of Radiology,* **43,** 576–577.

Laster, D. W., Moody, D. M., Ball, M. R. (1977) 'Epidermoid tumors with intraventricular and subarachnoid fat: report of two cases.' *American Journal of Roentgenology,* **128,** 504–507.

Lee, B. C. P., Gawler, J. (1978) 'Tuberous sclerosis: comparison of computed tomography and conventional neuroradiology.' *Radiology,* **127,** 403–407.

Lee, S. H., Rao, K. C. V. G. (1983) 'Primary tumors in adults.' *In:* Lee, S. H., Rao K. C. V. G. (Eds.) *Cranial Computed Tomography.* New York: McGraw-Hill. pp. 241–293.

Leo, J. S., Pinto, R. S., Hulvat, G. F., Epstein, F., Kricheff, I. I. (1979) 'Computed tomography of arachnoid cysts.' *Radiology,* **130,** 675–680.

Levine, H. L., Kleefield, J., Rao, K. C. V. G. (1982) 'The base of the skull.' *In:* Lee, S. H., Rao, K. C. V. G. (Eds.) *Cranial Computed Tomography.* New York: McGraw-Hill. pp. 371–459.

LeWald, L. T. (1933) 'Congenital absence of the superior orbital wall associated with pulsating exophthalmus: report of four cases.' *American Journal of Roentgenology,* **30,** 756–764.

Lind, W. A. T. (1924) 'Epiloia.' *Medical Journal of Australia,* **2,** 290–294.

Little, J. R., Gomez, M. R., MacCarty, C. S. (1973) 'Infratentorial arachnoid cysts.' *Journal of Neurosurgery,* **39,** 380–386.

Loeser, J. D., Alvord, E. C. (1968) 'Clinicopathological correlations in agenesis of the corpus callosum.' *Neurology,* **18,** 745–756.

Lynn, R. B., Buchanan, D. C., Fenichel, G. M., Freemon, F. R. (1980) 'Agenesis of the corpus callosum.' *Archives of Neurology,* **37,** 444–445.

McCormack, T. J., Plassche, W. M., Lin, S. R. (1978) 'Ruptured teratoid tumor in the pineal region.' *Journal of Computer Assisted Tomography,* **2,** 499–501.

McLaurin, R. L. (1964) 'Parietal cephaloceles.' *Neurology,* **14,** 764–772.

Manelfe, C., Rochiccioli, P. (1979) 'CT of septo-optic dysplasia.' *American Journal of Roentgenology,* **133,** 1157–1160.

Mann, H., Kozic, Z., Medinilla, O. R. (1983) 'Computed tomography of lambdoid calvarial defect in neurofibromatosis. A case report.' *Neuroradiology,* **25,** 175–176.

Marburg, O., Casamajor, L. (1944) 'Phlebostasis and phlebothrombosis of the brain in the newborn and early childhood.' *Archives of Neurology and Psychiatry,* **52,** 170–188.

Martin, G. I., Kaiserman, D., Liegler, D., Amorosi, E. D., Nadel, H. (1976) 'Computer assisted tomography in early diagnosis of tuberous sclerosis.' *Journal of the American Medical Association,* **235,** 2323–2324.

Menkes, J. H., Philippart, M., Clark, D. B. (1964) 'Hereditary partial agenesis of the corpus callosum.' *Archives of Neurology,* **11,** 198–208.

Mori, K., Hayashi, T., Handa, H. (1977) 'Infratentorial retrocerebellar cysts.' *Surgical Neurology,* **7,** 135–142.

Naidich, T. P. (1981) 'Cranial CT signs of the Chiari II malformation.' *Journal of Neuroradiology,* **8,** 207–227.

—— Leeds, N. E., Kricheff, I. I., Pudlowski, R. M., Naidich, J. B., Zimmerman, R. D. (1977) 'The tentorium in axial section. 1. Normal CT appearance and non-neoplastic pathology.' *Radiology,* **123,** 631–638.

—— Lin, J. P., Leeds, N. E., Kricheff, I. I., George, A. E., Chase, N. E., Pudlowski, R. M., Passalaqua, A. (1976) 'Computed tomography in the diagnosis of extra-axial posterior fossa masses.' *Radiology,* **120,** 333–339.

—— Pudlowski, R. M., Naidich, J. B., Gornish, M., Rodriquez, F. J. (1980*a*) 'Computed tomographic signs of the Chiari II malformation. Part 1: Skull and dural partitions.' *Radiology,* **134,** 65–71.

—— —— —— (1980*b*) 'Computed tomographic signs of Chiari II malformation. II: Midbrain and cerebellum.' *Radiology,* **134,** 391–398.

—— —— —— (1980*c*) 'Computed tomographic signs of the Chiari II malformation. III: Ventricles and cisterns.' *Radiology,* **134,** 657–663.

Norman, M. E. (1972) 'Neurofibromatosis in a family.' *American Journal of Diseases of Children,* **123,** 159–160.

Ohno, K., Enomoto, T., Inamoto, J., Takeshita, K., Arima, M. (1979) 'Lissencephaly (agyria) on computed tomography.' *Journal of Computer Assisted Tomography,* **3,** 92–95.

Pasternak, J. F., Mantovani, J. F., Volpe, J. J. (1980) 'Porencephaly from periventricular intracerebral hemorrhage in a premature infant.' *American Journal of Diseases of Children,* **134,** 673–675.

Patronas, N. J., Zeklowitz, M., Levin, K. (1982) 'Ventricular dilatation in neurofibromatosis.' *Journal of Computer Assisted Tomography,* **6,** 598–600.

Peach, B. (1964) 'Cystic prolongation of the fourth ventricle: an anomaly associated with the Arnold–Chiari malformation.' *Archives of Neurology,* **11,** 609–612.

—— (1965) 'Arnold–Chiari malformation. Anatomic features of 20 cases.' *Archives of Neurology,* **12,** 612–621.

Rakic, P., Yakovlev, P. I. (1968) 'Development of the corpus callosum and cavum septi in man.' *Journal of Comparative Neurology,* **132,** 45–72.

Ramsey, R. G., Huckman, M. S. (1977) 'Computed tomography of porencephaly and other cerebrospinal fluid-containing lesions.' *Radiology,* **123,** 73–77.

Rao, K. C. V. G., Harwood-Nash, D. C. (1983) 'Craniocerebral anomalies.' *In:* Lee, S. H., Rao, K. C. V. G. (Eds.) *Cranial Computed Tomography.* New York: McGraw-Hill. pp. 115–169.

Rengachary, S. S. (1981) 'Parasagittal arachnoid cyst: case report.' *Neurosurgery,* **9,** 70–75.

Riccardi, V. M., Kleiner, B. (1977) 'Neurofibromatosis: a neoplastic birth defect with two age peaks of severe problems.' *Birth Defects,* **13** (3c), 131–138.

Rumack, C. M., Johnson, M. L. (1984) *Perinatal and Infant Brain Imaging.* Chicago: Year Book Medical Publishers. pp. 1–248.

Russell, D. S., Rubinstein, L. J. (1963) *Pathology of Tumors of the Nervous System 2nd edn.* London: Edward Arnold, pp. 25–26.

—— —— (1971) *Pathology of Tumors of the Nervous System. 3rd edn.* Baltimore: Williams & Wilkins. p. 124.

Sarwar, M., Virapongse, C., Bhimani, S., Freilich, M. (1984) 'Interhemispheric fissure sign of dysgenesis of the corpus callosum.' *Journal of Computer Assisted Tomography,* **8,** 637–644.

Savoiardo, M., Harwood-Nash, D. C., Tadmore, R., Scotti, G., Musgrave, M. (1981) 'Gliomas of the intracranial anterior optic pathways in children: the role of computed tomography, angiography, pneumoencephalography and radionuclide brain scanning.' *Radiology,* **138,** 601–610.

Scarcella, G. (1960) 'Radiologic aspects of the Dandy–Walker syndrome.' *Neurology,* **10,** 260–266.

Schwalbe, E., Gredig, M. (1907) 'Uber Entwicklungsstörungen des Kleinhirns, Hirnstamms und Halsmarks bei Spina Bifida.' *Beiträge für pathologische Anatomie,* **40,** 132–194.

Scotti, G., Musgrave, M. A., Fitz, C. R., Harwood-Nash, D. C. (1980) 'The isolated fourth ventricle in children. CT and clinical review of 16 cases.' *American Journal of Neuroradiology,* **1,** 419–424.

Shaw, C. M., Alvord, E. C. (1969) 'Cava septi pellucidi et vergae: their normal and pathological states.' *Brain,* **92,** 213–224.

Shillito, J., Jr. (1982) 'Craniosynostosis.' *In:* Youmans, J. R. (Ed.) *Neurological Surgery Vol. 5.* Philadelphia: W. B. Saunders. pp. 1447–1466.

Solt, L. C., Deck, J. H. N., Baim, R. G., TerBrugge, K. (1980) 'Interhemispheric cyst of neuroepithelial origin in association with partial agenesis of the corpus callosum: case report.' *Journal of Neurosurgery,* **52,** 399–403.

Starkman, S. P., Brown, T. C., Linell, E. A. (1958) 'Cerebral arachnoid cysts.' *Journal of Neuropathology and Experimental Neurology,* **17,** 484–500.

Stevenson, A. C., Johnston, H. A., Steward, M. I. P., Goldring, D. R. (1966) 'Congenital malformations. A report of a series of consecutive births in 24 centers.' *Bulletin of the World Health Organization,* **34** (supplement), 1–127.

Stewart, R. M. Richman, D. P., Caviness, V. S. (1975) 'Lissencephaly and pachygyria: an architectonic and topographical analysis.' *Acta Neuropathologica,* **31,** 1–12.

Sturge, W. A. (1879) 'Case of rare vaso-motor disturbance in the leg.' *Transactions of the Clinical Society of London,* **12,** 156.

Sutton, J. B. (1887) 'The lateral recesses of the fourth ventricle: their relation to certain cysts and tumors of the cerebellum, and to occipital meningocele.' *Brain,* **9,** 352–361.

Taveras, J. M., Ransohoff, J. (1953) 'Leptomeningeal cysts of the brain following trauma with erosion of the skull.' *Journal of Neurosurgery,* **10,** 233–241.

Tilesius Von Tilenau, W. G. (1793) *Historia pathologica singularis cutis turpitudinus. Jo Godofredi Rheinhardi viri 50 Annorum.* Leipzig: S. L. Crusins.

Urich, H. (1976) 'Malformations of the nervous system, perinatal damage and related conditions in early life.' *In:* Blackwood, W., Corsellis, J. A. N. (Eds.) *Greenfield's Neuropathology. 3rd edn.* London: Edward Arnold. pp. 361–469.

Van der Hoeve, J. (1932) 'The Doyne memorial lecture: eye symptoms in phakomatoses.' *Transactions of the Ophthalmological Society U.K.,* **52,** 380–401.

Von Herzen, J. L., Benirschke, K. (1977) 'Unexpected disseminated herpes simplex infection in a newborn.' *Obstetrics and Gynecology,* **50,** 728–730.

von Recklinghausen, F. (1862) 'Ein Herz von einem Neugeborenen, welches mehrere, theils nach aussen, theils nach den hohlen prominirende tumoren (myomen) trug.' *Monatsschrift für Geburtshilfe und Gynäkologie,* **20,** 1–2.

—— (1882) *Uber die multiplen Fibrome der Haut und ihre Beziehung zu den multiplen Neuromen. Festschrift für Rudolph Virchow.* Berlin: August Hirschwald.

Walker, A. E. (1942) 'Lissencephaly.' *Archives of Neurology and Psychiatry,* **48,** 13–29.

Walsh, F. B., Lindenberg, R. (1961) 'Hypoxia in infants and children: a clinical-pathological study concerning the primary visual pathways.' *Bulletin of the Johns Hopkins Hospital,* **108,** 100–145.

Weber, F. P. (1922) 'Right sided hemi-hypertrophy, resulting from right sided congenital spastic hemiplegia with a morbid condition of the left side of the brain, revealed by radiograms.' *Journal of Neurology and Psychopathology,* **3,** 134–139.

Weichert, K. A., Dine, M. S., Benton, C., Silverman, F. N. (1973) 'Macrocranium and neurofibromatosis.' *Radiology,* **107,** 163–166.

Weisberg, L., Straberg, D., Meriwether, R. D., Robertson, H., Goodman, G. (1981) 'Computed tomography findings in the Arnold–Chiari Type I malformation.' *Computed Tomography,* **5,** 1–11.

Welsh, K., Naheedy, M. H., Abroms, I. F., Strand, R. D. (1980) 'Computed tomography of Sturge–Weber syndrome in infants.' *Journal of Computer Assisted Tomography,* **4,** 33–36.

Wenger, F. (1977) 'Venezuelan equine encephalitis.' *Teratology*, **16**, 359–362.
Wilkins, R. H., Brody, I. A. (1971) 'The Arnold–Chiari malformation.' *Archives of Neurology*, **25**, 376–379.
Wolpert, S. M., Haller, J. S., Rabe, E. F. (1970) 'The value of angiography in the Dandy–Walker syndrome and posterior fossa extra axial cysts.' *American Journal of Roentgenology*, **109**, 261–272.
Wright, F. S. (1982) 'Congenital structural defects.' *In:* Swaiman, K. F., Wright, F. S. (Eds.) *The Practice of Pediatric Neurology. 2nd edn.* St. Louis: C. V. Mosby. pp. 402–444.
Yakovlev, P. I. (1959) 'Pathoarchitectonic studies of cerebral malformations. III: Arrhinencephalies (holotelencephalies).' *Journal of Neuropathology and Experimental Neurology*, **18**, 22–55.
—— Wadsworth, R. C. (1946*a*) 'Schizencephalies. A study of the congenital clefts in the cerebral mantle I—Clefts with fused lips.' *Journal of Neuropathology and Experimental Neurology*, **5**, 116–130.
—— —— (1946*b*) 'Schizencephalies. A study of the congenital clefts in the cerebral mantle. II—Clefts with hydrocephalus and lips separated.' *Journal of Neuropathology and Experimental Neurology*, **5**, 169–206.
Yeates, A., Enzmann, D. (1979) 'An intraventricular arachnoid cyst.' *Journal of Computer Assisted Tomography*, **3**, 697–700.
Zatz, L. M. (1968) 'Atypical choroid plexus calcifications associated with neurofibromatosis.' *Radiology*, **91**, 1135–1139.
Zimmerman, R. A., Bilaniuk, L. T., Gallo, E. (1978) 'Computed tomography of the trapped fourth ventricle.' *American Journal of Roentgenology*, **130**, 503-506.
—— —— Dolinskas, C. (1979*a*) 'Cranial computed tomography of epidermoid and congenital fatty tumors of maldevelopmental origin.' *Computed Tomography*, **3**, 40–47.
—— Breckbill, D., Dennis, M. W., Davis, D. O. (1979*b*) 'Cranial CT findings in patients with meningomyelocele.' *American Journal of Roentgenology*, **132**, 623–629.
—— Bilaniuk, L. T. (1982) 'The orbit.' *In:* Lee, S. H., Rao, C. V. G. (Eds.) *Cranial Computed Tomography.* New York: McGraw-Hill. pp. 71–113.
—— —— Metzger, R. A., Grossman, R. I., Schut, L., Bruce, D. A. (1983) 'Computed tomography of orbital-facial neurofibromatosis.' *Radiology*, **146**, 113–116.

5
HYDROCEPHALUS

Hydrocephalus is defined as the pathologic condition in which part or all of the ventricular system is dilated due to imbalance in production and absorption of cerebrospinal fluid. The increased volume of cerebrospinal fluid is not a result of either cerebral dysgenesis or destruction (Harwood-Nash and Fitz 1976). Hydrocephalus may result from oversecretion, obstruction, or impaired absorption of cerebrospinal fluid.

Active hydrocephalus is progressive and is associated with increased intraventricular pressure. Arrested hydrocephalus means that intraventricular pressure has returned to normal, and is thus not a stimulus for further ventricular enlargement. Hydrocephalus *ex vacuo* represents an increase in cerebrospinal fluid volume under normal pressure following the loss of brain tissue (Fishman 1980).

Normal cerebrospinal fluid (CSF) formation (Fig. 5.1)
The major portion of CSF production is from the choroid plexus, although limited amounts may also be produced extrachoroidally in the cerebral ventricles, aqueduct of Sylvius and subarachnoid space (Pollay and Curl 1967, Milhorat *et al.* 1971).

The choroid plexus includes the choroidal epithelium, blood vessels and interstitial connective tissue. There are no morphologic changes between the choroid plexus of the lateral, third or fourth ventricles, although functional differences have been postulated (Pappenheimer *et al.* 1961).

The rate of CSF production in humans is 0.35ml/min, or approximately 500ml/day (Davson and Segal 1976, Fishman 1980).

CSF produced by the choroid plexus of lateral ventricles passes through the foramina of Monro into the third ventricle, aqueduct of Sylvius and fourth ventricle. From paired lateral foramina of Luschka or the midline foramen of Magendie, CSF passes into the basal cisterns and then anteriorly through the chiasmatic cisterns, Sylvian fissures and pericallosal cisterns, laterally over the cerebral hemispheres, posteriorly around the cerebellum *via* the quadrigeminal plate cistern and posterior callosal cistern, and then over the cerebral hemispheres.

In addition there is downward flow of CSF into the spinal subarachnoid space (Harwood-Nash and Fitz 1976).

Absorption of CSF occurs primarily at the arachnoid villi and granulations (Pacchionian bodies). The villi represent herniations of the arachnoid membrane which penetrate into the dura and protrude into the lumen of the superior sagittal sinus and other venous structures (Fishman 1980). The villi are only seen microscopically.

The larger granulations composed of multiple villi are visible from the age of

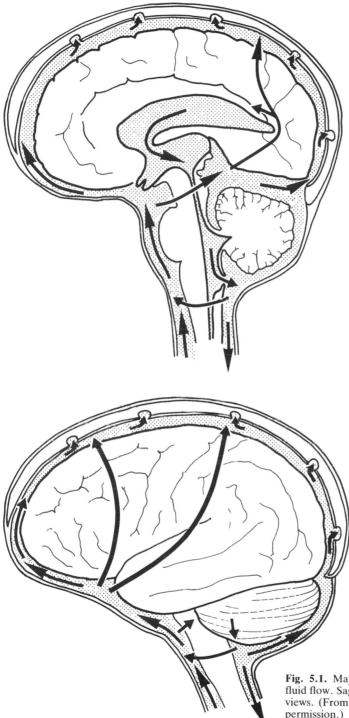

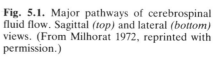

Fig. 5.1. Major pathways of cerebrospinal fluid flow. Sagittal *(top)* and lateral *(bottom)* views. (From Milhorat 1972, reprinted with permission.)

TABLE 5.1

Hydrocephalus: etiology

1. Overproduction of CSF
   Choroid plexus papilloma

2. Obstruction to CSF flow
   Intraventricular (IVOH)
      Congenital anomalies
      Post-inflammatory
      Post-hemorrhagic
      Tumors
   Extraventricular (EVOH)
      Congenital anomalies
      Post-inflammatory
      Subarachnoid hemorrhage
      Dural venous thrombosis
      Tumors and non-neoplastic mass lesions

3. Impaired absorption of CSF
   Defective arachnoid villi
   Impaired venous drainage

six months (Millen and Woollam 1962). The exact mechanism of absorption is unknown. Weed (1923) concluded that CSF absorption occurred by filtration across an intact membrane. Welch and Friedman (1960) and Welch and Pollay (1963) attributed a valve-like function to the villi. Multiple vacuoles in the membrane of the arachnoid villi have been described by Tripathi and Tripathi (1974) and Tripathi (1977) as permitting vesicular transport of CSF.

Classification

Extraventricular obstructive hydrocephalus (EVOH) (communicating hydrocephalus)
The site of obstruction is located beyond the outlet foramina of the fourth ventricle, within compartments of the subarachnoid spaces, or at the arachnoid villi or venous sinuses.

Intraventricular obstructive hydrocephalus (IVOH) (non-communicating hydrocephalus)
The site of obstruction is located between the lateral ventricles and outlet foramina of the fourth ventricle.

Etiology

The various etiologic factors are classified in Table 5.1.

In the period between birth and two years the usual cause is a developmental abnormality. Aqueduct stenosis is the commonest of the developmental abnormalities to produce hydrocephalus (Harwood-Nash and Fitz 1976, O'Brien 1982), and may be associated with an encephalocele, spina bifida, or Arnold-Chiari malformation.

Intra-uterine infection, hemorrhage, arachnoid cysts, arteriovenous malform-

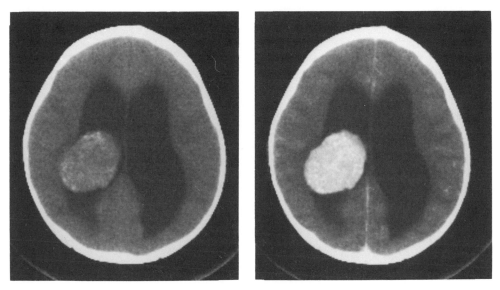

Fig. 5.2. Choroid plexus papilloma. 18-month-old boy. Non-contrast head CT scan *(left)* and contrast-enhanced head CT scan *(right)* demonstrate large soft tissue mass within dilated lateral ventricle. Contrast enhancement is demonstrated within tumor mass.

ations and tumors may also result in hydrocephalus. These conditions are discussed in greater detail in the appropriate chapters.

In early to later childhood (two to 10 years) posterior fossa tumors and aqueduct stenosis are the most common causes of hydrocephalus (O'Brien 1982).

Pathophysiology of hydrocephalus
The development of hydrocephalus is related to four mechanisms.
1. Overproduction of CSF
2. Obstruction to CSF flow (intraventricular or extraventricular)
3. Impaired CSF absorption at the arachnoid villi
4. Venous obstruction

1. Overproduction of CSF
Choroid plexus papilloma (Fig. 5.2) is the only condition responsible for increased CSF formation sufficient to permit intracranial hypertension (Fishman 1980). The resultant hydrocephalus may be due to mass effect with subsequent ventricular obstruction, intraventricular hemorrhage produced by the tumor, or oversecretion of CSF by the tumor. Eisenberg *et al.* (1974) measured CSF production in a child with choroid plexus papilloma, pre- and post-operatively. The pre-operative CSF formation rate was increased fourfold and fell to the normal rate after surgical removal.

2. Obstruction of CSF pathways
Obstruction to CSF flow is the commonest form of hydrocephalus. The blockage

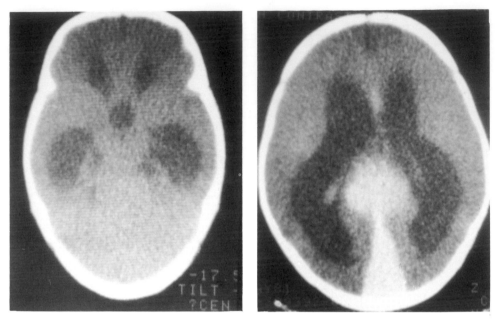

Fig. 5.3. Vein of Galen aneurysm. Six-month-old boy. *Left:* non-contrast head CT scan demonstrates obstructive hydrocephalus. There is marked dilatation of lateral and third ventricles. *Right:* contrast-enhanced head CT scan shows large vein of Galen aneurysm.

may occur in intraventricular or extraventricular locations. There is dilatation of the ventricular system proximal to the site of obstruction, with normal ventricular size distally. However, there are exceptions (Naidich 1980):

(a) The fourth ventricle may not be dilated in 25 to 35 per cent of patients, with EVOH thus resembling aqueduct stenosis.

(b) Second and third sites of obstruction develop in 20 per cent of patients with EVOH. Only the lowest obstruction will be demonstrated by CT.

(c) The dilated third or fourth ventricle which is obstructed may be indistinguishable from intraventricular space-occupying lesions (*e.g.* lucent epidermoid tumor, cysticercus cyst, arachnoid cyst).

Intraventricular obstructive hydrocephalus (IVOH) (internal hydrocephalus/non-communicating hydrocephalus)
The site of obstruction may occur between the lateral ventricles and the outlet foramina of the fourth ventricle.

LATERAL VENTRICLES
Congenital coarctation is a rare form of obstruction, occurring usually at the trigone or within the temporal horn. The narrowing may be a congenital maldevelopment or a consequence of intra-uterine ventriculitis with adhesion formation (Harwood-Nash and Fitz 1976). Obstruction of the atrium by an

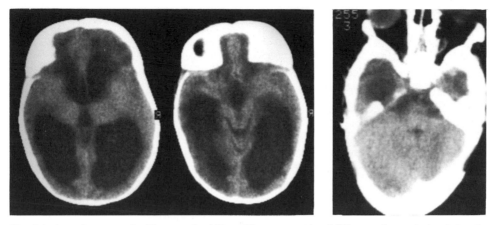

Fig. 5.4. Aqueduct stenosis. Five-month-old boy. Non-contrast head CT scans demonstrate obstructive hydrocephalus with dilated lateral and third ventricles *(left)* and small fourth ventricle *(right)*.

intraventricular tumor produces enlargement of the temporal horn (Naidich and Gado 1978).

FORAMEN OF MONRO

Developmental occlusion of the foramen of Monro is rare (Skultety and Hardy 1956). The most common cause of obstruction is tumor. The foramen of Monro may be partially obstructed by extra-axial suprasellar masses or intraventricular tumors and cysts, and arachnoid cysts of the suprasellar cistern (Fitz 1982).

Other causes are intraventricular hemorrhage (following trauma, hemophilia, arteriovenous malformation) and infection (Fitz 1982).

Unilateral or bilateral dilatation of the lateral ventricles will be demonstrated on CT depending on the site of obstruction. Both foramina may be compressed by a single large tumor; the ipsilateral ventricle is usually compressed with contralateral ventricular dilatation (Fitz 1982).

THIRD VENTRICLE

The commonest obstructive lesions are extrinsic to the third ventricle (Harwood-Nash and Fitz 1976). These include craniopharyngioma and paraventricular glioma (thalamus, optic chiasm, hypothalamus) and mass lesions related to the posterior third ventricle (gliomas of the posterior hypothalamus and thalamus), tumors of the pineal region, arteriovenous malformations (Fig. 5.3), and arachnoid cysts, and chordomas.

Aneurysms of the basilar and internal carotid arteries which are rare in childhood may be sufficiently large to obstruct the third ventricle (Thompson *et al.* 1973).

AQUEDUCT STENOSIS

Aqueduct stenosis (Fig 5.4) is the commonest cause of IVOH.

Intrinsic lesions. Congenital aqueduct stenosis more commonly occurs with the Chiari II malformation.

The etiology is unknown but has been attributed to maldevelopment, intra-uterine vascular abnormality, infection of hypoxia (Harwood-Nash and Fitz 1976).

Four main types of anomaly have been described by Russell (1949):

1. Stenosis. Narrowing occurs without abnormal gliosis in the surrounding tissue.
2. Forking. Two main channels of greatly reduced dimension are found behind each other in the mid-sagittal plane of the brainstem, separated by normal tissue.
3. Septum formation. A thin neuroglial membrane produces partial or total occlusion of the aqueduct. There may be an association with ventricular ependymitis suggesting an intra-uterine infection.
4. Gliosis. Narrowing of the aqueduct or sub-division into two or more channels is present in association with proliferation of fibrillary glia.

Extrinsic lesions. Extrinsic mass lesions producing both distortion and displacement of the aqueduct are commoner in older children.

Neoplastic lesions in the brainstem, tentorial hiatus, cerebellopontine angle, quadrigeminal plate and cerebellum may be involved. Other causes include dilated vein of Galen, aneurysm, quadrigeminal arachnoid cyst, and brainstem edema.

CT appearances of aqueduct stenosis (Fig. 5.4)

1. The lateral and third ventricles are moderately or severely dilated. The fourth ventricle is usually normal in size if the Chiari malformation is absent, but may be small if the malformation is present. The presence of the fourth ventricle may be missed if CT sections are 10mm or thicker (Fitz 1982).
2. Chiari II malformation. The CT appearances have been described in detail in Chapter 4.
3. Mass lesions producing aqueduct stenosis. The extrinsic causes of aqueduct stenosis, as described above, may be readily demonstrated on CT. Intravenous contrast medium administration is mandatory to exclude both inflammatory and neoplastic masses.

FOURTH VENTRICULAR OBSTRUCTION

This may be congenital (*e.g.* Dandy-Walker cyst) or acquired in origin. Acquired causes include hemorrhage, infection, and mass lesions. The mass lesions are diverse, including extraventricular intra-axial neoplasms (astrocytoma, medulloblastoma, exophytic brainstem glioma), abscess, cerebellar edema, and extra-axial masses such as arachnoid cyst, chordoma and subdural hematoma (Harwood-Nash and Fitz 1976).

Extraventricular obstructive hydrocephalus (EVOH) (external hydrocephalus/ communicating hydrocephalus)

The site of obstruction to CSF flow lies within the subarachnoid space between the outlet foramina of the fourth ventricle and arachnoid granulations.

The most common causes of EVOH are hemorrhage and infection of and within

TABLE 5.2

Causes of EVOH

Hemorrhage
  Subarachnoid hemorrhage
  Post-hemorrhagic arachnoiditis
  Dural mass hemorrhage

Infection
  Bacterial (common)
  Fungal and parasitic (rare)

Infiltration of the meninges
  Seeding by cerebral neoplasm
  Leukemia
  Lymphoma
  Leptomeningeal sarcoma
  Nonmalignant infiltration
    Histiocytosis X
    Gargoylism

Excess CSF protein content

Congenital lesions
  Intra-uterine infection and hemorrhage
  Arnold Chiari malformation
  Lissencephaly
  Congenital absence of arachnoid granulations

Skull abnormalities
  Achondroplasia
  Basilar impression

From Harwood-Nash and Fitz (1976) *Neuroradiology in Infants and Children* (reprinted with permission).

the meninges and subarachnoid space, although a wide spectrum of lesions may be responsible (Harwood-Nash and Fitz 1976, Naidich and Gado 1978). Table 5.2 lists the many varied causes.

CT appearances
The basic appearance of EVOH is constant and is not affected by the level of obstruction. The findings of Fitz (1982) are:
1. Moderate dilatation of the lateral ventricles with mild dilatation of the third and fourth ventricles. Marked dilatation of all ventricles may occur, however, or only the lateral and third ventricles may be involved (Fig. 5.5)
2. Dilatation of the subarachnoid space over the hemisphere may be commonly encountered in EVOH of childhood. This has been found by Fitz (1982) to be a reliable sign of extraventricular obstruction.
3. Specific appearances due to the underlying etiology may be demonstrated. Contrast enhancement of a membrane may be visible in patients with subdural empyema. Contrast-enhancement of the meninges due to primary tumor of the subarachnoid space is extremely rare, and must be differentiated from a similar appearance due to inflammation or metastasis (Flodmark *et al.* 1979).

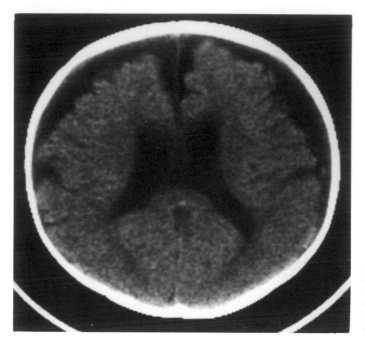

Fig. 5.5. Extraventricular obstructive hydrocephalus. Eight-month-old girl. Non-contrast head CT scan reveals evidence of a dilated subarachnoid space.

Effects of untreated hydrocephalus on brain parenchyma
Three main effects of untreated hydrocephalus which may become irreversible have been described (Naidich *et al.* 1976, Naidich 1980):

PERIVENTRICULAR EDEMA (Fig. 5.6)
Periventricular lucency seen on CT is believed to be due to extension of CSF into the white matter across the ependyma. The periventricular blurring is usually noted first adjacent to the superolateral angles of the frontal horns where it is most severe, due to marked ependymal disruption (Milhorat *et al.* 1970, Page 1975). This effect may also be noted along the occipital horns, atria, and other parts of the ventricle underlying white matter.

DISPROPORTIONATE DILATATION OF THE ATRIA AND OCCIPITAL HORNS (Fig 5.7)
The atria and occipital horns may be dilated to a greater extent in comparison with the frontal horns. This has been attributed to the varying effects of hydrocephalus on gray and white matter and the variable distensibility of the vertex and skull base (Hochwald *et al.* 1972, Rubin *et al.* 1975, Naidich *et al.* 1976). The relative rigidity of the skull base restrains expansion of the frontal horns, whereas the vertex is distensible and thus permits dilatation of the atria and occipital horns. The gray matter surrounding the frontal horns is only slightly affected by the axonal fragmentation, myelin destruction and gliosis which occur with severe hydrocephalus. The atria and occipital horns are surrounded by white matter and are more subject to the effects of hydrocephalus with subsequent ventricular enlargement.

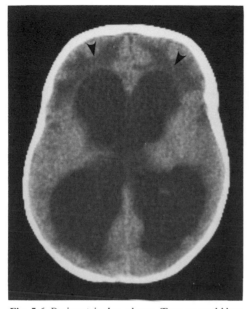

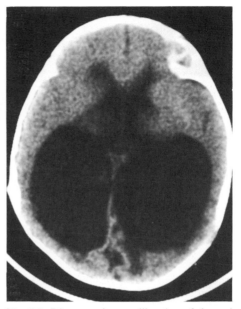

Fig. 5.6. Periventricular edema. Two-year-old boy with medulloblastoma. Non-contrast head CT scan demonstrates areas of low density *(arrowheads)* surrounding the frontal horns due to periventricular edema.

Fig. 5.7. Disproportionate dilatation of the atria and occipital horns. Five-month-old boy. The atria and occipital horns appear markedly dilated in relation to the frontal horns.

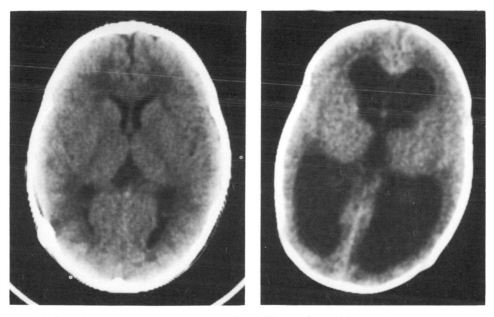

Fig. 5.8. Post-shunt appearances. Non-contrast head CT scans in an eight-month-old boy with marked hydrocephalus. Post-shunt *(left)* and pre-shunt appearance *(right)*. Post-shunt appearance shows considerable decrease in ventricular size.

91

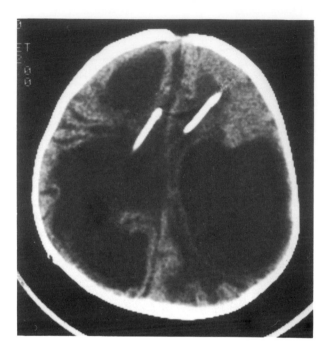

Fig. 5.9. Shunt malfunction. Two-year-old girl with ventriculitis and subsequent adhesion formation. Non-contrast head CT scan reveals evidence of residual hydrocephalus and ventricular loculation due to adhesions. Two ventricular shunt tubes are in place.

THINNING OF THE CEREBRAL MANTLE

Progressive thinning of the cerebral mantle occurs with increasing ventricular dilatation. This change is attributed to stretching of axon fibers and sheaths passing around the dilated ventricles (Rubin *et al.* 1975).

Treated hydrocephalus

The post-shunt appearances described in detail by Naidich (1980), include:

1. Regression of periventricular edema. This occurs within one to several weeks after shunting.

2. Decrease in ventricular size (Fig. 5.8) The shunt-containing ventricle is usually smaller (Kaufman *et al.* 1973). The reduction in size of the frontal horns is often greater than that of the atria and occipital horns, as the relatively spared gray matter returns to normal rapidly compared with the more severely damaged white matter (Rubin *et al.* 1975, Naidich *et al.* 1976)

3. The thalami move superomedially. The corpus callosum folds downwards. These changes result in small ventricles with sharpened lateral angles and an acute callosal angle.

4. The lateral ventricles may be barely visible as slits or not visualized. In such instances there is absence of cortical sulci and formation of a diamond-shaped CSF space at the apex of the incisura, composed of the dilated confluent superior vermian and velum interpositum cisterns.

5. The cerebral mantle may increase in thickness after shunting in early hydrocephalus, due to thickening and shortening of axon fibers as they surround

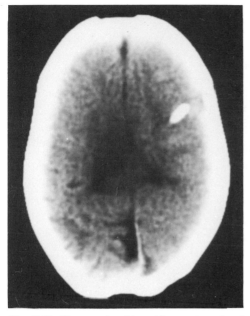 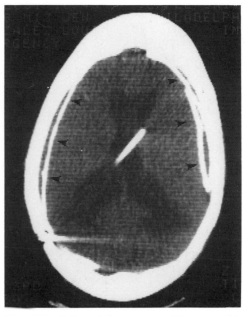

Fig. 5.10. Shunt malposition. Non-contrast head CT scan in a two-year-old girl with shunt blockage. Note position of the shunt tube within the cerebral cortex.

Fig. 5.11. Subdural hematomas. Nine-year-old boy with hydrocephalus. Non-contrast head CT scan reveals evidence of calcified subdural membranes bilaterally *(arrowheads)*.

the small vessels. (This may not occur, however, in later hydrocephalus.)

6. Fissures and sulci may appear to be widened, with focal or diffuse invagination of the cortical surfaces (Emery 1965). The interhemispheric fissure widens just above the corpus callosum.

Intracranial complications of shunts

Shunt complications are fairly common and are readily assessed by CT.

1. *Shunt blockage* is the most commonly encountered problem (Harwood-Nash and Fitz 1976). Obstruction of the cerebral ventricular end occurs in a quarter to a third of all cases. The causes for this include pressure across the ependyma, perforation of brain, hemorrhage, inspissated CSF debris or adhesions following ventriculitis (Fig. 5.9).

2. *Infection.* Shunt infection occurs in 2 to 15 per cent of patients (Naidich *et al.* 1982). Intense choroiditis and ependymitis with rarefaction and cyst formation has been demonstrated by these authors in the periventricular white matter. Ventriculitis and meningitis may also occur with subsequent development of brain abscess, thromboses of cortical vessels and infarction, ventricular adhesions and loculations, and porencephaly.

3. *Shunt malposition* is a common complication. Catheters entering the cortex and ventricular system at the wrong site may cross vital neural pathways with consequent neurologic problems (Fig. 5.10).

93

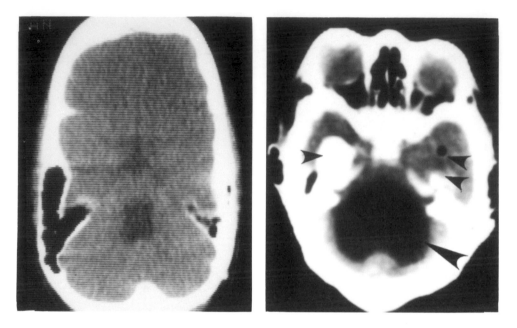

Fig. 5.12. Trapped fourth ventricle. *Left:* 10-year-old girl with increasing fourth ventricular size following shunt placement. Non-contrast head CT scan demonstrates an isolated dilated fourth ventricle. *Right:* three-month-old boy with previous history of neonatal intraventricular hemorrhage. The fourth ventricle was normal on ultrasound examination at birth. Increasing fourth ventricular size was subsequently documented by ultrasound and CT. This head CT scan was performed after metrizamide (amipaque) introduction into the ventricular system. Positive contrast medium is noted to fill right temporal horn *(left arrowhead)* and left temporal horn, which also contains air *(double arrowheads)* but fails to fill markedly enlarged fourth ventricle *(large arrowhead)*.

4. *Subdural hematoma.* Rapid collapse of the ventricles may cause rupture of bridging veins with the ensuing development of small or large subdural hematomas. These are often bilateral, and may subsequently calcify (Fig. 5.11).

5. *Premature closure of sutures* may follow decreased intracranial pressure and ventricular size.

6. *Shunt dependence* (slit ventricle syndrome). Shunt dependence occurs when the ventricles become very small following shunting. There is loss of ventricular compliance with inability to re-expand (Fitz 1982).

7. *The trapped fourth ventricle.* Entrapment of the fourth ventricle is a condition due to obstruction of the aqueduct and the outlet foramina of Luschka and Magendie (Zimmerman *et al.* 1978). This entity has also been referred to as double compartment hydrocephalus (DeFeo *et al.* 1975), isolated fourth ventricle (Hawkins *et al.* 1978, Scotti *et al.* 1980) and encysted fourth ventricle (Raimondi *et al.* 1969, DeFeo *et al.* 1975).

Entrapment has been shown to occur after shunting for communicating hydrocephalus, aqueduct stenosis and obstruction of the fourth ventricle. Subsequent mechanical or inflammatory changes within the aqueduct or outlet foramina of the fourth ventricle isolate the fourth ventricle from the ventricular system and subarachnoid space (Scotti *et al.* 1980).

As this is a potentially curable entity, CT is the modality of choice in patients with shunted hydrocephalus who show progressive neurological deficits or develop new posterior fossa signs. The need for other studies such as metrizamide ventriculography will be obviated. The CT appearance is that of marked dilatation of the fourth ventricle (Fig. 5.12).

Normal pressure hydrocephalus
Normal pressure hydrocephalus (NPH) is a condition first described by Hakim (1964) with the clinical triad of ataxia, dementia and urinary incontinence. This diagnosis is not made in children, but in older adults. Considerable ventricular enlargement may be present without elevated intraventricular pressure (Adams *et al.* 1965). The condition may be idiopathic, or may follow subarachnoid hemorrhage (Foltz and Ward 1956, Kibler *et al.* 1961).

Cerebral atrophy
The normal subarachnoid spaces
The sulci of infants under the age of six months have been found by Harwood-Nash and Fitz (1976) to be normally fairly large. The study of Kleinman *et al.* (1983), who used a high-resolution CT scanner, confirmed that the size of the subarachnoid space is variable during the first two years of life. Increased size of the subarachnoid space accompanies enlargement of the brain and development of the gyral pattern. Because of the variability of the subarachnoid spaces which may appear much larger than anticipated, the CT appearances should be correlated with head circumference measurements and other clinical data.

Cerebral atrophy
Cerebral atrophy is defined as a loss of brain substance, involving gray matter, white matter, or both (Fitz 1982). This may be focal or diffuse.

Focal atrophy
This may follow decreased vascular supply to an area (due to vascular anomalies, infarction) trauma or infection. The cerebrum and cerebellum may be involved. The CT manifestations are local ventricular or sulcal enlargement, or a combination of both.

Hemiatrophy
Cerebral hemiatrophy (Dyke *et al.* 1933) follows neonatal or intra-uterine vascular occlusion. The onset is usually during adolescence but may rarely also occur in childhood.

The calvarium on the affected side is usually thickened. There is evidence of atrophy of the cerebral hemisphere with a ventricular shift toward the atrophic side. Prominence of the mastoid and paranasal sinuses and elevation of the orbit roof on the affected side may also be demonstrated by CT.

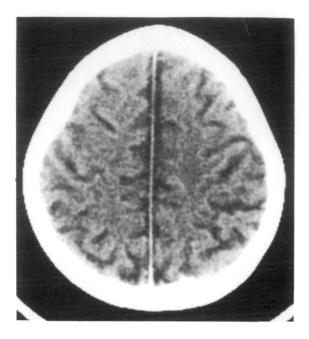

Fig. 5.13. Diffuse cortical atrophy. 10-year-old girl with leukemia, receiving steroid therapy. Contrast-enhanced head CT scan demonstrates generalized increase in sulcal size.

Central atrophy

The clinical signs are of delayed development or brain injury. The CT appearance is that of mild ventricular enlargement without evidence of enlarged sulci.

Cortical atrophy

Enlargement of the sulci is present without accompanying increase in ventricular size (Fig. 5.13).

Benign subdural collections of infancy (benign subdural effusions)

In addition to the subdural effusions due to trauma and infection there exists an entity of benign subdural effusion (Robertson and Gomez 1978, Robertson *et al.* 1979, Ment *et al.* 1981). Although this abnormality is of unknown etiology the frequency is probably higher than previously recognized (Ment *et al.* 1981). Robertson and Gomez (1978) consider this abnormality to occur during the first stage of communicating internal hydrocephalus, as half of their patients subsequently developed significant ventriculomegaly. The initial clinical presentation in most cases is that of abnormally increasing head circumference (Robertson and Gomez 1978, Robertson *et al.* 1979, Ment *et al.* 1981).

The CT appearances in patients with benign subdural effusions consist of enlarged subarachnoid spaces, prominent basilar cisterns, and normal or minimally increased ventricular size (Robertson and Gomez 1978, Robertson *et al.* 1979, Ment *et al.* 1981).

Subdural hematoma is an important disorder to be differentiated from a benign subdural effusion. The larger size of the extra-axial fluid collection, loss of the prominent sulcal pattern, and lack of enlargement of the basilar cisterns are features of a subdural hematoma (Ment *et al.* 1981). Dilated subarachnoid spaces may also be encountered in patients suffering from malnutrition (Marks *et al.* 1978), patients receiving chemotherapy (Enzmann and Lane 1978) and in premature infants following intracranial hemorrhage (Papile *et al.* 1978).

REFERENCES

Adams, R. D., Fisher, C. M., Hakim, S., Ojemann, R. G., Sweet, W. H. (1965) 'Symptomatic occult hydrocephalus with "normal" cerebrospinal-fluid pressure.' *New England Journal of Medicine*, **273**, 117–126.

Davson, H., Segal, M. B. (1976) 'Homeostasis in the nervous system.' *In: Introduction to Physiology, Volume 3; Control Mechanisms.* New York: Grune & Stratton. pp. 576–621.

DeFeo, D., Foltz, E. L., Hamilton, A. E. (1975) 'Double compartment hydrocephalus in a patient with cysticercosis meningitis.' *Surgical Neurology*, **4**, 247–251.

Dyke, C. G., Davidoff, L. M., Masson, C. B. (1933) 'Cerebral hemiatrophy with homolateral hypertrophy of the skull and sinuses.' *Surgery, Gynecology and Obstetrics*, **57**, 588–600.

Eisenberg, H. M., McComb, J. G., Lorenzo, A. V. (1974) 'Cerebrospinal fluid overproduction and hydrocephalus associated with choroid plexus papilloma.' *Journal of Neurosurgery*, **40**, 381–385.

Emery, J. L. (1965) 'Intracranial effect of longstanding decompression of the brain in children with hydrocephalus and meningomyelocele.' *Developmental Medicine and Child Neurology*, **7**, 302–309.

Enzmann, D. R., Lane, B. (1978) 'Enlargement of subarachnoid spaces and lateral ventricles in pediatric patients undergoing chemotherapy.' *Journal of Pediatrics*, **92**, 535–539.

Fishman, R. A. (1980) *Cerebrospinal Fluid in Diseases of the Nervous System.* Philadelphia: W. B. Saunders. pp. 1–384.

Fitz, C. R. (1982) 'The ventricles and subarachnoid spaces in children.' *In:* Lee, S. H., Rao, K. C. V. G. (Eds.) *Cerebral Computed Tomography.* New York: McGraw-Hill. pp. 201–239.

Flodmark, O., Fitz, C. R., Harwood-Nash, D. C., Chuang, S. (1979) 'Neuroradiological findings in a child with primary leptomeningeal melanoma.' *Neuroradiology*, **18**, 153–156.

Foltz, E. L., Ward, A. A., Jr. (1956) 'Communicating hydrocephalus from subarachnoid bleeding.' *Journal of Neurosurgery*, **13**, 546–566.

Hakim, S. (1964) 'Some observations on CSF pressure: hydrocephalic syndrome in adults with "normal" CSF pressure.' *Thesis No 957, Javeriana University, School of Medicine, Bogota, Colombia.*

Harwood-Nash, D. C., Fitz, C. R. (1976) 'Hydrocephalus.' *In: Neuroradiology in Infants and Children.* St. Louis: C. V. Mosby. pp. 609–667.

Hawkins, J. C., Hoffman, H. J., Humphreys, R. P. (1978) 'Isolated fourth ventricle as a complication of ventricular shunting; report of three cases.' *Journal of Neurosurgery*, **49**, 910–913.

Hochwald, G. M., Epstein, F., Malhan, C. (1972) 'The role of the skull and dura in experimental feline hydrocephalus.' *Developmental Medicine and Child Neurology*, Supplement **27**, 65–69.

Kaufman, B., Weiss, M. H., Young, H. F., Nulsen, F. E. (1973) 'Effects of prolonged cerebrospinal fluid shunting on the skull and brain.' *Journal of Neurosurgery*, **38**, 288–297.

Kibler, R. F., Couch, R. S. C., Crompton, M. R. (1961) 'Hydrocephalus in the adult following spontaneous subarachnoid hemorrhage.' *Brain*, **84**, 45–61.

Kleinman, P. K., Zito, J. L., Davidson, R. I., Raptopoulos, V. (1983) 'The subarachnoid spaces in children: normal variations in size.' *Radiology*, **147**, 455–457.

Marks, H. G., Borns, P., Steg, N. L., Stine, S. B., Stroud, H. H., Yates, T. S. (1978) 'Catch-up brain growth—demonstration by CAT scan.' *Journal of Pediatrics*, **93**, 254–256.

Ment, L. R., Duncan, C. C., Geehr, R. (1981) 'Benign enlargement of the subarachnoid spaces of the infant.' *Journal of Neurosurgery*, **54**, 504–508.

Milhorat, T. H. (1972) *Hydrocephalus and the Cerebrospinal Fluid.* Baltimore: Williams and Wilkins.

—— Clark, R. G., Hammock, M. K., McGrath, P. P. (1970) 'Structural, ultrastructural, and permeability changes in the ependyma and surrounding brain favoring equilibrium in progressive hydrocephalus.' *Archives of Neurology*, **22**, 397–407.

—— Hammock, M. K., Fenstermacher, J. D., Rall, D. P., Levin, V. A. (1971) 'Cerebrospinal fluid production by the choroid plexus and brain.' *Science*, **173**, 330–332.

Millen, J., Woollam, D. H. M. (1962) *The Anatomy of the Cerebrospinal Fluid.* London: Oxford University Press.

Naidich, T. P. (1980) 'Hydrocephalus.' *In:* Moss, A. A. (Ed.) *Computed Tomography, Ultrasound and X-Ray: an Integrated Approach.* Academic Press. pp. 509–530.

—— Epstein, F., Lin, J. P., Kricheff, I. I., Hochwald, G. (1976) 'Evaluation of pediatric hydrocephalus by computed tomography.' *Radiology,* **119,** 337–345.

—— T. P., Gado, M. (1978) 'Hydrocephalus.' *In:* Newton, T. H., Potts, D. G. (Eds.) *Radiology of the Skull and Brain, Volume 4: Ventricles and Cisterns.* St. Louis: C. V. Mosby. pp. 3764–3834.

—— Schott, L. H., Baron, R. L. (1982) 'Computed tomography in evaluation of hydrocephalus.' *Radiologic Clinics of North America,* **20,** 143–167.

O'Brien, M. S. (1982) 'Hydrocephalus in children.' *In:* Youmans, J. R. (Ed.) *Neurological Surgery.* Philadelphia: W. B. Saunders. pp. 1381–1422.

Page, R. B. (1975) 'Scanning electron microscopy of the ventricular system in normal and hydrocephalic rabbits. Preliminary report and atlas.' *Journal of Neurosurgery,* **42,** 646–664.

Papile, L. A. Burstein, J., Burstein, R., Koffler, H. (1978) 'Incidence and evolution of subependymal and intraventricular hemorrhage: a study of infants with birthweights less than 1500gm.' *Journal of Pediatrics,* **92,** 529–534.

Pappenheimer, J. R., Heisey, S. R., Jordan, E. F. (1961) 'Active transport of diodrast and phenolsulfonephthalein from cerebrospinal fluid to blood.' *American Journal of Physiology,* **200,** 1–10.

Pollay, M., Curl, F. (1967) 'Secretion of CSF by the ventricular ependyma of the rabbit.' *American Journal of Physiology,* **213,** 1031–1038.

Raimondi, A. J., Samuelson, G., Yarzagaray, L., Norton, T. (1969) 'Atresia of the foramina of Luschka and Magendie: the Dandy–Walker cyst.' *Journal of Neurosurgery,* **31,** 202–216.

Robertson, W. C. Jr., Gomez, M. R. (1978) 'External hydrocephalus.' *Archives of Neurology,* **35,** 541–544.

—— Chun, R. W. M., Orrison, W. W., Sackett, J. F. (1979) 'Benign subdural collections of infancy.' *Journal of Pediatrics,* **94,** 382–385.

Rubin, R. C., Hochwald, R. G., Tiell, M., Liwnicz, B., Epstein, F. (1975) 'Reconstruction of the cerebral cortical mantle in shunt corrected hydrocephalus.' *Developmental Medicine and Child Neurology,* **17,** Suppl. 35, 151–156.

Russell, D. S. (1949) *Observations on the Pathology of Hydrocephalus. M.R.C. Special Report Series No. 265,* London: H.M.S.O. p. 138.

Scotti, G., Musgrave, M. A., Fitz, C. R., Harwood-Nash, D. C. (1980) 'The isolated fourth ventricle in children: CT and clinical review of 16 cases.' *American Journal of Roentgenology,* **135,** 1233–1238.

Skultety, F. M., Hardy, R. G. (1956) 'Congenital obliteration of the anterior portion of the lateral ventricle.' *Neurology,* **6,** 478–483.

Thompson, J. R., Harwood-Nash, D. C., Fitz, C. R. (1973) 'Cerebral aneurysms in children.' *American Journal of Roentgenology,* **118,** 163–175.

Tripathi, B. S., Tripathi, R. C. (1974) 'Vacuolar transcellular channels as a drainage pathway for cerebrospinal fluid.' *Journal of Physiology (London),* **239,** 195–206.

Tripathi, R. C. (1977) 'The functional morphology of the outflow systems of ocular and cerebrospinal fluids.' *In:* Bito, L. Z., Davson, H., Fenstermacher, J. D. (Eds.) *The Ocular and Cerebrospinal Fluids.* New York: Academic Press. pp. 65–116.

Weed, L. H. (1923) 'The absorption of cerebrospinal fluid into the venous system.' *American Journal of Anatomy,* **31,** 191–221.

Welch, K., Friedman, V. (1960) 'The cerebrospinal fluid valves.' *Brain,* **83,** 454–469.

—— Pollay, M. (1963) 'The spinal arachnoid villi of the monkeys, *Cercopithecus aethiops, Sabaeus* and *Macaca irus.*' *Anatomical Record,* **145,** 43–48.

Zimmerman, R. A., Bilaniuk, L. T., Gallo, E. (1978) 'Computed tomography of the trapped fourth ventricle.' *American Journal of Roentgenology,* **130,** 503–506.

6
TRAUMA

Trauma is the major cause of death in children after one year of age, and is second only to respiratory infection as the commonest reason for hospital admission (Craft 1975). The epidemiology of head injuries in children has been classified into main age categories by McLaurin and McLennan (1982). The peak incidence of head injury occurs under one year of age, with half the cases due to 'birth trauma'. Many injuries may be attributed to the carelessness of a parent or guardian who has dropped the infant or failed to prevent him falling from a height. It is also in this age-group that the 'battered child' may be discovered, requiring the astuteness of both clinician and radiologist. The toddler is at risk because of a desire to explore new frontiers without the benefit of any previous experience. In children under the age of three, most head injuries are sustained at home. A second peak incidence occurs between three and four years. Between the ages of four and eight, injury due to moving vehicles is a major cause of head trauma; this decreases as the child becomes more aware of the dangers. After the age of 13 years, there are no specific epidemiologic factors. In the later teenage years, injuries following the driving of motor vehicles under the influence of alcohol have resulted in a highly significant cause of morbidity and mortality. Head injuries in infants and children are different from those in adults (Milhorat 1978). There is greater lability in the physiologic response of a child to head trauma. The skull at a young age is readily expansile, so it may accommodate serious intracranial bleeding without the usual neurologic signs.

The advent of CT has revolutionized the early assessment and diagnosis in head injuries, and obviated the need in most cases for more invasive diagnostic studies. CT should be the initial imaging modality when significant brain injury is suspected in order to define the nature and severity of the injury, provided that clinical examination does not reveal a neurosurgical emergency, e.g. epidural hematoma, which requires immediate evacuation (Zimmerman and Bilaniuk 1981).

However, cerebral angiography may be needed in some circumstances (Faerber 1979), e.g. when there is a plateau in neurologic signs (due to carotid occlusion or vasospasm), suspected traumatic aneurysm, isodense subdural hematoma not shown by CT, head injury due to subarachnoid hemorrhage or seizure, and suspected carotid-cavernous fistula.

Edema
Generalized cerebral edema, which occurs immediately after trauma, has been found to be the most frequent finding on CT in children with acute head injury (Zimmerman et al. 1978a). The cause of brain swelling has been attributed to increased cerebral blood volume and the subsequent development of cerebral

edema (Lewis 1976).

The CT features, as described by Zimmerman *et al.* (1978*a*), are:

1. Slight increase in the density of the brain, which may be due to the addition of increased blood. The density returns to normal with the resolution of edema and decreased bloodflow. The authors did not note this appearance in adults, in whom cerebral bloodflow tends to be low immediately following trauma.

2. Absence or compression of the lateral and third ventricles and perimesencephalic cisterns (Fig. 6.1). The increased blood volume produces a decrease in intracranial compliance thereby forcing cerebrospinal fluid out of the subarachnoid spaces and ventricles. The changes of ventricular size may be more apparent on review of serial CT examinations as the ventricles are normally small in the pediatric age-group.

Contusion

A contusion is a focal lesion containing macerated hemorrhagic tissue (Merino-de Villasante and Taveras 1976, Peyster and Hoover 1982). This is the commonest parenchymal abnormality found after injury, frequently associated with skull fractures and other lesions, usually extracerebral collections of blood (Dublin *et al.* 1977). The superficial cortex is most frequently involved (Zimmerman *et al.* 1977*a*). Hemorrhagic contusions occur more commonly in older children than infants and young children, This is attributed to the greater pliability of the pediatric skull, and possibly the pediatric brain (Zimmerman and Bilaniuk 1981).

The initial post-injury CT appearance of a contusion (Fig. 6.2) is composed of (i) increased density, higher than surrounding brain due to the extravasated blood, and (ii) low density of the swollen brain substance, producing a non-homogeneous appearance (Merino-de Villasante and Taveras 1976).

There is associated mass effect, which increases because of edema at the site of contusion, and becomes maximal between the third and sixth days after the injury (Zimmerman and Bilaniuk 1978). Further bleeding at the site of contusion results in the formation of a contusional hematoma. In the absence of clot formation the combination of edema fluid and hemorrhagic tissue produces an area of variable density ranging from hypodense to hyperdense (Zimmerman *et al.* 1977*a*). Administration of contrast medium a week after the injury results in enhancement of the margins of the contusion (Zimmerman *et al.* 1977*a*). There is ultimate resorption of the contusion resulting in cortical encephalomalacia.

Shearing injuries

Shearing (diffuse impact) injuries of the white matter were described by Zimmerman *et al.* (1978*b*) in young children (mean age eight years) involved as passengers in high speed vehicular collisions. The underlying mechanism is attributed to the abrupt cranial acceleration at the time of impact when one cerebral hemisphere is placed in motion relative to the other (Zimmerman *et al.* 1978*b*).

The areas most commonly involved are the corpus callosum, septum pellucidum, medullary pyramids, third ventricular region and deep white matter

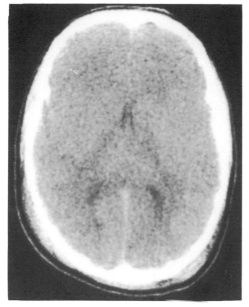

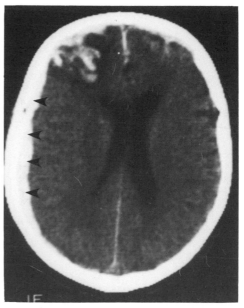

Fig. 6.1. Central edema. 10-year-old girl. Non-contrast head CT scan demonstrates diffuse cerebral edema with ventricular compressions. (Courtesy of Joel Swartz MD, Philadelphia).

Fig. 6.2a. Cerebral contusion. 14-year-old boy. Non-contrast head CT scan demonstrates right frontal contusion, composed of mixed densities. An acute subdural hematoma is also present (*arrowheads*). (Courtesy of Gary DeFillip MD, Philadelphia.)

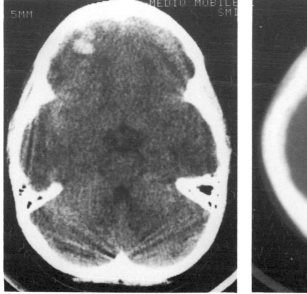

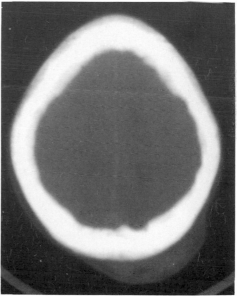

Fig. 6.2b. Contre-coup injury. Two-year-old boy. *Left:* non-contrast head CT scan shows a right frontal hematoma. *Right:* non-contrast head CT scan (higher section) demonstrates left occipital soft tissue swelling.

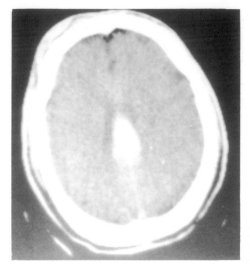

Fig. 6.3. Shearing injury. 14-year-old male. Non-contrast head CT scan demonstrates a large hemorrhage within the corpus callosum.

(Shalen and Handel 1981).

The CT findings as originally described by Zimmerman *et al.* (1978*b*) consist of:

1. Bilateral cerebral swelling with cisternal and ventricular compression, eccentric hemorrhage in the corpus callosum (Fig. 6.3), subarachnoid hemorrhage and the absence of specific focal mass lesions.

2. Small focal areas of hemorrhage, less commonly identified, adjacent to the third ventricle or within the white matter of the cerebral hemisphere.

3. Atrophic enlargement of the lateral ventricles and focal areas of decreased density within the cerebral hemisphere white matter appear two to three weeks after the injury.

Intracerebral hematoma

Acute intracerebral hematomas are most commonly found in the frontal and temporal lobes in contrast to the basal ganglia involvement with spontaneous hemorrhages (Dolinskas *et al.* 1977*a*). They are commonly associated with traumatic lesions, especially contusions. Multiple lesions may be present.

The CT appearance is that of a well-defined area of increased density within the brain parenchyma, associated with mass effect and surrounded by a zone of lower density representing macerated tissue and edema (Merino-de Villasante and Taveras 1976). The ability of CT to localize and measure the volume of a loculation of blood within the brain provides critical information, also available from cerebral angiography, as to whether there is a discrete accumulation of blood or merely swollen hemorrhagic brain tissue (French and Dublin 1977). An isodense lesion is usually noted after two to four weeks. The associated mass effect usually does not diminish as rapidly as the change in density (Pinto and Kricheff 1979). A contrast-enhanced CT scan may demonstrate 'ring' enhancement with central

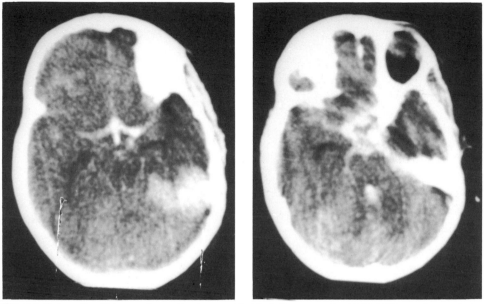

Fig. 6.4. Subarachnoid hemorrhage. Four-year-old girl. *Left:* non-contrast head CT scan demonstrates hemorrhage within suprasellar cistern. There is also blood within fourth ventricle. *Right:* non-contrast head CT scan demonstrates hemorrhage within suprasellar cistern. Associated parenchymal contusions are also present.

isodensity. This non-specific appearance may be confused with abscess or tumor; but in the latter lesions there is no mass effect and there is a prominent surrounding area of edema and usually a central area of decreased density (Dolinskas *et al.* 1977b, Zimmerman *et al.* 1977b).

Most hematomas develop immediately after the episode of trauma; however, there may be a delay in the appearance (Morin and Pitts 1970). In the series of Gudeman *et al.* (1979) most delayed hematomas occurred during the first 48 hours after injury and were usually associated with a poor prognosis.

The size and density of hematomas will gradually decrease with time. The duration of resolution will vary with the initial size of the lesion. A small hematoma will rapidly heal with a small residual scar; a large lesion may take months to heal (Romanul 1970).

Subarachnoid hemorrhage
Subarachnoid hemorrhage is manifested by bands of increased density along the interhemispheric fissure, tentorium, basal cisterns, Sylvian fissures and sulci (Fig. 6.4). The basal cisterns may be obliterated by subarachnoid hemorrhage. The increased density seen on CT rarely persists for more than a few days (Kishore and Lipper 1983).

Intraventricular hemorrhage
Post-traumatic intraventricular hemorrhage is now readily identified by CT, having

previously been diagnosed by more invasive methods. It would appear that some patients, especially infants and children in whom intraventricular hemorrhage was unsuspected, may tolerate this form of hemorrhage without drainage (Dublin *et al.* 1977).

The hemorrhages are identified as lesions of increased density conforming to the configuration of the ventricles involved (Merino-de Villasante and Taveras 1976) (Fig.6.5). Intraventricular hemorrhages may be associated with the traumatic lesions and may result from extension of an intracerebral hematoma (Zimmerman and Bilaniuk 1978).

Hydrocephalus of varying degrees which may be transient or permanent has been described in one third of the patients who survived (Dublin *et al.* 1977).

Extracerebral collections
Subdural hematoma
Subdural hematoma is a collection of blood between the dura mater and arachnoid dura. Acute, subacute and chronic types are recognized on a chronologic basis.

ACUTE SUBDURAL HEMATOMA (SDH)
This is the usual result of severe head injury. Rarer causes are birth injury due to the birth process or application of forceps (Abroms *et al.* 1977), osteogenesis imperfecta where the poorly ossified skull affords less protection (Harwood-Nash and Fitz 1976), or too rapid shunt decompression of hydrocephalus (Illingworth 1970).

The hematoma may be located over the convexity, and tentorium, in the middle or posterior cranial fossae or within the interhemispheric fissure. In the series of Harwood-Nash and Fitz (1976), 90 per cent of subdural hematomas were supratentorial in location with 10 per cent in the posterior fossa. Location of a subdural hematoma within the posterior fossa is more common in children than adults (Ciembronkiewicz 1965). The underlying etiology is attributed to birth injury in many instances (McKissock *et al.* 1960). Bilateral lesions were found to be more common (61 per cent) by Harwood-Nash and Fitz (1976).

The usual CT appearance of an acute subdural hematoma is a crescentic concavo-convex lesion located against the calvarium laterally, and the cerebral cortex medially (Fig. 6.6).

The density of the hematoma will vary with its age and is of greater density than surrounding brain parenchymal in the acute phase. This is readily apparent on an unenhanced CT scan. The increased density is directly related to the hemoglobin protein component within the hematoma (Bergstrom *et al.* 1977, Scotti *et al.* 1977).

When the hemorrhage occurs in patients with abnormalities of the calvarium subdural space or cerebral parenchyma, atypical configurations are encountered (Zimmerman and Danziger 1982). Extensive parenchymal damage may thus compress the subdural space with resultant localization of the subdural hematoma. Lentiform collections may result from the bulge of a localized collection into the adjacent cortex or may also be secondary to loculation of the subdural space by fibrotic bands from previous inflammation or trauma.

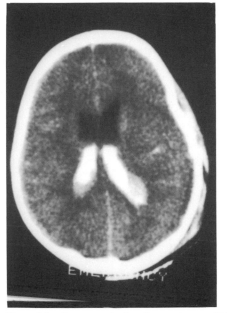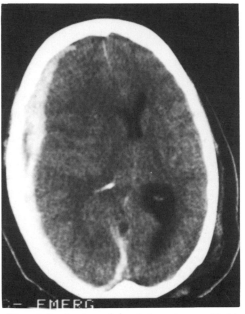

Fig. 6.5. Intraventricular hemorrhage. Four-year-old girl. Non-contrast head CT scan demonstrates hemorrhage within both lateral ventricles. This patient also had hemorrhage within fourth ventricle, subarachnoid hemorrhage and parenchymal contusions (see Fig. 6.4).

Fig. 6.6. Acute subdural hematoma. Eight-year-old boy. Non-contrast head CT scan demonstrates contralateral ventricular shift. There is a concave-convex lesion of increased density which is an acute subdural hematoma. (Courtesy of Gary DeFilipp MD, Philadelphia.)

Although less common in adults, acute interhemispheric subdural hematomas are common in the pediatric age-group, and especially in abused children (Zimmerman *et al.* 1979). These hematomas occur predominantly in the parieto-occipital region and are frequently associated with parenchymal injury. Associated skull fractures are infrequent (Zimmerman *et al.* 1979). The interhemispheric subdural hematoma is a distinct entity from interhemispheric subarachnoid hemorrhage, also occurring in infants and children (Dolinskas *et al.* 1978). In the latter condition the stripe of increased density representing blood is thinner and often extends over the entire distance of the fissure ('the falx sign').

The appearances within the posterior fossa are variable. In addition to the usual crescentic configuration (Fig. 6.7), there may be a lentiform collection or a lesion with a sharp lateral margin where it abuts the tentorium (Zimmerman and Danziger 1982).

The mass effect exerted by the space-occupying lesion will produce a contralateral shift of the lateral ventricles and midline structures. This effect will thus not be present if there are bilateral subdural hematomas.

Hemorrhagic contusions or lacerations were associated with acute subdural hematomas in half of the patients in the series of Zimmerman *et al.* (1978a).

105

SUBACUTE SUBDURAL HEMATOMA

The density of the subdural hematoma decreases and closely approximates that of the brain (isodense lesion) two to four weeks after the injury, although this has been reported as early as the first week after injury and up to three months later (Pinto and Kricheff 1979).

Additional CT appearances which are helpful in establishing the diagnosis include compression of the ipsilateral ventricle, pineal and subfalcine shift. Obliteration of cortical sulci, medial displacement of sulci or a cortical vein away from the inner table of the skull (following contrast infusion) are additional signs (Kim *et al.* 1978). Non-visualization of sulci is however more important in adults suggesting mass effect. Administration of contrast medium may demonstrate enhancement on the medial side of the isodense SDH (Tsai *et al.* 1978) (Fig. 6.7). Delayed enhancement of the hematoma itself may occur after four to six hours (Messina 1976).

CHRONIC SUBDURAL HEMATOMA

Progressive decrease in the density of the subdural hematoma occurs following the isodense phase described above. The density approaches that of cerebrospinal fluid approximately 22 to 30 days after the episode of trauma (Scotti *et al.* 1977, Pinto and Kricheff 1979). The lesion is hypodense relative to brain parenchyma (Fig. 6.8); but the hematoma may also be hyperdense, due to a recent but clinically unsuspected rehemorrhage (Zimmerman and Danziger 1982).

The layering phenomenon or 'hematocrit effect' may be seen following liquefaction of clotted blood within either the subacute or chronic phases. There is an anterior hypodense antedependent portion, well demarcated from a hyperdense dependent portion located posteriorly (Forbes *et al.* 1978, Shalen and Handel 1981).

Epidural hematoma

An epidural (extradural) hematoma is a collection of blood between the dura mater and the inner table of the skull. The hematoma may be arterial or venous in origin. In most cases, arterial rupture involves the middle meningeal artery or its branches, but it may also arise from the anterior or posterior meningeal branches of the vertebral artery (Fisher *et al.* 1958, Brillman 1979).

Venous epidural hematomas occur from tears in the superior sagittal sinus at the cranial apex, transverse sinus, torcula, and also from the occipital sinus around the foramen magnum (Lindenberg 1977, McLaurin and McLennan 1982).

Extradural hematomas are uncommon in infants and children. In the series of Harwood-Nash and Fitz (1976) only 0.1 per cent of all children presenting with craniocerebral trauma had extradural hematomas. The male to female ratio in this series was 3:1.

The hematomas are uncommon under the age of one year. This lower incidence has been attributed to the greater degree of adherence of the dura to the inner table, and the lack of bony vascular grooves for the meningeal vessels (Harwood-Nash and Fitz 1976). Sharp fractures in this age-group are unusual,

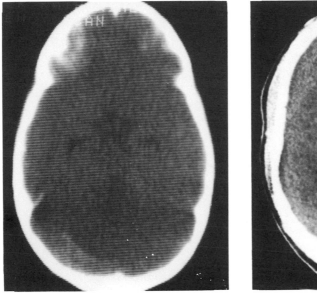

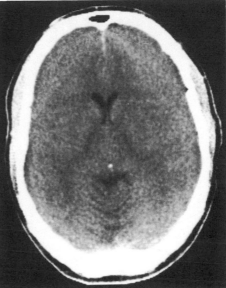

Fig. 6.7 *Above left:* acute subdural hematoma. 18-month-old girl. Non-contrast head CT scan demonstrates an acute subdural hematoma within the posterior fossa. The patient made an uneventful recovery after surgical evacuation of the hematoma. *Above right:* isodense subdural hematoma. 17-year-old male. Non-contrast head CT scan demonstrates compression of the ventricles, without shift. *Below left:* contrast-enhanced head CT scan displays the membranes of the bilateral isodense subdural hematomas (*arrowheads*). (Courtesy of Joel Swartz MD, Philadelphia.)

Fig. 6.8 *(below).* Chronic subdural hematoma. Four-year-old male. Non-contrast head CT scan shows a biconcave low density, representing a chronic subdural hematoma, and ventricular shift.

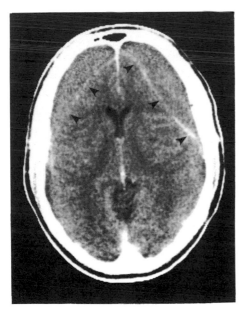

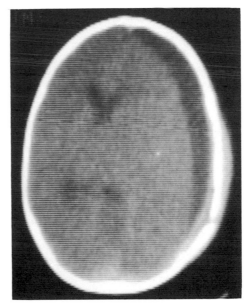

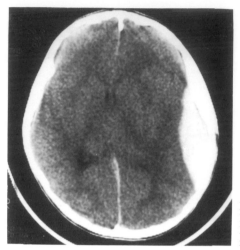

Fig. 6.9. Extradural hematoma. 10-year-old girl. Non-contrast head CT scan demonstrates contralateral ventricular shift. There is a biconvex lesion of increased density, which is an epidural hematoma.

Subdural hygroma

Subdural hygroma is a collection of clear, xanthochromic or blood-tinged fluid which is located within the subdural space following head injury (Cooper 1982). The lesion may be supra or infratentorial in location, and may coexist with epidural locations are thus adjacent to the middle fossa floor, temporal squamosa or frontal bone (Zimmerman and Danziger 1982). This lesion constitutes a neurosurgical emergency, as the expanding force of the mass will produce impaction of the mass on the midbrain.

Epidural hematomas may also be located within the posterior fossa, following hemorrhage from the anterior or posterior branches of the vertebral artery (Kim *et al.* 1978, Brillman 1979).

CT appearances

1. The epidural hematoma, as visualized in the acute phase, is a well-defined biconvex (lenticular) lesion which is hyperdense in relation to the surrounding brain (Figs. 6.9, 6.10). The firm dural attachment to the inner table of the skull limits peripheral expansion of the hematoma, thus accounting for the convex medial margin. The attenuation values are higher than those encountered with subdural hematoma (Kishore 1982). 10 per cent of epidural hematomas in children may have a subacute or chronic presentation (Bruce 1982). In patients in whom hematomas present five to 20 days after the trauma, the lesions have mildly increased density with an enhancing inner membrane representing the dura and granulation tissue. The density of the hematoma after late presentation may approach that of brain (isodensity) or mixed values may be observed (Peyster and Hoover 1982). Venous epidural hematomas resulting from rupture of large dural sinuses may produce occlusion with subsequent thrombosis, infarction and hydrocephalus (Zimmerman and Danziger 1982).
2. Midline shift. This is relatively small compared to that found with subdural hematoma, unless there is associated parenchymal injury (Kishore 1982).

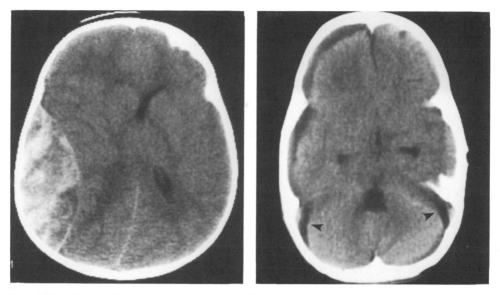

Fig. 6.10. *Above left:* extradural hematoma. Two-year-old boy. Non-contrast head CT scan demonstrates a biconvex extracerebral collection of mixed density. There is mass effect on the ipsilateral lateral ventricle, with contralateral ventricular shift and bowing of the falx. *Above right:* subdural hygroma. Four-year-old girl with previous severe head injury. Non-contrast head CT scan demonstrates supratentorial subdural fluid collection which is of low density, in addition to infratentorial accumulation of fluid *(arrowheads)*. *Below left:* fluid is also noted over the tentorium cerebelli *(arrowhead)*.

Fig. 6.11 *(below)*. Hydrocephalus. Four-year-old boy. Post-traumatic hydrocephalus is demonstrated in this patient three months after head injury. Multiple areas of infarction (low density areas) are evident.

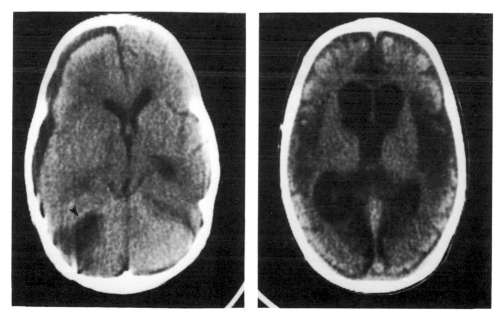

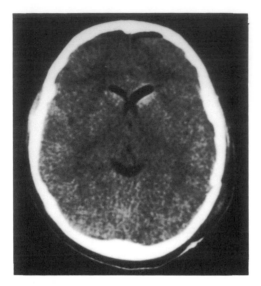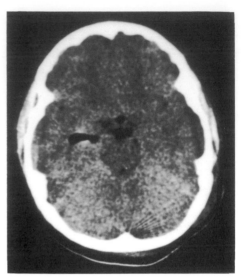

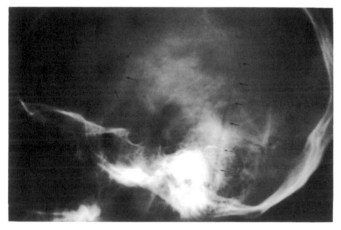

Fig. 6.12. Pneumocephalus. Six-year-old boy with head trauma. Non-contrast head CT scans demonstrate air in the frontal horns *(above left)* and right temporal horn *(above right)* of the lateral ventricles. *Left:* Lateral skull radiograph demonstrates a non-depressed vertical skull fracture *(arrows)*.

which may be an additional reason for this lower incidence (McLaurin and McLennan 1982).

Acute epidural hematomas occur most frequently in the temporal region, as the hemorrhage arises from the middle meningeal artery or its branches in the majority of cases (Lindenberg 1977, McLaurin and McLennan 1982). The various and subdural hematomas (Stone *et al.* 1981). The earliest theory of pathogenesis is that of Naffziger (1924) who speculated that a tear in the arachnoid permits the escape of cerebrospinal fluid into the subdural space. The hygroma increases in size due to a flap valve effect as the cerebrospinal fluid is trapped (DaCosta and Adson 1941). Hygromas may also result from effusions into the subdural space from damaged capillaries within the underlying brain (Stone *et al.* 1981). CT scanning is the modality of choice for the diagnosis. An extracerebral collection is demonstrated, with density similar to that of cerebrospinal fluid (Fig. 6.10). Contrast enhancement is usually not observed (Stone *et al.* 1981).

Hydrocephalus

Ventricular enlargement may result from closed head trauma. The presence of blood within the subarachnoid space may lead to obstruction of cerebrospinal fluid with resultant communicating hydrocephalus; less commonly, hemorrhage within the ventricular system or around the aqueduct may result in an obstructive non-communicating hydrocephalus (Fig. 6.11).

Hydrocephalus was noted by Kishore *et al.* (1978) in 40 per cent of patients who had head CT scans at least 14 days after injury. 8 per cent of patients surviving severe head injury will have hydrocephalus after three months (Gudeman *et al.* 1981).

The pathogenesis of delayed-onset hydrocephalus is attributed to shearing of nerve fibers immediately after impact; there is subsequent degeneration, which reduces the bulk of cerebral white matter and results in reciprocal expansion of the ventricles (Levin *et al.* 1981).

Atrophy

Post-traumatic cerebral atrophy may be focal or diffuse, and may be located above or below the tentorium. Focal atrophy is especially found in the frontal and temporal areas (Lindenberg 1977).

The CT appearances consist of increased ventricular and sulcal size, and there may also be associated porencephaly (Harwood-Nash and Fitz 1976).

Pneumocephalus

Pneumocephalus is uncommon in children. Fractures involving the frontal, ethmoid, and sphenoid sinuses, as well as the mastoid air cells, may result in the entry of air into the epidural, subdural, subarachnoid spaces, parenchyma or the ventricles.

The characteristic CT appearance of intracranial air is a region of low-absorption values (-1000 Hounsfield units). A surrounding halo effect, which appears as a white rim, is due to the abrupt change in attenuation between the air and surrounding brain parenchyma (Davis *et al.* 1977) (Fig. 6.12).

Minute volumes of air as low as 0.5cc can be identified on CT; the presence of small amounts of intracranial air in patients with a history of trauma should alert the clinician to the possibility of an underlying basal skull fracture (Osborn *et al.* 1978).

Fractures and foreign bodies

Skull fractures which are compound or depressed, and associated soft-tissue swelling, are readily demonstrated by CT (Fig. 6.13). Linear fractures, however, may not always be visualized.

Penetrating radiopaque foreign bodies such as bullet fragments and bone are

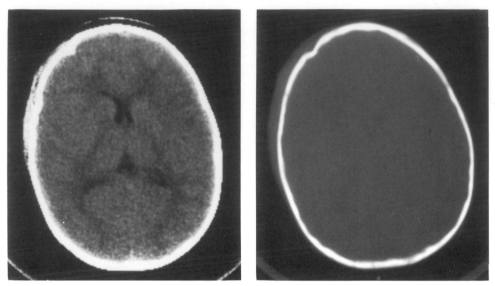

Fig. 6.13. Fracture. Three-year-old girl. Non-contrast head CT scans demonstrate a depressed skull fracture. There is no evidence of extracerebral fluid collection or intracranial contusion. The fracture is optimally visualized at appropriate bone window settings.

easily visualized (Figs. 6.14, 6.15). Foreign bodies within the orbit are well demonstrated by CT. This modality is more sensitive in the display of many objects not well visualized on conventional radiographs (Davis *et al.* 1977). The relationship of foreign bodies to surrounding anatomic structures is also well demonstrated.

Cerebrospinal fluid fistula
Cerebrospinal fistulae usually follow fractures of the skull base with associated meningeal injury resulting in communication of the subarachnoid space and the paranasal sinuses or middle ear.

Cerebrospinal rhinorrhea
Communication between the subarachnoid space and one of the paranasal sinuses produces a flow of cerebrospinal fluid through the nose or down the pharynx. Trauma is the commonest cause, although congenital anomalies, hydrocephalus, osteomyelitis, tumor and spontaneous fistulae have all been described in the etiology (Lantz *et al.* 1980).

Post-traumatic rhinorrhea is uncommmon in children, occurring in 0.5 per cent of all head injuries and in 2 per cent of children with skull fractures (Harwood-Nash and Fitz 1976). The possibility of CSF rhinorrhea is very low in children below the age of six years, because the paranasal sinuses are less well developed at this age (Bakay and Glasauer 1980).

The leak either begins immediately or within 48 hours of the injury (Lewin 1954, Robinson 1970), and most stop in less than a week (Lewin 1954). The risk of

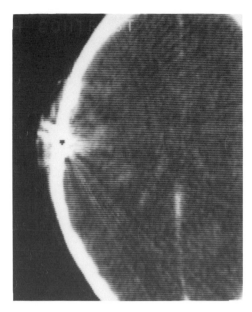

Fig. 6.14. Foreign body. 10-year-old boy. Contrast-enhanced head CT scan shows evidence of multiple radiopaque foreign bodies (corresponding to shrapnel) within the scalp and medial to the inner table. There is considerable artifact from the foreign bodies. A small area of increased density is noted intracranially, around the shrapnel, representing contusion.

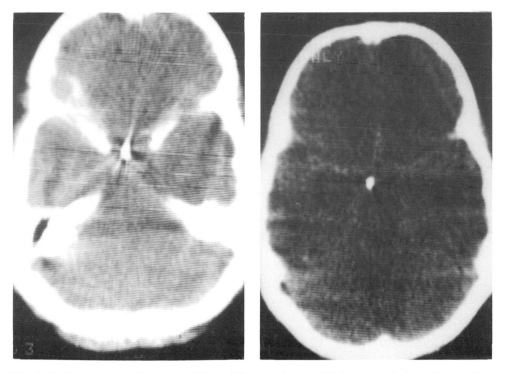

Fig. 6.15. Foreign body. Four-year-old boy. Migratory intracranial foreign body following previous plastic surgery. *Left:* lateral skull radiograph demonstrates a radiopaque traversing the suprasellar region. *Right:* non-contrast head CT scan shows the pin within the suprasellar region.

113

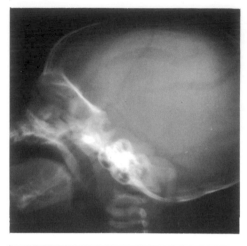

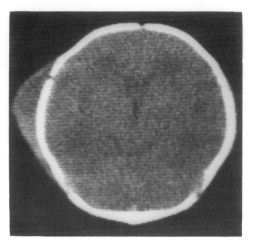

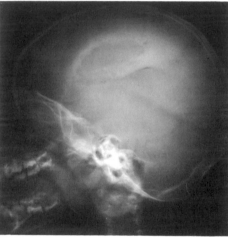

Fig. 6.16. Leptomeningeal cyst. One-month-old girl with severe head injury. *Above left:* lateral skull radiograph demonstrates non-depressed frontoparietal fracture. *Above right:* non-contrast head CT scan demonstrates the fracture. *Left:* lateral skull radiograph obtained 11 months later demonstrates diastasis of the fracture. *Below left:* non-contrast head CT scan performed at this time demonstrates cerebral herniation through the fracture site. *Below right:* non-contrast head CT scan (bone detail) demonstrates the widened fracture site.

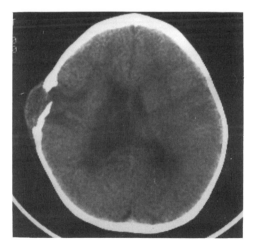

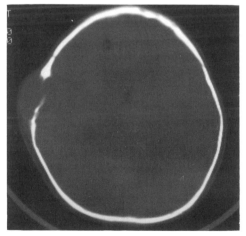

intracranial infection developing in untreated patients is high, occurring in 50 per cent of patients in the series of Robinson *et al.* (1967).

Cerebrospinal otorrhea
Communication between the subarachnoid space and the petrous bone produces a flow of cerebrospinal fluid through the ear.

The most frequent cause is trauma with a similar incidence in children to that of cerebrospinal rhinorrhea (Harwood-Nash and Fitz 1976). In addition to external leaks, the cerebrospinal fluid may also loculate within the middle ear or leak through the Eustachian tube (McLaurin and McLennan 1982). Most fistulae close spontaneously (Raaf 1967).

Accurate localization of cerebrospinal fluid fistula has in the past included plain film radiography, conventional tomography, positive contrast ventriculography, isotope cisternography and ventriculography. Computed tomography now appears to be the ideal modality. Conventional CT may demonstrate the presence of intracranial air, or may demonstrate opacification or air-fluid levels in the sinuses or middle ear. High resolution thin coronal sections are required for demonstration of fractures. Metrizamide cisternography is a relatively easy procedure and is the best examination for precise anatomic delineation of the fistulous tract (Ghoshhajra 1982).

Growing skull fractures of childhood (enlarging skull fractures of childhood, leptomeningeal cyst)
A growing skull fracture of childhood follows skull trauma which is of sufficient force to tear the underlying dura. There is concurrent subarachnoid hemorrhage which impairs the local circulation of cerebrospinal fluid. Protrusion of the arachnoid occurs through the dural tear into the fracture site. Gradual erosion of the bone edges follows as a result of protrusion, which is aided by normal brain pulsation. Arachnoidal adhesions around the margin of the lesion also serve to trap cerebrospinal fluid locally (Taveras and Ransohoff 1953).

90 per cent of these fractures have been found by Lende and Erickson (1961) to occur under the age of three years, with over half under the age of 12 months.

The shortest interval between head injury and observation of the cranial defect has been found to be two months (Harwood-Nash and Fitz 1976, Kingsley *et al.* 1978). The evolution of a leptomeningeal cyst is depicted in Figure 6.16.

Battered child syndrome (Caffey-Kemp syndrome, abused child syndrome, whiplash-shaker infant syndrome)
Although this syndrome was originally recognized and described by Tardieu in 1860 and West in 1888, the subsequent radiologic findings of John Caffey in 1946 produced a marked medical and social impact. In view of the high incidence and significant morbidity and mortality, this syndrome has been considered by Caffey to be the most important infantile disease ever detected by radiologic examination.

In most cases, radiologic examination is performed because of a previous history of trauma; the lesions which are found may be more extensive than

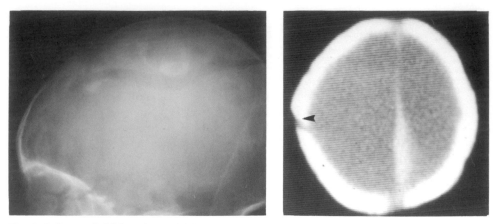

Fig. 6.17. Battered child syndrome. Eight-month-old girl who was initially found to be 'unresponsive' by her parents. *Left:* lateral skull radiograph demonstrates a non-depressed diastatic frontoparietal fracture. *Right:* non-contrast head CT scan demonstrates the fracture *(arrowhead)* and interhemispheric subdural hematoma.

anticipated or there may be features of both acute and chronic lesions, indicative of repetitive trauma. In some instances, the lesions found may be incidental to the present clinical history, and these should alert the radiologist and clinician to the underlying cause. In the original description by Caffey (1946) the main features described are subdural hematomas, intra-ocular hemorrhages and multiple traction changes in the long bones.

Subdural hematoma is the commonest lesion in this syndrome, and is the most frequent cause of death (Caffey 1974). Despite the absence of external signs of trauma in the physical examination, or an absence of history of trauma, the possibility of a subdural hematoma should never be excluded. The advent of CT widened the scope of cranial imaging, previously mainly limited to skull radiographs. CT now plays a major rôle in the assessment of head trauma in these patients (Ellison *et al.* 1978, Zimmerman *et al.* 1979). The findings in these two series includes:

1. Intracerebral hematoma and contusion
2. Cerebral edema
3. Cerebral atrophy
4. Acute subdural hematoma

In 58 per cent of the cases described by Zimmerman *et al.* (1979), the location was in the posterior (parieto-occipital) portion of the interhemispheric fissure on either side of the falx at the site of drainage of the cerebral veins attached to the superior sagittal sinus. A similar appearance is produced by an interhemispheric subarachnoid hemorrhage (Dolinskas *et al.* 1978) but the stripe of blood is thinner and may extend over the entire length of the fissure.

Skull fractures were found by Zimmerman *et al.* (1979) in only 13 per cent of patients with acute interhemispheric subdural hematoma (Fig. 6.17).

Retinal hemorrhage is not detected by CT, but in one patient in the series of

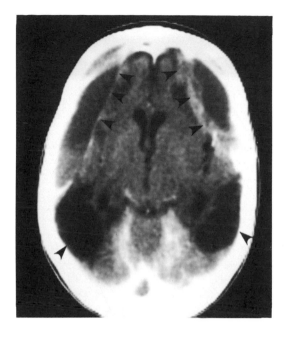

Fig. 6.18. Battered child syndrome. 11-month-old boy. Contrast-enhanced head CT scan reveals evidence of bilateral acute-on-chronic subdural hematomas. The medial borders are well demonstrated *(multiple arrowheads)* following administration of iodinated contrast medium. Areas of infarction (low-density areas) are present posteriorly *(single arrowheads)*.

Zimmerman *et al.* (1979) with suspected massive retinal hemorrhage, a follow-up CT scan demonstrated a smaller eye on the affected side.

Cephalhematoma

A cephalhematoma is a subperiosteal hematoma which is sharply limited to the bone edges that it overlies. The commonest cause is trauma to the fetal head which occurs during labor. The application of forceps to the head may be an additional cause of trauma. Cephalhematomas may also result from skull trauma sustained in infancy and later childhood. Fractures in the parietal bones underlying cephalhematomas were found in 25 per cent of the series of Kendall and Woloshin (1952).

The CT appearances correlate with the plain film radiographs of the skull: (i) During the first two weeks of life, the lesion is composed of fluid blood. This is manifested by soft tissue swelling on both CT and plain skull radiographs. (ii) Towards the end of the second week, a rim of bone starts to form beneath the elevated pericranium. The increased density of bone will be noted in contrast to that of the blood-containing soft tissue mass.

REFERENCES

Abroms, I. F., McLennan, J. E., Mandell, F. (1977) 'Acute neonatal subdural hematoma following breech delivery.' *American Journal of Diseases of Children,* **131,** 192–194.
Bakay, L., Glausauer, F. E. (1980) *Head Injury.* Boston: Little, Brown. pp. 278–292.
Bergström, M., Ericson, K., Levander, B., Swendsen, P. (1977) 'Computed tomography of cranial subdural and epidural hematomas: variation of attenuation related to time and clinical events such as rebleeding.' *Journal of Computerized Assisted Tomography,* **1,** 449–455.

Brillman, J. (1979) 'Acute hydrocephalus and death one month after surgical treatment of acute epidural hematoma.' *Journal of Neurosurgery*, **50**, 374–376.

Bruce, D. A. (1982) 'Special considerations of the pediatric age group.' *In:* Cooper, P. R. (Ed.) *Head Injury.* Baltimore: Williams & Wilkins. pp. 315–325.

Caffey, J. (1946) 'Multiple fractures in the long bones of infants suffering from chronic subdural hematoma.' *American Journal of Roentgenology*, **56**, 163–173.

—— (1974) 'The whiplash-shaken infant syndrome: manual shaking by the extremities with whiplash-induced intracranial and intraocular bleedings, linked with residual permanent brain damage and mental retardation.' *Pediatrics*, **54**, 396–403.

Ciembroniewicz, J. E. (1965) 'Subdural hematoma of the posterior fossa; review of the literature with addition of three cases.' *Journal of Neurosurgery*, **22**, 465–473.

Cooper, P. R. (1982) 'Post traumatic intracranial mass lesions.' *In:* Cooper, P. R. (Ed.) *Head Injury.* Baltimore: Williams & Wilkins. pp. 185-232.

Craft, A. W. (1975) 'Head injury in children.' *In:* Vinken, P. J. Bruyn, G. W. (Eds.) *Handbook of Clinical Neurology, Volume 23. Injuries of the Brain and Skull, Part I.* Amsterdam: Elsevier-North Holland. pp. 445–458.

DaCosta, D. G., Adson, A. W. (1941) 'Subdural hydroma.' *Archives of Surgery*, **43**, 559–567.

Davis, K. R., Taveras, J. M., Roberson, G. H., Ackerman, R. H., Dreisbach, J. N. (1977) 'Computed tomography in head trauma.' *Seminars in Roentgenology*, **12**, 53–62.

Dolinskas, C. A., Bilaniuk, L. T., Zimmerman, R. A., Kuhl, D. E. (1977*a*) 'Computed tomography of intracerebral hematomas. 1: Transmission CT observations on hematoma resolution.' *American Journal of Roentgenology*, **129**, 681–688.

—— —— —— —— Alavi, A. (1977*b*) 'Computed tomography of intracerebral hematomas. II: Radionuclide and transmission CT studies of the perihematoma region.' *American Journal of Roentgenology*, **129**, 689–692.

—— Zimmerman, R. A., Bilaniuk, L. T. (1978) 'A sign of subarachnoid bleeding in cranial computed tomograms of pediatric head trauma patients.' *Radiology*, **126**, 409–411.

Dublin, A. B., French, B. N., Rennick, J. M. (1977) 'Computed tomography in head trauma.' *Radiology*, **122**, 365–369.

Ellison, P. H., Tsai, F. Y., Largent, J. A. (1978) 'Computed tomography in child abuse and cerebral contusion.' *Pediatrics*, **62**, 151–154.

Faerber, E. N. (1979) *Cerebral Trauma in Central Nervous System: Approaches to Radiologic Diagnosis.* New York: Grune & Stratton. pp. 95–108.

Fisher, R. G., Kim, J. K., Sachs, E. (1958) 'Complications in posterior fossa due to occipital trauma—their operability.' *Journal of the American Medical Association*, **167**, 176–182.

Forbes, G. S., Sheedy, P. F., Piepgras, D. G., Houser, O. W. (1978) 'Computed tomography in the evaluation of subdural hematomas.' *Radiology*, **126**, 143–148.

French, B. N., Dublin, A. B. (1977) 'The value of computerized tomography in the management of 1000 consecutive head injuries.' *Surgical Neurology*, **7**, 171–183.

Ghoshhajra, K. (1982) 'Craniofacial trauma and CSF fistula.' *In:* Lee, S. H., Rao, K. C. V. G. (Eds.) *Cranial Computed Tomography.* New York: McGraw-Hill. pp. 461–478.

Gudeman, S. K., Kishore, P. R. S., Miller, J. D., Girevendulis, A. K., Lipper, M. H., Becker, D. P. (1979) 'The genesis and significance of delayed traumatic intracerebral hematoma.' *Neurosurgery*, **5**, 309–313.

—— —— Becker, D. P., Lipper, M. H., Girevendulis, A. K., Jeffries, B. F., Butterworth, J. (1981) 'Computerized tomography in the evaluation of incidence and significance of post-traumatic hydrocephalus.' *Radiology*, **141**, 397–402.

Harwood-Nash, D. C., Fitz, C. R. (1976) 'Craniocerebral trauma.' *In: Neuroradiology in Infants and Children.* St. Louis: C. V. Mosby. pp. 789–854.

Illingworth, R. D. (1970) 'Subdural hematoma after treatment of chronic hydrocephalus by ventriculocaval shunts.' *Journal of Neurology, Neurosurgery and Psychiatry*, **33**, 95–99.

Kendall, N., Woloshin, H. (1952) 'Cephalohematomas associated with fracture of the skull.' *Journal of Pediatrics*, **41**, 125–132.

Kim, K. S., Hemmati, M., Weinberg, P. E. (1978) 'Computed tomography in isodense subdural hematoma.' *Radiology*, **128**, 71–74.

Kingsley, D., Till, K., Hoare, R. (1978) 'Growing fractures of the skull.' *Journal of Neurology, Neurosurgery and Psychiatry*, **41**, 312–318.

Kishore, P. R. S. (1982) 'Head injury. Radiographic evaluation.' *In:* Cooper, P. R. (Ed.) *Head Injury.* Baltimore: Williams & Wilkins. pp. 43–64.

—— Lipper, M. H., Miller, J. D., Girevendulis, A. K., Becker, D. P., Vines, F. S. (1978)

118

'Post-traumatic hydrocephalus in patients with severe head injury.' *Neuroradiology*, **16**, 261–265.
—— —— (1983) 'Craniocerebral trauma.' *In:* Lee, S. H., Rao, K. C. V. G. (Eds.) *Cranial Computed Tomography*. New York: McGraw-Hill. pp. 479–504.
Lantz, E. J., Forbes, G. S., Brown, M. L., Laws, E. R. (1980) 'Radiology of cerebrospinal fluid rhinorrhea.' *American Journal of Neuroradiology*, **1**, 391–398.
Lende, R. A., Erickson, T. C. (1961) 'Growing fractures of childhood.' *Journal of Neurosurgery*, **18**, 479–489.
Levin, H. S., Myers, C. A., Grossman, R. G., Sarwar, M. (1981) 'Ventricular enlargement after closed head injury.' *Archives of Neurology*, **38**, 623–629.
Lewin, N. (1954) 'Cerebrospinal fluid rhinorrhea in closed head injuries.' *British Journal of Surgery*, **42**, 1–18.
Lewis, A. J. (1976) *Mechanisms of Neurological Disease*. Boston: Little, Brown. pp. 1–540.
Lindenberg, R. (1977) 'Pathology of craniovertebral injuries.' *In:* Newton, T. H., Potts, D. G. (Eds.) *Radiology of the Skull and Brain. Vol. 3: Anatomy and Pathology*. St. Louis: C. V Mosby. pp. 3049–3087.
McKissock, W., Richardson, A., Broom, W. H. (1960) 'Subdural hematoma; a review of 389 cases.' *Lancet*, **1**, 1365–1369.
McLaurin, R. J., McLennan, J. E. (1982) 'Diagnosis and treatment of head injury in children.' *In:* Youmans, J. R. (Ed.) *Neurological Surgery, Volume 4*. Philadelphia: W. B. Saunders. pp. 2084–2136.
Merino-de Villasante, J., Taveras, J. (1976) 'Computerized tomography (CT) in acute head trauma.' *American Journal of Roentgenology*, **126**, 765–778.
Messina, A. V. (1976) 'Computed tomography: contrast media within hematomas (a preliminary report).' *Radiology*, **119**, 725–726.
Milhorat, T. H. (1978) 'Trauma.' *In: Pediatric Neurosurgery*. Philadelphia: F. A. Davis. pp. 41–89.
Morin, M. A., Pitts, P. W. (1970) 'Delayed apoplexy following head injury ("traumatische spät-apoplexie").' *Journal of Neurosurgery*, **33**, 542–547.
Naffziger, H. C. (1924) 'Subdural fluid accumulations following head injury.' *Journal of the American Medical Association*, **82**, 1751–1752.
Osborn, A. G., Daines, J. H., Wing, S. D., Anderson, R. E. (1978) 'Intracranial air on computerized tomography.' *Journal of Neurosurgery*, **48**, 355–359.
Peyster, R. G., Hoover, E. D. (1982) 'CT in head trauma.' *Journal of Trauma*, **22**, 25–38.
Pinto, R. S., Kricheff, I. I. (1979) 'CT in head trauma.' *In:* Buenger, R. E. (Ed.) *Syllabus for Categorial Course in Computed Tomography. Course 209A*. Chicago: Radiological Society of North America. pp. 1–31.
Raaf, J. (1967) 'Post traumatic CSF leaks.' *Archives of Surgery*, **95**, 648–651.
Robinson, A. E., Meares, B. M., Goree, J. A. (1967) 'Traumatic sphenoid sinus effusion: an analysis of 50 cases.' *American Journal of Roentgenology, Radium Therapy and Nuclear Medicine*, **101**, 795–801.
Robinson, R. G. (1970) 'Cerebrospinal fluid rhinorrhea, meningitis and pneumocephalus due to non-missile injuries.' *Australian and New Zealand Journal of Surgery*, **39**, 328–334.
Romanul, F. C. A. (1970) 'Examination of the brain and spinal cord.' *In:* Tedeschi, C. G. (Ed.) *Neuropathology. Methods and Diagnosis*. Boston: Little, Brown. pp. 131–215.
Scotti, G., Terbrugge, K., Melancon, D., Belanger, G. (1977) 'Evaluation of the age of subdural hematomas by computed tomography.' *Journal of Neurosurgery*, **47**, 311–315.
Shalen, P. R., Handel, S. F. (1981) 'Diagnostic challenges in closed head trauma.' *Radiologic Clinics of North America*, **19**, 53–68.
Stone, J. L., Lang, R. G. R., Sugar, O., Moody, R. A. (1981) 'Traumatic subdural hygroma.' *Journal of Neurosurgery*, **8**, 542–550.
Tardieu, A. (1860) 'Etude médico-légale sur les services et mauvais traitements exercés sur des enfants.' *Annales de la Hygiène Publique et Médicine Légale*, **13**, 361–398.
Taveras, J. M., Ransohoff, J. (1953) 'Leptomeningeal cysts of the brain following trauma with erosion of the skull.' *Journal of Neurosurgery*, **10**, 233–241.
Tsai, F. Y., Huprich, J. E., Gardner, F. G., Segall, H. D., Teal, J. S. (1978) 'Diagnostic and prognostic implications of computed tomography of head trauma.' *Journal of Computed Assisted Tomography*, **2**, 323–331.
West, S. (1888) 'Acute periosteal swelling in several young infants of the same family, probably rickety in nature.' *British Journal of Medicine*, **1**, 856–857.
Zimmerman, R. A., Bilaniuk, L. T., Dolinskas, C., Gennarelli, T., Bruce, D., Uzzel, B. (1977a) 'Computed tomography of acute intracerebral hemorrhagic contusion.' *Computed Axial Tomogra-*

phy, **1,** 271–280.
—— Leeds, N. E., Naidich, T. P. (1977*b*) 'Ring blush associated with intracerebral hematoma.' *Radiology,* **122,** 707–711.
—— Bilaniuk, L. T. (1978) 'Computed tomography of traumatic intracerebral hemorrhagic lesions: the change in density and mass effect with time.' *Neuroradiology,* **16,** 320–321.
—— —— Bruce, D., Dolinskas, C., Obrist, W., Kutz, D. (1978*a*) 'Computed tomography of pediatric head trauma. Acute general cerebral swelling.' *Radiology,* **126,** 403–408.
—— —— Genneralli, T. (1978*b*) 'Computed tomography of shearing injuries of the cerebral white matter.' *Radiology,* **127,** 393–396.
—— —— Bruce, D., Schut, L., Uzzell, B., Goldberg, H. I. (1979) 'Computed tomography of craniocerebral injury in the abused child.' *Radiology,* **130,** 687–690.
—— —— (1981) 'Computed tomography in pediatric head trauma.' *Journal of Neuroradiology,* **8,** 257–271.
—— Danziger, A. (1982) 'Extracerebral trauma.' *Radiologic Clinics of North America,* **20,** 105–121.

7
VASCULAR DISORDERS

Cerebrovascular disease in infants and children is well documented, dating back to the seventeenth century (Willis 1667). Traditionally angiography has been employed for the demonstration of extracranial vascular compromise and intracranial vascular abnormalities. Radionuclide imaging has been utilized in the diagnosis of cerebral infarction, but is not able to demonstrate the morphologic changes occurring in evolving and resolving infarcts and hematomas (Chiu *et al.* 1976). Computed tomography has emerged as the prime modality for the initial evaluation and follow-up of intracranial cerebrovascular disease.

Vascular disorders of infancy and childhood may be subdivided into two major groups: intracranial hemorrhage (intracerebral and subarachnoid), and occlusive vascular disease. Table 7.1 lists the spectrum of causes.

Intracranial hemorrhage
Intracranial hemorrhage may result from extravasation of blood into numerous sites which include the subarachnoid, subdural or epidural spaces, ventricular system or cerebral parenchyma.

The most common cause is trauma, although other causes are arteriovenous malformations, aneurysms, blood dyscrasias (Fig. 7.1), tumors, and infections. The numerous causes are listed in Table 7.1.

Cerebrovascular malformations
Cerebrovascular malformations are the most common cause of primary subarachnoid hemorrhage in children. These lesions were originally classified by Cushing and Bailey (1928) into arterial, venous and arteriovenous types but have subsequently been classified into the following four types based on microscopic features by Russell and Rubinstein (1974): (i) arteriovenous malformations (AVMs), (ii) venous malformations, (iii) cavernous angiomas or hemangiomas, and (iv) capillary telangiectasias.

Rôle of CT
Computed tomography is useful primarily as a screening procedure to confirm the presence or absence of cerebral abnormalities, to demonstrate hemorrhage, and determine if other associated intracranial abnormalities associated with AVMs are present (Norman 1983). Angiography is mandatory for precise anatomic delineation and characterization of the abnormality prior to treatment, and also to demonstrate associated abnormalities (*e.g.* aneurysms).

121

TABLE 7.1
Classification of cerebrovascular diseases

Intracranial hemorrhage (includes intracerebral and subarachnoid)
  Arteriovenous malformation or angioma
  Blood dyscrasias
    Anaphylactoid purpura, aplastic anemia,hemophilia, leukemia, thrombocytopenic purpura,
      complications of anticoagulant therapy
    Deficiency syndromes
    Vitamin B_1 deficiency (Wernicke encephalopathy), vitamin C deficiency (scurvy), vitamin K
      deficiency (hemorrhagic disease of the newborn)
  Hypertension
  Intracranial aneurysm
  Intracranial neoplasms
  Liver disease
  Toxic or infectious encephalopathy
  Trauma
    Cavernous sinus fistula, epidural hemorrhage, subdural hemorrhage

Occlusive vascular diseases
  Dural sinus and cerebral venous thomboses, associated with:
    Congenital heart disease; debilitating states (marantic), dehydration or hyperosmolarity: infections
      of face, ears, or paranasal sinuses; inflammatory bowel disease; lead encephalopathy; leukemia;
      meningitis; metastatic neoplasms (e.g. neuroblastoma); sickle cell disease; Sturge-Weber-
      Dimitri syndrome (trigeminal encephalo-angiomatosis)
  Arterial thrombosis
    Idiopathic or spontaneous
    Symptomatic or associated with:
      Arteriosclerosis (progeria)
      Blood dyscrasias:
        Polycythemia, sickle cell disease, thrombotic thrombocytopenia
      Cerebral arteritis
        Acute infectious diseases, granulomatous disease (Takayasu disease), syphilis
      Collagen disease
        Lupus erythematosus, polyarteritis nodosa
      Complications of arteriography
      Cyanotic congenital heart disease
      Dissecting cerebral aneurysm
      Extra-arterial disease
        Craniometaphyseal dysplasia, mucormycosis, retropharyngeal abscess, tumors of the base of
          the skull
      Fibromuscular dysplasia
      Inflammatory bowel disease
      Metabolic
        Diabetes mellitus, homocystinuria
      Radiation
      Trauma to the carotid vertebrobasilar or cerebral arteries
  Cerebral embolism associated with:
    Air: complications of cardiac, neck, or thoracic surgery
    Cardiac:
      atrial fibrillation or other arrhythmias, congenital heart disease with right-to-left shunt.
        severe cardiac failure, atrial myxoma, bacterial endocarditis (acute or subacute)
    Fat: complications of fractures and IV fat infusions
    Placenta: complications of infarcted tissue
    Septic: complications of pneumonia or lung abscess
    Tumor
    Umbilical vein catheterization

From: Pediatrics (17th edn.). Edited by Abraham Rudolph; reprinted with permission, Appleton-
Century-Crofts.

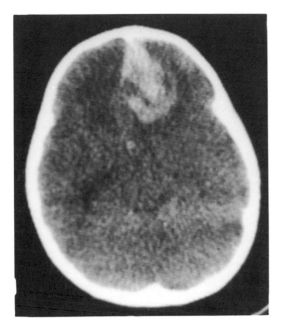

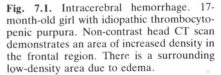

Fig. 7.1. Intracerebral hemorrhage. 17-month-old girl with idiopathic thrombocytopenic purpura. Non-contrast head CT scan demonstrates an area of increased density in the frontal region. There is a surrounding low-density area due to edema.

Arteriovenous malformation (AVM)

Arteriovenous malformations are the commonest vascular malformations in childhood. They arise at an early stage of fetal development (about three weeks) when there is differentiation into primitive arteries, capillaries and veins. Direct arteriovenous communication results from an arrest of normal development (Newton and Troost 1974, Stein and Wolpert 1980). With subsequent development of the child's brain, additional arterial contributions are acquired (Hook and Johanson 1958, Waltimo 1973). The increased bloodflow, repeated small hemorrhages and attenuation of distended venous channels is considered responsible for the occurrence of symptoms which are more common in the second and third decades of life than in childhood (Stein and Wolpert 1980).

The commonest location is supratentorial, mostly cortical but often with deep extension (Harwood-Nash and Fitz 1976). They are most frequent in the middle cerebral artery distribution but any cerebral artery may be involved (Russell and Rubinstein 1974). The lesions may also occur less commonly within the posterior fossa and extremely rarely in the choroid plexus (Britt *et al.* 1980). The incidence of brainstem arteriovenous malformations in childhood was found by Perret and Nishioka (1966) to exceed that within the cerebellum, in contrast to adults where the reverse is found. Some malformations are microscopic and are thus referred to as 'cryptic'.

The common presenting signs and symptoms are focal headache, hemiplegia and cranial nerve palsies, and subarachnoid hemorrhage. Macrocephaly and cardiac failure may occur as a result of large malformations. Seizures were found in 19 per cent of the series of Harwood-Nash and Fitz (1976).

123

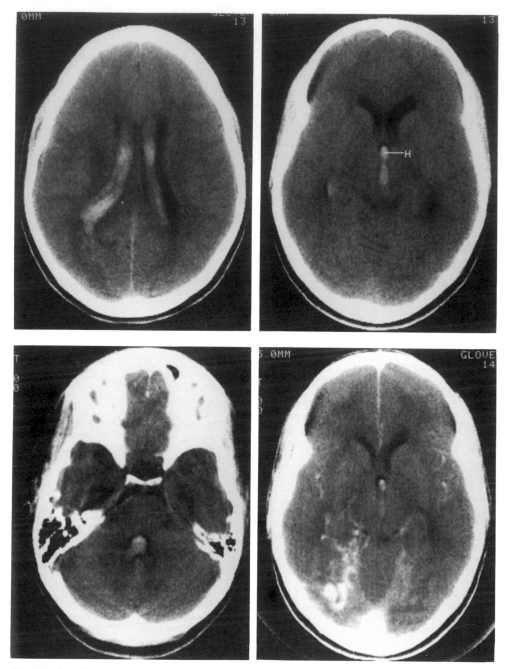

Fig. 7.2. Arteriovenous malformation (AVM) in a one-year-old with headache and meningismus. Non-contrast head CT scans demonstrate hemorrhage (H) within the lateral *(top left)*, third *(top right)* and fourth ventricles *(bottom left)*. A large contrast-enhancing AVM with a serpiginous configuration is demonstrated on the contrast-enhanced head CT scan *(bottom right)*. (Courtesy of Joel Swartz MD, Philadelphia.)

CT appearances

The non-contrast CT scan may be normal or may have increased density, low density or mixed density (Terbrugge *et al.* 1977, LeBlanc *et al.* 1979).

If there has been hemorrhage, the clot will be demonstrated with or without cisternal or ventricular blood (Fig. 7.2). Low-density areas may also be identified, following previous bleeds or infarcts. Tubular calcification within the vessel wall and punctate dystrophic calcification may also be indicative of an arteriovenous malformation (Norman 1983).

Following administration of contrast medium, most arteriovenous malformations will demonstrate abnormal enhancement unless there is thrombosis of the lesion (Terbrugge *et al.* 1977). The increased density has been attributed to mural thrombosis or calcification within the vessels involved, presence of an associated hematoma, calcification, or gliosis in the intervening brain tissue (Pressman *et al.* 1975). The arteries supplying the malformation together with draining veins may be clearly visualized in some instances (Fig. 7.2), but angiography is required for precise delineation of the lesion.

Associated features will also be demonstrated, such as intracerebral hematoma, intraventricular hemorrhage, ventricular compression, ipsilateral ventricular enlargement usually with ipsilateral shift or generalized hydrocephalus (Pressman *et al.* 1975, LeBlanc *et al.* 1979). Hemorrhage from an arteriovenous malformation is most often situated in the cortex or adjacent white matter, in contrast to the hypertensive hemorrhage in the older patient which is situated deeply in the lentiform nucleus, thalamus or dentate nucleus. The hemorrhage may be isodense if between one and three weeks of age, and may only be detected in the pre-contrast scan by the mass effect (Norman 1983).

Liquefaction of the hematoma of an AVM may produce a low-attenuation area simulating a cyst. Rim enhancement may be present on the post-contrast scan. An appropriate clinical history of severe headaches and the CT appearance should suggest the possibility of an AVM, although the differential diagnosis includes abscess, tumor, ependymal cyst, encephalomalacia and subacute infarction. Angiography is required to confirm the vascular abnormality (Daniels *et al.* 1979).

Angiographically occult AVMs may exhibit heterogeneous increased density on the pre-contrast scan, with subsequent enhancement after administration of contrast medium (Kramer and Wing 1977, LeBlanc *et al.* 1979).

Dural arteriovenous malformation

Arteriovenous malformations that mainly or exclusively involve the intracranial dura are rare, accounting for 10 to 15 per cent of all intracranial AVMs (Newton and Cronqvist 1969). The CT findings of limited cases reported in the literature (Bitoh *et al.* 1980, Miyasaka *et al.* 1980, Norman 1983) include:
1. Areas of decreased density, due to edema resulting from raised venous sinus pressure
2. Hydrocephalus
3. Vermiform or patchy enhancement following contrast administration. This is a result of retrograde venous drainage through collateral channels, including cortical

and diploic veins.
4. Enlarged straight and transverse sinuses
5. Enlarged venous varices in the dural sinus at the site of primary drainage
6. Intraparenchymal and subarachnoid hemorrhage
7. Prominent vascular grooves on the inner table of the skull. This will be detected by attention to bone windows at the time of the scan.

Vein of Galen aneurysm
Midline arteriovenous malformations involving the vein of Galen have been divided by Litvak *et al.* (1960) into three main categories:
1. Aneurysm of the great vein of Galen. There is dilatation of the great cerebral vein which is contiguous with a dilated straight sinus and torcula. The malformation is supplied directly by branches of the carotid and basilar circulations.
2. Racemose conglomerations of blood vessels with dilated deep venous drainage.
3. Arteriovenous shunts which are transitional between the true aneurysm of the great vein of Galen and the racemose angiomas.

Although the separation into separate entities may be helpful for surgical management, the underlying pathogenesis is based on a single embryologic defect (O'Brien and Schechter 1970). The primitive Galenic system and choroidal arteries are in close contact. A congenital fistula develops between the two systems. This communication may persist as a fistula or may be accompanied by secondary dilatation elsewhere. Regression after the initiation of a secondary arteriovenous malformation may also occur.

The clinical syndromes produced by primary aneurysms of the vein of Galen have been divided by Amacher and Shillito (1973) into four groups:
1. Neonatal. The presenting signs are severe cardiac failure, and cranial bruit. Most patients in this group were found to be male.
2. Neonatal or infancy. Mild cardiac failure is detected in the neonatal period followed by craniomegaly one to six months later with the detection of a cranial bruit.
3. Infancy (one to 12 months). Craniomegaly, with a cranial bruit is present.
4. Late (3½ to 27 years). Headache and syncope on exercise are the main presenting signs. Rim-like calcification within the pineal region may be present on skull radiographs.

Radiologic diagnosis has been established in the past by cerebral angiography (Gold *et al.* 1964, Heinz *et al.* 1968, Weir *et al.* 1968), and less frequently by plain skull radiographs (Russell and Newton 1964) and pneumo-encephalography (Sansregret *et al.* 1964).

The CT appearances have been described by Macpherson *et al.* (1979) and Spallone (1979):
1. A sharply outlined mass, rounded or triangular in configuration, of increased density. This is situated in the region of the vein of Galen. There is homogeneous enhancement after contrast medium. The above appearances, together with the triangular complex of straight sinus and torcula herophili, is highly suggestive of vein of Galen aneurysm (Figs. 7.3, 7.4).

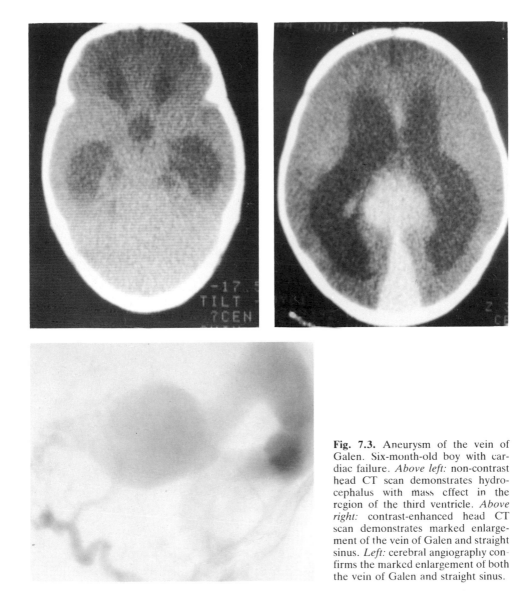

Fig. 7.3. Aneurysm of the vein of Galen. Six-month-old boy with cardiac failure. *Above left:* non-contrast head CT scan demonstrates hydrocephalus with mass effect in the region of the third ventricle. *Above right:* contrast-enhanced head CT scan demonstrates marked enlargement of the vein of Galen and straight sinus. *Left:* cerebral angiography confirms the marked enlargement of both the vein of Galen and straight sinus.

2. Hydrocephalus is usually present (Figs. 7.3, 7.5).

Thrombosis within a vein of Galen aneurysm has been demonstrated on CT and surgically confirmed by Rix *et al.* (1980) (Fig. 7.5). Peripheral enhancement of the lesion occurred after contrast medium administration ('target' sign), attributed to enhancement of vascular granulation tissue.

Post-operative CT scans are valuable for the assessment of aneurysm size, thrombosis, hydrocephalus and the presence of subdural effusions which commonly occur after surgery (Amacher and Shillito 1973) (Fig. 7.6).

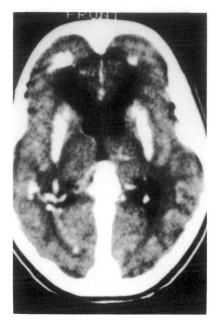

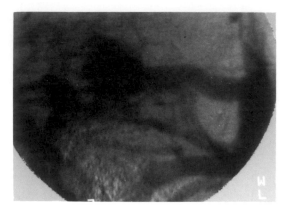

Fig. 7.4. Vein of Galen aneurysm. 14-year-old girl with seizure disorder and headaches. *Left:* contrast-enhanced head CT scan demonstrates marked engorgement of vein of Galen and straight sinus. Calcification within basal ganglia and cerebral cortex is consistent with Fahr's disease (see Chapter 10). *Above:* prominent vein of Galen and straight sinus are demonstrated by cerebral digital venous subtraction angiography.

Venous angioma

Venous angioma is a malformation composed of a single enlarged tortuous vein or a group of veins. The commonest site is the spinal cord and its meninges. The cerebrum and cerebellum are infrequently involved. This condition is rare in childhood, with most lesions occurring above the age of 20 (Russell and Rubenstein 1971).

The CT appearance of the few cases in the literature (Michels *et al.* 1977, Fierstein *et al.* 1979, Moritake *et al.* 1980) is of a normal or hyperdense area on pre-contrast scan, with subsequent rounded or linear area of enhancement not associated with edema or mass effect on the post-contrast scan (Fig. 7.7).

Cavernous angioma (cavernoma)

The cavernous angioma is a hamartoma characterized by blood-filled spaces which are separated by fine fibrous strands without intervening neural tissue (Russell and Rubinstein 1971, Rubinstein 1972). The cerebral hemispheres are most frequently involved, followed by the pons, although the basal ganglia, ventricular system, pineal and sellar regions, cerebellum, orbit, and spinal cord are other sites described (Ramina *et al.* 1980). The peak age incidence of these lesions is between the third and sixth decades of life but they may also occur in childhood occasionally (Russell and Rubenstein 1971, Pozzati *et al.* 1980). Calcification within the malformation has been noted in 11 to 40 per cent of cases (Ramina *et al.* 1980).

CT appearances

1. The typical appearance of a well-demarcated collection of rounded densities on

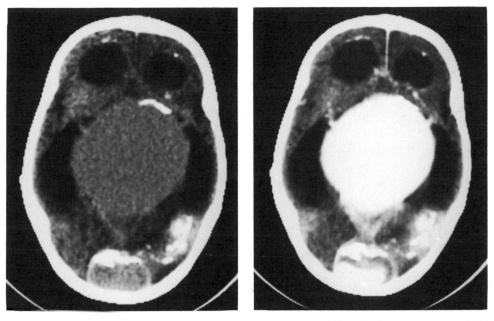

Fig. 7.5. Thrombosis within a vein of Galen aneurysm. Three-year-old boy. *Left:* non-contrast head CT scan demonstrates marked hydrocephalus with mass effect distorting the ventricular system. Note peripheral calcification within the vein of Galen and straight sinus. *Right:* contrast-enhanced head CT scan demonstrates partial thrombosis within the enhancing vein of Galen and straight sinus.

the pre-contrast scan followed by minimal contrast enhancement was described by Bartlett and Kishore (1977). Marked contrast enhancement has been noted by Ito *et al.* (1978) and Numaguchi *et al.* (1979).

2. Dense areas of calcification 'hemangioma calcificans' (DiTullio and Stern 1979)
3. Cyst formation with calcification (Ramina *et al.* 1980).

Capillary telangiectasis
Capillary telangiectases are composed of pathologically enlarged and varicose capillaries which drain into enlarged venous channels (Russell and Rubenstein 1974). The pons is the commonest location although the cerebral cortex is less frequently involved.

They are rarely symptomatic except for the hereditary form, Rendu-Osler-Weber disease, which is often symptomatic. The central lesions are telangiectases, arteriovenous malformations and angiomas. The clinical features may include convulsions, neurologic abnormalities, cerebrovascular accidents and subarachnoid hemorrhages.

CT appearances (Assencio-Ferreira *et al.* 1981, Terbrugge *et al.* 1983) include:
1. Cerebellar atrophy
2. Small hyperdense lesions on pre-contrast scan, with slight enhancement after contrast administration.

129

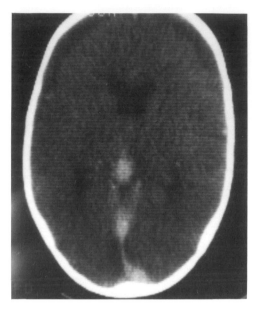

Fig. 7.6. Vein of Galen aneurysm. Post-operative effusion. 18-month-old boy with increasing head circumference and vein of Galen aneurysm. Postoperative contrast-enhanced head CT scan reveals evidence of bilateral subdural effusions.

Cryptic cerebrovascular malformations

The term cryptic or occult cerebrovascular malformation was introduced by Crawford and Russell in 1956 to describe small vascular malformations not detected by angiography. Cavernous angiomas account for most cryptic malformations; the remainder are due to capillary telangiectasis which rarely produces clinical symptoms, venous and arteriovenous malformations.

The lesion may be demonstrated on pre-contrast CT as a non-homogeneous high-density area with subsequent contrast enhancement in most cases and minimal mass effect. Ring-type enhancement may occasionally be encountered, indicating old or resolving hematoma (Becker *et al.* 1979).

Aneurysms

Cerebral aneurysms are uncommon in infants and children. They are of three etiologic types: congenital, traumatic, and inflammatory (bacterial or fungal).

Congenital aneurysms are commonest and may be associated with other lesions such as coarctation of the aorta (Schwartz and Baronofsky 1960), polycystic kidneys (Bigelow 1953). Ehler's-Danlos syndrome (Rubinstein and Cohen 1964) and a persistent trigeminal artery (Wolpert 1966, George *et al.* 1971).

Two cases have been described associated with agenesis of the corpus callosum (Garcia-Chavez and Moosy 1965) and multiple congenital anomalies (Pool and Potts 1965).

These aneurysms are very rare within the newborn period, with few reported cases in the literature (Lee *et al.* 1978*b*). Although they may be diagnosed in young children, most present in the teenage years. In a series of 300 ruptured intracranial aneurysms, 58 cases were found in patients under the age of 19 years (Patel and

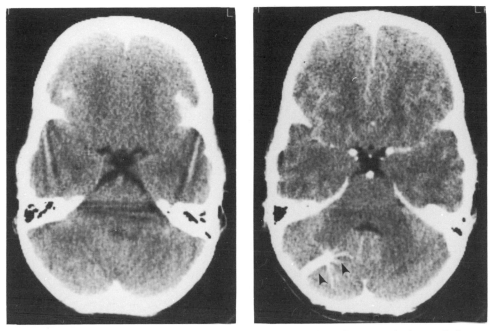

Fig. 7.7. Venous angioma. Five-year-old boy with increased head circumference and seizures. *Left:* non-contrast scan, and *right:* contrast-enhanced scan which demonstrates linear enhancement with terminal branching in the posterior fossa *(arrowheads)*. There is no mass effect or edema.

Richardson 1971).

The arterior circulation is involved more commonly than the posterior circulation, with the internal carotid and middle cerebral arteries being the most frequent sites (Shucart and Wolpert 1974).

Mycotic aneurysms may be secondary to congenital heart disease with septic emboli, cavernous sinus thrombophlebitis, osteomyelitis of the skull, and meningitis (Suwanela *et al.* 1972). These are most commonly situated along more distal arteries; they may rupture, producing intracerebral or subarachnoid hemorrhage (Bailey 1971).

Traumatic aneurysms are rare. These may be located on large basal arteries, primarily the extradural or supraclinoid portions of the internal carotid artery, or on distal peripheral arteries, especially the cortical branches of the middle cerebral artery (Benoit and Wortzman 1973).

Dissecting aneurysms usually follow trauma (Wolpert and Schechter 1966). They occur most frequently in the middle cerebral artery distribution (Shucart and Wolpert 1974).

CT appearance

Detection of cerebral aneurysms depends on their size and location. Aneurysms larger than 5mm in diameter may be detected by high-resolution CT scans with thin

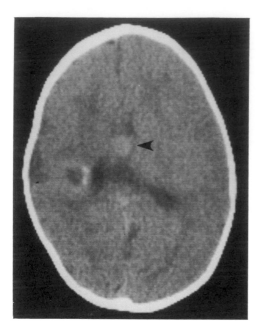

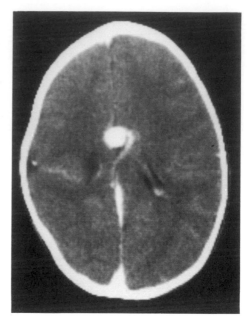

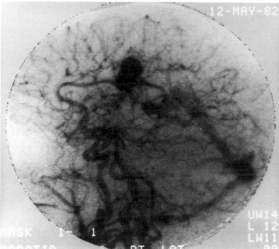

Fig. 7.8. Aneurysm and arteriovenous malformation. 11-month-old girl with left hemiparesis. *Above left:* non-contrast head CT scan demonstrates a soft tissue mass of slightly increased density *(arrowhead)* within the midline. There is no associated mass effect. *Above right:* contrast-enhanced head CT scan reveals marked enhancement within the midline mass. A prominent draining vein is noted. *Left:* cerebral digital venous subtraction angiogram (lateral projection) demonstrates filling of a pericallosal artery aneurysm and vascular malformation.

sections; for aneurysms less than 5mm in diameter the modality of choice is angiography (Terbrugge *et al.* 1983).

In the absence of thrombus within the lumen, the lesion appears as a rounded area of slightly increased density on the pre-contrast scan, then homogeneous enhancement is noted on the post-contrast scan (Fig. 7.8). Partially thrombosed aneurysms are noted on the pre-contrast scan to display a central or eccentric hyperdense region, contained within an isodense area which may contain calcium.

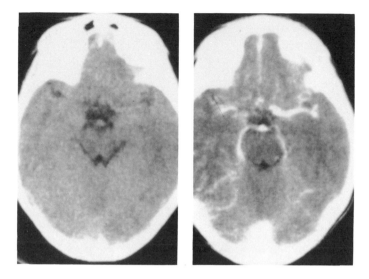

Fig. 7.9. Internal carotid artery occlusion. Six-year-old boy with sickle cell disease. *Far left:* non-contrast head CT scan, and *left:* contrast-enhanced head CT scan. There is occlusion of the left lateral carotid artery. Cerebral digital subtraction angiography demonstrated occlusion of the internal carotid artery above the carotid bifurcation.

Enhancement of the central and peripheral areas is noted on the post-contrast scan (Pinto *et al.* 1979). The completely thrombosed aneurysm has a ring-shaped hyperdense area on the pre-contrast scan which is noted to enhance after contrast medium administration. Central enhancement does not occur (Pinto *et al.* 1979).

Cerebrovascular occlusive disease
The incidence of cerebrovascular accidents in infants and children is less than in the elderly. However, the magnitude is greater than previously realized, as demonstrated by the study of a Minnesota pediatric population in which the incidence was 2.52 individuals per 100,000, approximately one half of the incidence of pediatric intracranial tumors (Schoenberg *et al.* 1978).

Cerebral thrombosis
The majority of cerebrovascular accidents in children are due to thrombotic occlusion of the intracranial arteries, primarily in the middle cerebral artery distribution or extracranial portion of the internal carotid artery. The basilar artery is less frequently involved (Golden 1982).

Arterial occlusion tends to occur more commonly in a previously healthy child but may also occur as a complication of systemic diseases (Gold and Michelsen 1983) (Fig. 7.9). These numerous disorders are listed in Table 7.1.

Extracranial occlusive disease is most often due to trauma involving the cervical portion of the internal carotid artery which is compressed against the transverse process of the second cervical vertebra, or trauma to the vertebral artery with repeated subluxation of the first cervical vertebra on the second cervical vertebra, resulting in vertebral artery occlusion which may be complicated by embolization into the basilar artery (Singer *et al.* 1975, Gold and Michelsen 1983).

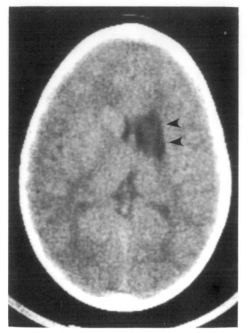 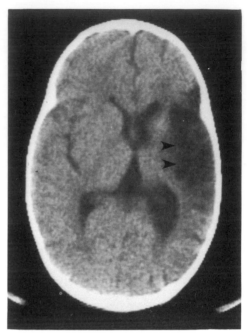

Fig. 7.10. Cerebral infarction. Three-year-old girl with right hemiparesis. Non-contrast head CT scan demonstrates a low-density area *(arrowheads)* corresponding to infarction in the distribution of the lenticulostriate branch of the left middle cerebral artery.

Fig. 7.11. Non-hemorrhagic cerebral infarction. 18-month-old girl with right hemiparesis. Non-contrast head CT scan demonstrates low-density area *(arrowheads)* representing infarction in distribution of left middle cerebral artery. There is ipsilateral dilatation of left lateral ventricle.

CT appearances of non-hemorrhagic infarcts

The appearances of vaso-occlusive infarcts are first evident between 24 and 48 hours after the onset of symptoms (Davis *et al.* 1975), although abnormalities have been demonstrated between three to six hours after the ictus (Inoue *et al.* 1980). Approximately half of all infarcts are visualized within 48 hours (Houser *et al.* 1982).

DENSITY, SHAPE AND SIZE

There is a focal poorly defined hypodense area which involves both cortex and underlying white matter (Figs. 7.10, 7.11). The low density is due to intracellular edema and tissue necrosis (Alcala *et al.* 1978). The hypodense area is confined to the vascular supply area of the occluded artery. The lesion becomes more sharply delineated as edema increases by the third to fourth day with increasing hypodensity (Houser *et al.* 1982). Density increases after seven to 10 days with subsiding of edema (Campbell *et al.* 1978).

Differentiation from tumors and abscesses is made by location and distribution of the lesion (Goldberg 1983). Infarcts are usually located within both gray and white matter, unlike tumors and abscesses which are within white matter with possible extension to the cortex. Infarcts develop sharply demarcated margins and lie within or between arterial territories. The low-density lesions of tumor or abscess have poorly defined margins and are not limited to arterial distributions, spreading diffusely within white matter.

The size and shape of an infarct does not accurately reflect the complete distribution of single or multiple major of minor branch occlusions (Bradac and Oberson 1980, Houser *et al.* 1982). The appearances will depend on which vessels are occluded, availability of collateral channels and the structures affected.

During the second week irregular and normodense bands appear within the low-density areas, mostly in gray matter. They are due to the hyperemia following improved collateral circulation and new capillary ingrowth (Inoue *et al.* 1980, Goldberg 1983).

Between the fourth week and the third month, the hypodense area becomes more clearly defined with ipsilateral ventricular dilatation. The low-density area may revert to normal density temporarily or permanently in some instances (Becker *et al.* 1979, Houser *et al.* 1982), but there is cystic change in many cases, so the density values are equivalent to that of cerebrospinal fluid (Davis *et al.* 1975, Houser *et al.* 1982).

Sulcal enlargement may be the only abnormality with some cortical infarcts (Goldberg 1983).

MASS EFFECT
Mass effect is minimal during the first 24 hours of onset (Goldberg 1983) but is maximal by the fifth day (Clasen *et al.* 1980). This gradually subsides and is usually absent after the third week (Masdeu *et al.* 1977, Houser *et al.* 1982).

CONTRAST ENHANCEMENT
The vast majority of infarcts display contrast enhancement 14 to 21 days after the ictus (Inoue *et al.* 1980, Pullicino and Kendall 1980) (Fig. 7.12). There have been reports of enhancement occurring in the first week (Lee 1978*a*, Weisberg 1980), but this is attributed to embolic causes (Goldberg 1983).

Enhancement is maximal during the third week; thereafter it decreases rapidly and is unusual after the second month (Houser *et al.* 1982). Persistent enhancement has, however, been noted nine months after the ictus although this is rare (Norton *et al.* 1978).

The postulated pathophysiologic mechanisms for contrast enhancement include breakdown of the blood-brain barrier (Blahd 1971, Fishman 1975), new capillary growth (Blahd 1971, DiChiro *et al.* 1974), and luxury perfusion (Soin and Burdine 1976). Ischemic injury to the blood-brain barrier mechanism of the capillary endothelium allows large molecules to escape into the extravascular space (Goldberg 1983).

Confluent gyral, homogeneous and ring-enhancement patterns have been observed closer to the third week, when maximal enhancement occurs with streaky, amorphous, stippled or patchy enhancement noted earlier or later than this period (Houser *et al.* 1982).

135

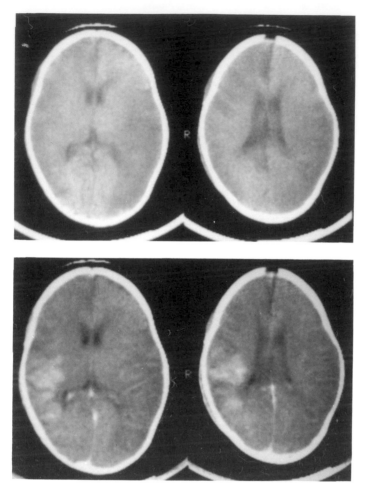

Fig. 7.12.
Non-hemorrhagic
cerebral infarction. Female
neonate with left hemi-
paresis. *Top:* non-contrast
head CT scan demonstrates
low density corresponding
to infarction in the
distribution of the right
middle cerebral artery.
Bottom: contrast-enhanced
head CT scan demonstrates
prominent enhancement in
a gyral pattern.

The use of contrast media has been shown to increase the diagnostic yield of infarcts. In some instances where the pre-contrast scan was normal, contrast enhancement of the infarct may be the only abnormality demonstrated (Wing *et al.* 1976, Norton *et al.* 1978). The converse is also applicable in a small number of cases; in the series of Wing *et al.* (1976), the low-density lesions seen on the pre-contrast scan were subsequently obscured after the injection of contrast medium.

Contrast enhancement occurs mainly in cortex and deep gray matter (Inoue *et al.* 1980). Enhancement tends to occur earliest in the cortex at the margins of the infarct as collateral circulation is increased to this region initially (Goldberg 1983). Enhancement into the underlying white matter may be noted on delayed scans (Goldberg 1983).

A large number of infarcts have been noted to develop a contrast blush on the post-contrast scan, occurring during the second week after infarction (Yock and

Marshall 1975).

The patterns of enhancement are variable and may be predominantly peripheral, central, homogeneous or heterogeneous (Norton *et al.* 1978). Heterogeneous enhancement was noted to be more common than the homogeneous type in Norton's series. The different types as described above have been analysed in greater detail by Goldberg (1983), as follows:

1. The heterogeneous appearance represents avascular areas of coagulation necrosis or the varying amount of collateral recirculation to different areas of the infarct.
2. The homogeneous pattern is thought to be due to incomplete necrosis and more uniform reperfusion of the infarct.
3. The linear band and central patterns represent areas of enhancement in the cortical ribbon which lies within and surrounding the infarct.
4. The peripheral enhancing pattern is noted as an enhancing rim, developing in areas of hemispheric infarction with both gray and white matter necrosis.
5. Ring enhancement, which is most common in the necrotic infarcts found within the basal ganglia and also around infarcts in the white matter with varying involvement of the overlying cortex.

The appearances of contrast enhancement described above may simulate those of tumor or abscess. Mass effect is usually absent when contrast enhancement occurs in an infarct and the lesion usually has a vascular distribution. Follow-up CT scans will help to exclude tumors and abscesses (Goldberg 1983).

The rôle of angiography in primary cerebral arterial thrombosis

Although CT is established as the primary modality for the examination of intracranial cerebrovascular disease, angiography is required in the investigation of primary cerebral arterial thrombosis. There are five main categories (Hilal *et al.* 1971, Gold and Michelsen 1983):

1. Extracranial occlusive disease.
2. Basal occlusive disease without telangiectasia. Vasculitis, encasement by tumor, and radiation therapy have been suggested as etiologic factors.
3. Basal occlusive disease with telangiectasia (Moyamoya disease). Although there are CT descriptions of this disease (see below) angiography will be required for precise arterial delineation.
4. Distal branch occlusion over the convexity. Diabetes mellitus, sickle cell disease, intravenous drug abuse, and neurocutaneous symptoms have all been implicated.
5. Small artery disease.

Occlusion of the small perforating arteries have been demonstrated in homocystinuria and peri-arteritis nodosa.

Cerebral embolism

Cerebral embolic disease is not common in infants and children. Vascular occlusion may follow emboli from thrombus, air, fat, tumor or bacteria, with the middle cerebral artery or one of its branches being most commonly involved (Gold and Michelsen 1983). Emboli usually are of cardiac (cyanotic congenital heart disease,

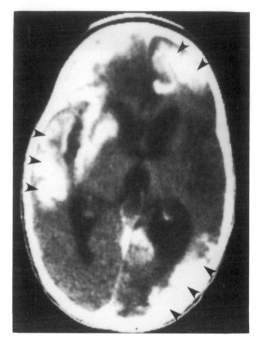

Fig. 7.13. Hemorrhagic cerebral infarction. Two-year-old girl with previously demonstrated bilateral infarcts. Contrast-enhanced head CT scan demonstrates prominent contrast enhancement in a gyral pattern *(arrowheads)*.

rheumatic valvular disease) or pulmonary origin. Air embolism may occur as a complication of cardiopulmonary bypass surgery. Fat embolism released from fracture sites is rare.

CT appearances

Emboli have been demonstrated as focal hyperdense lesions near bifurcations of the anterior and middle cerebral arteries (Yock 1981). The CT appearance will vary with the temporal sequence of the embolic infarct (Goldberg 1983).

1. A scan performed prior to lysis of the embolus will be similar to that of vaso-occlusive infarct. There may be evidence of infarcts of about the same age in more than one vascular territory.

2. Following lysis and fragmentation of the embolus, which occurs between one and three days later, the vascular occlusion has been removed and thus the infarcted area is perfused at a higher pressure with increased bloodflow. There is a resultant hyperemic luxury perfusion pattern due to loss of the normal autoregulatory pattern. There are two distinct patterns which occur after lysis and fragmentation:

(1) Previous mild-to-moderate ischemia results in a pre-contrast scan which may appear normal or may exhibit slight increase in density in the cortical area of infarction. There is a corresponding diffuse homogeneous blush noted on the post-contrast scan.

(2) With more severe ischemia initially the pre-contrast scan displays an area of low density of the white matter, with the overlying cortex appearing either isodense or minimally hyperdense. A hyperdense cortical blush is noted on the post-contrast

138

scan with enhancement extending into the white matter. A cortical gyral pattern of enhancement may occur following lysis of the embolus frequently involving the basal ganglia. Brain swelling is a frequent accompaniment of the enhancement developing with embolic infarcts, as both features are present between days two and five.

Hemorrhagic infarction is usually a further complication after the onset of embolic infarction and is more prone to develop when tissue necrosis is marked (Goldberg 1983). The initial pre-contrast scan may only demonstrate an area of decreased density. Cortical hemorrhage which develops with clinical deterioration appears as a band-like region of mild or moderately increased density, with ill-defined margins, assuming the gyral configuration of the cortex. The surrounding cortex is hypodense (Fig. 7.13).

Following contrast administration the area of infarction will develop increased density, without enhancement of the area of hemorrhage. There may be considerable mass effect.

Dural sinus and cerebral venous thromboses
Cerebral edema and infarction may result from obstruction of the dural sinus and cerebral venous occlusion. This may commonly occur as a complication of pyogenic infections, dehydration and debilitating states, trauma, sickle cell disease and polycythemia. Less frequent causes are leukemia, metastatic disease, lead encephalopathy, inflammatory bowel disease, thrombotic thrombocytopenia and Sturge-Weber disease. The CT appearances are described in Chapter 8.

Moyamoya disease
Moyamoya disease is a condition of unknown etiology which develops in childhood. Although earlier reports involved children of Japanese ancestry (Kudo 1968, Nishimoto and Takeuchi 1968) other races may be similarly afflicted (Taveras 1969). The disease is hereditary in some cases, but may follow other disorders such as neurofibromatosis (Tomsick *et al.* 1976), tuberculosis, sickle cell disease, bacterial meningitis, head trauma, Fanconi anemia and radiation therapy (Gold and Michelsen 1983).

The term moyamoya is a Japanese expression to describe 'something hazy just like a puff of smoke drifting in the air' (Suzuki and Takaku 1969). This refers to the collateral network of dilated intraparenchymal arteries arising proximal to the occlusion of the middle and anterior cerebral arteries and supraclinoid portion of the internal carotid artery.

The CT appearances as described by Handa *et al.* (1977) and Takahashi *et al.* (1980) include:
1. Parenchymal areas of hypodensity due to ischemia
2. Cerebral atrophy
3. Hemorrhage which may have intraventricular, subarachnoid, or basal ganglionic location
4. Curvilinear densities in the region of the basal ganglia representing parenchymal collateral vessels.

REFERENCES

Alcalá, H., Gado, M., Torack, R. M. (1978) 'The effect of size, histologic elements, and water content on the visualization of cerebral infarcts.' *Archives of Neurology,* **35,** 1–7.

Amacher, A. L., Shillito, J., Jr. (1973) 'The syndromes and surgical treatment of aneurysms of the great vein of Galen.' *Journal of Neurosurgery,* **39,** 89–98.

Assencio-Ferreira, V. J., Bancovsky, I., Diament, A. J., Dias, A. J., Gherpelli, J. L., Morreira, F. A. (1981) 'Computed tomography in ataxia telangiectasia.' *Journal of Computer Assisted Tomography,* **5,** 660–662.

Bailey, O. T. (1971) *In:* Minckler, J. (Ed.) *Pathology of the Nervous System. Vol. 2.* New York: McGraw-Hill.

Bartlett, J. E., Kishore, P. R. (1977) 'Intracranial cavernous angioma.' *American Journal of Roentgenology,* **128,** 653–656.

Becker, D. H., Townsend, J. J., Kramer, R. A., Newton, T. H. (1979) 'Occult cerebrovascular malformations.' *Brain,* **102,** 249–287.

Benoit, B. G., Wortzman, G. (1973) 'Traumatic cerebral aneurysms.' *Journal of Neurology, Neurosurgery and Psychiatry,* **36,** 127–138.

Bigelow, N. H. (1953) 'The association of polycystic kidneys with intracranial aneurysms and other related disorders.' *American Journal of Medical Science,* **225,** 485–494.

Bitoh, S., Arita, N., Fujiwara, M., Ozaki, K., Nakao, Y. (1980) 'Dural arteriovenous malformation near the left sphenoparietal sinus.' *Surgical Neurology,* **13,** 345–349.

Blahd, W. H. (1971) *Nuclear Medicine. 2nd edn.* New York: McGraw-Hill. pp. 262–267.

Bradac, G. B., Oberson, R. (1980) 'CT and angiography in cases with occlusive disease of supratentorial cerebral vessels.' *Neuroradiology,* **19,** 193–200.

Britt, R. H., Silverberg, G. D., Enzmann, D. R., Hanbery, J. W. (1980) 'Third ventricular choroid plexus arteriovenous malformation simulating a colloid cyst.' *Journal of Neurosurgery,* **52,** 246–250.

Campbell, J. K., Houser, O. W., Stevens, J. C., Wahner, H. W., Baker, H. L., Folger, W. N. (1978) 'Computed tomography and radionuclide imaging in the evaluation of ischemic stroke.' *Radiology,* **126,** 695–702.

Chiu, L. C., Fodor, L. B., Cornell, S. H., Christie, J. H. (1976) 'Computed tomography and brain scintigraphy in ischemic stroke.' *American Journal of Roentgenology,* **127,** 481–486.

Clasen, R. A., Huckman, M. S., Von Roenn, K. A., Pandolfi, S., Laing, I., Lobick, J. J. (1980) 'Time course of cerebral swelling in stroke: a correlative autopsy and CT study.' *Advances in Neurology,* **28,** 395–412.

Crawford, J. V., Russell, D. S. (1956) 'Cystic arteriovenous and venous hamartomas of the brain.' *Journal of Neurology, Neurosurgery and Psychiatry,* **19,** 1–11.

Cushing, H., Bailey, P. (1928) *Tumors Arising from the Blood Vessels of the Brain: Angiomatous Malformations and Hemangioblastomas.* Springfield, Ill.: C. C. Thomas.

Daniels, D. L., Haughton, V. M., Williams, A. L., Strother, C. M. (1979) 'Arteriovenous malformation simulating a cyst on computed tomography.' *Radiology,* **133,** 393–394.

Davis, K. R., Ackerman, R. H., Kistler, J. P., Mohr, J. P. (1975) 'Computed tomography of cerebral infarction: hemorrhage, contrast enhancement, and time of appearance.' *Computerized Tomography,* **1,** 71–86.

DiChiro, G., Timins, E. L., Jones, A. E., Johnston, G. S., Hammock, M. K., Swan, S. J. (1974) 'Radionuclide scanning and microangiopathy of evolving and completed brain infarction. A correlative study in monkeys.' *Neurology,* **24,** 418–423.

DiTullio, M. V., Stern, W. E. (1979) 'Hemangioma calcificans.' *Journal of Neurosurgery,* **50,** 110–114.

Fierstein, S. B., Pribram, H. W., Hieshima, G. (1979) 'Angiography and computed tomography in the evaluation of cerebral venous malformations.' *Neuroradiology,* **17,** 137–148.

Fishman, R. A. (1975) 'Brain edema.' *New England Journal of Medicine,* **293,** 706–711.

Garcia-Chavez, C., Moossy, J. (1965) 'Cerebral artery aneurysm in infancy: association with agenesis of the corpus callosum.' *Journal of Neuropathology and Experimental Neurology,* **24,** 492–501.

George, A. E., Lin, J. P., Morantz, R. A. (1971) 'Intracranial aneurysm on a persistent primitive trigeminal artery.' *Journal of Neurosurgery,* **35,** 601–604.

Gold, A. P., Ransohoff, J., Carter, S. (1964) 'Vein of Galen malformation.' *Acta Neurologica Scandinavica,* **40** [Suppl. 11], 1–31.

—— Michelsen, W. J. (1983) 'Cerebrovascular diseases.' *In:* Rudolph, A. M., Hoffman, J. I. E. (Eds.) *Pediatrics. 17th edn.* East Norwalk, Connecticut: Appleton–Century–Crofts. pp. 1637–1645.

Goldberg, H. I. (1983) 'Stroke.' *In:* Lee, S. H., Rao, K. C. V. G. (Eds.) *Cranial Computed Tomography.* New York: McGraw-Hill. pp. 583–657.

140

Golden, G. S. (1982) 'Cerebrovascular disease.' *In:* Swaiman K. F., Wright, F. S. (Eds.) *The Practice of Pediatric Neurology, Vol. 2. 2nd edn.* St. Louis: C. V. Mosby. pp. 772–793.

Handa, J., Handa, H., Nakano, Y., Okuno, T. (1977) 'Computed tomography in moyamoya: analysis of 16 cases.' *Journal of Computerized Axial Tomography,* **1,** 165–174.

Harwood-Nash, D. C., Fitz, C. H. (1976) *Neuroradiology in Infants and Children.* St. Louis: C. V. Mosby.

Heinz, E. R., Schwartz, J. F., Sears, R. A. (1968) 'Thrombosis in the vein of Galen malformation.' *British Journal of Radiology,* **41,** 424–428.

Hilal, S. K., Solomon, G. E., Gold, A. P., Carter, S. (1971) 'Primary cerebral arterial occlusive disease in children. Part I: Acute acquired hemiplegia.' *Radiology,* **99,** 71–86.

Hook, O., Johanson, C. (1958) 'Intracranial arteriovenous aneurysms: a follow-up study with particular attention to their growth.' *Archives of Neurology and Psychiatry,* **80,** 39–54.

Houser, O. W., Campbell, J. K., Baker, H. L., Sundt, T. S. (1982) 'Radiologic evaluation of ischemic cerebrovascular syndromes with emphasis on computed tomography.' *Radiologic Clinics of North America,* **20,** 123–142.

Inoue, Y., Takemoto, K., Miyamoto, T., Yoshikawa, N., Taniguchi, S., Saiwai, S., Nishimura, Y., Komatsu, T. (1980) 'Sequential computed tomography scans in acute cerebral infarction.' *Radiology,* **135,** 655–662.

Ito, J., Sato, I., Tanimura, K. (1978) 'Angiographic manifestations of a convexity cavernous hemangioma.' *Japanese Journal of Clinical Radiology,* **23,** 204–205.

Kramer, R. A., Wing, J. D. (1977) 'Computed tomography of angiographically occult cerebral vascular malformations.' *Radiology,* **123,** 649–652.

Kudo, T. (1968) 'Spontaneous occlusion of the Circle of Willis. A disease apparently confined to Japanese.' *Neurology,* **18,** 485–496.

LeBlanc, R., Ethier, R., Little, J. R. (1979) 'Computerized tomography findings in arteriovenous malformations of the brain.' *Journal of Neurosurgery,* **51,** 756–772.

Lee, K. F., Chambers, R. A., Diamond, C., Park, C. H., Thompson, N. L., Schnapf, D., Pripstein, S. (1978a) 'Evaluation of cerebral infarction by computed tomography with special emphasis on microinfarction.' *Neuroradiology,* **16,** 156–158.

Lee, Y. J., Kandall, S. R., Ghali, V. S. (1978b) 'Intracerebral arterial aneurysm in a newborn.' *Archives of Neurology,* **35,** 171–172.

Litvak, J., Jahr, M. D., Ransohoff, J. (1960) 'Aneurysms of the great vein of Galen amd midline cerebral arteriovenous anomalies.' *Journal of Neurosurgery,* **17,** 945–954.

MacPherson, P., Teasdale, G. M., Lindsay, K. W. (1979) 'Computed tomography in diagnosis and management of aneurysm of the vein of Galen.' *Journal of Neurology, Neurosurgery, and Psychiatry,* **42,** 786–789.

Masdeu, J. C., Azar-Kia, B., Rubino, F. A. (1977) 'Evaluation of recent cerebral infarction by computerized tomography.' *Archives of Neurology,* **34,** 417–421.

Michels, L. G., Bentson, J. R., Winter, J. (1977) 'Computed tomography of cerebral venous angiomas.' *Journal of Computer Assisted Tomography,* **1,** 149–154.

Miyasaka, K., Takei, H., Nomura, M., Sugimoto, S., Aida, T., Abe, H., Tsuru, M. (1980) 'Computerized tomographic findings in dural arteriovenous malformations.' *Journal of Neurosurgery,* **53,** 698–702.

Moritake, K., Handa, H., Mori, K., Ishikawa, M., Morimoto, M., Takebe, Y. (1980) 'Venous angiomas of the brain.' *Surgical Neurology,* **14,** 95–105.

Newton, T. H., Cronqvist, S. (1969) 'Involvement of dural arteries in intracranial arteriovenous malformations.' *Radiology,* **93,** 1071–1078.

—— Troost, B. T. (1974) 'Arteriovenous malformation and fistula.' *In:* Newton, T. H., Potts, D. G. (Eds.) *Radiology of the Skull and Brain: Vol. 2, Book 4. Angiography.* St. Louis: C. V. Mosby. pp. 2490–2565.

Nishimoto, A., Takeuchi, S. (1968) 'Abnormal cerebrovascular network related to the internal carotid arteries.' *Journal of Neurosurgery,* **29,** 255–260.

Norman, D. (1983) 'Computed tomography of cerebrovascular malformations.' *Paper presented at the Neuroradiology Conference, Vail, Colorado. March 21–25.*

Norton, G. A., Kishore, P. R. S., Lin, J. (1978) 'CT contrast enhancement in cerebral infarction.' *American Journal of Roentgenology,* **131,** 881–885.

Numaguchi, Y., Kishikawa, T., Fukui, M., Sawada, K., Kitamura, K., Matsuura, K., Russell, W. J. (1979) 'Prolonged injection angiography for diagnosing intracranial cavernous hemangiomas.' *Radiology,* **131,** 137–138.

O'Brien, M., Schechter, M. M. (1970) 'Arteriovenous malformations involving the Galenic system.'

American Journal of Roentgenology, **110,** 50–55.

Patel A. N., Richardson, A. E. (1971) 'Ruptured intracranial aneurysms in the first two decades of life.' *Journal of Neurosurgery,* **35,** 571–576.

Perret, G., Nishioka, H. (1966) 'Report on the cooperative study of intracranial aneurysms and subarachnoid hemorrhage. Section VI: Arteriovenous malformations.' *Journal of Neurosurgery,* **25,** 467–490.

Pinto, R. S., Kricheff, I. I., Butler, A. R., Murali, R. (1979) 'Correlation of computed tomographic, angiographic and neuropathological changes in giant cell aneurysms.' *Radiology,* **132,** 85–92.

Pool, J. L., Potts, D. G. (1965) *Aneurysms and Arteriovenous Anomalies of the Brain: Diagnosis and Treatment.* New York: Harper & Row. p. 57.

Pozzati, E., Padovani, R., Marrone, B., Finizio, F., Gaist, G. (1980) 'Cerebral cavernous angiomas in children.' *Journal of Neurosurgery,* **53,** 826–832.

Pressman, B. D., Kirkwood, J. R., Davis, D. O. (1975) 'Computerized transverse tomography of vascular lesions of the brain. Part I: Arteriovenous malformations.' *American Journal of Roentgenology, Radium Therapy and Nuclear Medicine,* **124,** 208–214.

Pullicino, P., Kendall, B. E. (1980) 'Contrast enhancement in ischemic lesions. 1: Relationship to prognosis.' *Neuroradiology,* **19,** 235–239.

Ramina, R., Ingunza, W., Vonofakos, D. (1980) 'Cystic cerebral cavernous angioma with dense calcification.' *Journal of Neurosurgery,* **52,** 259–262.

Rix, E. G., Cowley, A. R., Kelly, D. L., Jr., Laster, D. W. (1980) 'Thrombosed aneurysm of the vein of Galen.' *Neurosurgery,* **7,** 274–278.

Rubinstein, L. J. (1972) 'Tumors of the central nervous system.' *In: Atlas of Tumor Pathology, Second Series, Fascicle 6.* Washington, D.C.: Armed Forces Institute of Pathology.

Rubinstein, M. K., Cohen, N. H. (1964) 'Ehlers–Danlos syndrome associated with multiple intracranial aneurysms.' *Neurology,* **14,** 125–132.

Russell, D. S., Rubinstein, L. J. (1971) 'Vascular tumors and hamartomas.' *In: Pathology of Tumors of the Nervous System. 3rd edn.* Baltimore: Williams & Wilkins. pp. 85–108.

—— —— (1974) *Pathology of Tumors of the Nervous System. 4th edn.* Baltimore: Williams & Wilkins.

Russell, W., Newton, T. H. (1964) 'Aneurysm of the vein of Galen. Case report and review of the literature.' *American Journal of Roentgenology,* **92,** 756–760.

Sansregret, A., LeBlanc, P., Archambault, R. (1964) 'Signes cisternographiques et iodoventriculographies d'un anevrysme artérioveineux de l'ampoule de Galein.' *Journal of the Canadian Association of Radiologists,* **15,** 34–37.

Schoenberg, B. S., Mellinger, J. F., Schoenberg, D. G. (1978) 'Cerebrovascular disease in infants and children: a study of incidents, clinical features and survival.' *Neurology,* **28,** 763–768.

Schwartz, M. J., Baronofsky, I. D. (1960) 'Ruptured intracranial aneurysm associated with coarctation of the aorta.' *American Journal of Cardiology,* **6,** 982–988.

Shucart, W. A., Wolpert, S. N. (1974) 'Intracranial arterial aneurysms in childhood.' *American Journal of Diseases of Children,* **127,** 288–293.

Singer, W. D., Haller, J. S., Wolpert, S. N. (1975) 'Occlusive vertebrobasilar artery disease associated with cervical spine anomaly.' *American Journal of Diseases of Children,* **129,** 492–495.

Soin, J. S., Burdine, J. A. (1976) 'Acute cerebral vascular accident associated with hyperperfusion.' *Radiology,* **118,** 109–112.

Spallone, A. (1979) 'Computed tomography in aneurysms of the vein of Galen.' *Journal of Computer Assisted Tomography,* **3,** 779–782.

Stein, B. M., Wolpert, S. N. (1980) 'Arteriovenous malformations of the brain. I: Current concepts and treatment.' *Archives of Neurology,* **37,** 1–5.

Suwanwela, C., Suwanwela, N., Chruchinda, S., Hongsaprabhas, C. (1972) 'Intracranial aneurysms of extravascular origin.' *Journal of Neurosurgery,* **36,** 552–557.

Suzuki, J., Takaku, A. (1969) 'Cerebrovascular "Moyamoya" disease.' *Archives of Neurology,* **20,** 288–299.

Takahashi, M., Saito, Y., Konno, K. (1980) 'Intraventricular hemorrhage in childhood moyamoya disease.' *Journal of Computer Assisted Tomography,* **4,** 117–120.

Taveras, J. M. (1969) 'Multiple progressive intracranial arterial occlusions: a syndrome of children and young adults.' *American Journal of Roentgenology,* **106,** 235–268.

Terbrugge, K., Scotti, G., Ethier, R., Melancon, D., Tchang, S., Milner, C. (1977) 'Computed tomography in intracranial arteriovenous malformation.' *Radiology,* **122,** 703–705.

—— Rao, K. C. V. G., Lee, S. H. (1983) 'Cerebral vascular anomalies.' *In:* Lee, S. H., Rao, K. C. V. G. (Eds.) *Cranial Computed Tomography.* New York: McGraw-Hill. pp. 547-581.

Tomsick, T. A., Lukin, R. R., Chambers, A. A. Benton, C. (1976) 'Neurofibromatosis and intracranial

142

arterial occlusive disease.' *Neuroradiology*, **11**, 229–234.

Waltimo, O. (1973) 'The change in size of intracranial arteriovenous malformations.' *Journal of the Neurological Sciences*, **19**, 21–27.

Weir, B. K. A., Allen, P. B. R., Miller, J. D. R. (1968) 'Excision of thrombosed vein of Galen aneurysm in an infant: case report.' *Journal of Neurosurgery*, **29**, 619–622.

Weisberg, L. A. (1980) 'Computerized tomographic enhancement patterns in cerebral infarction.' *Archives of Neurology*, **37**, 21–24.

Willis, T. (1667) *Pathologiae cerebri et nervosi generis specimen. In quo agitur de morbis convulsivis et de scorbuto.* Oxonii, excudebat Guild Hall, Impensis Ja, Allestry, p. 49.

Wing, S. D., Norman, D., Pollock, J. A., Newton, J. H. (1976) 'Contrast enhancement of cerebral infarcts in computed tomography.' *Radiology*, **121**, 89–92.

Wolpert, S. N. (1966) 'The trigeminal artery and associated aneurysms.' *Neurology*, **16**, 610–614.

—— Schechter, M. M. (1966) 'Traumatic middle cerebral artery occlusion.' *Radiology*, **87**, 671–677.

Yock, D. H., Jr. (1981) 'CT demonstration of cerebral emboli.' *Journal of Computer Assisted Tomography*, **5**, 190–196.

—— Marshall, W. H. (1975) 'Recent ischemic brain infarcts at computed tomography: appearances pre- and postcontrast infusion.' *Radiology*, **117**, 559–608.

8

CENTRAL NERVOUS SYSTEM INFECTION AND IMMUNE DEFICIENCY DISORDERS

Infection of the central nervous system is a common problem in the pediatric age-group, requiring early diagnosis and management to ensure a favorable prognosis. The advent of modern therapeutic agents, coupled with major clinical and radiologic advances, has made a significant impact in decreasing the morbidity and mortality associated with this form of disease.

Computed tomography (CT) has become the modality of choice in the radiologic evaluation of infection of the central nervous system. The ease and simplicity of this procedure is particularly well suited to the patient who may have a life-threatening disease. In selected cases other diagnostic radiologic studies may be needed, *e.g.* cerebral angiography for the demonstration of an arteritis.

A wide variety of organisms may infect the central nervous system including bacterial (acute and chronic), viral, protozoal, rickettsial, parasitic, and fungal agents. The organisms may originate from direct penetrating skull injuries, contiguous spread from a localized infected source such as osteomyelitis, otitis media or sinusitis, and direct hematogenous spread to the meninges with subsequent cortical involvement.

Acute bacterial infections
Bacterial meningitis
The pathophysiologic sequence during acute bacterial meningitis may be divided into three stages (Adams *et al.* 1948, Berman and Banker 1966).
1. *First week* (acute stage): there is inflammatory cell invasion of the meninges, with a predominance of polymorphonuclear leukocytes. The brain and ependymal surfaces are intact.
2. *Second and third weeks* (subacute stage): there is microglial proliferation of the subpial surfaces and cortex, with destruction of the ependymal cells. Purulent exudate may collect around the skull base, producing cranial-nerve palsies and obstruction of cerebrospinal fluid circulation with consequent hydrocephalus. Vasculitis and phlebitis which may be present in the acute stage, are most prominent at this stage. Thromboses and cerebral infarctions may occur as sequelae.
3. *Fourth week* (chronic stage): the basilar exudate becomes organized, undergoing fibroblastic change. The hydrocephalus increases in severity. Large areas of cortical necrosis may be present.

During an uncomplicated course of meningitis there is usually no head CT scan performed. In cases which are successfully treated or in the early stages of meningitis there are no abnormalities found on CT (Zimmerman *et al.* 1976). But if

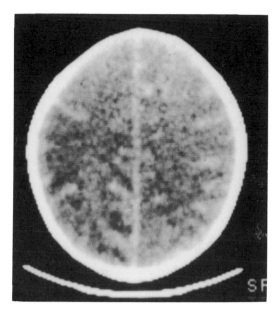
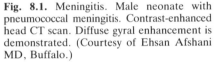

Fig. 8.1. Meningitis. Male neonate with pneumococcal meningitis. Contrast-enhanced head CT scan. Diffuse gyral enhancement is demonstrated. (Courtesy of Ehsan Afshani MD, Buffalo.)

there is subsequent clinical deterioration, the presence of complications are best demonstrated by CT.

Enlargement and occasional contrast enhancement of the subarachnoid spaces have been described in the evolution of meningitis (Bilaniuk *et al.* 1978) (Figs. 8.1, 8.2). The enhancement of meningitis is attributed to vascular enlargement and dilatation, perivascular inflammation in the leptomeninges and extravasation of contrast medium into the subarachnoid space from newly formed capillaries (Bilaniuk *et al.* 1978). Obliteration of cisterns may also be demonstrated (Bonstelle 1983).

Complications of meningitis
HYDROCEPHALUS
Hydrocephalus as a complication of meningitis may be of the communicating type due to impaired CSF flow through basal cisterns or absorption over the brain surface, or obstructive with involvement of the outlets of the ventricles at any or all levels (Shultz and Leeds 1973) (Fig. 8.3).

Post-meningitic hydrocephalus is common in the neonatal period, occurring in almost a third of patients who survive the acute illness (Lorber and Pickering 1966).

SUBDURAL EFFUSION
A subdural effusion which is of clinical significance should be suspected in children with meningitis developing focal neurologic signs, head enlargement and an abnormal response to treatment (Butler and Johnson 1974). Effusions are most commonly seen during the course of treatment of Haemophilus influenzae meningitis. They contain proteinaceous yellow fluid and are usually sterile

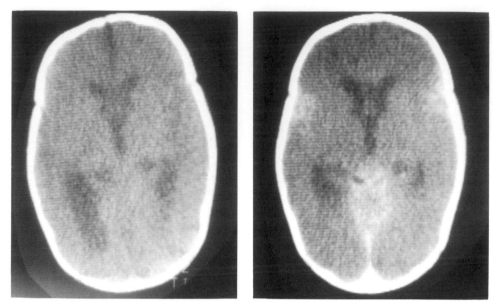

Fig. 8.2. Meningitis. Two-year-old boy with H. influenzae meningitis. *Left:* non-contrast head CT scan, and *right:* contrast-enhanced CT scan, demonstrating cisternal enhancement due to inflammatory exudate.

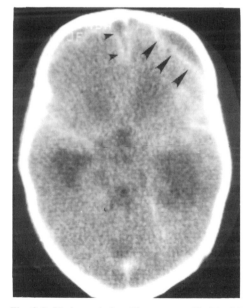

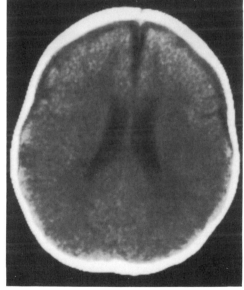

Fig. 8.3. Hydrocephalus. Three-year-old girl with H. influenzae meningitis. Contrast-enhanced head CT scan demonstrates evidence of hydrocephalus. A subdural empyema is noted anteriorly in the left frontal region *(arrowheads)*.

Fig. 8.4. Subdural effusion. 14-month-old boy with H. influenzae meningitis. Non-contrast head CT scan reveals evidence of bilateral low-density areas anteriorly. Subdural effusions were evacuated.

146

(Harwood-Nash and Fitz 1976). Aspiration of the subdural space will establish the presence of the effusion, but this procedure is usually reserved for patients with significant or progressive neurologic abnormalities, or in whom empyema is suspected clinically.

The CT appearance is that of a low-density area over the surface of the cerebral hemisphere (Fig. 8.4). This may be unilateral or bilateral. Extension may occur into the interhemispheric fissure. Membrane formation is uncommon, but when present it may be detected by contrast enhancement on its medial aspect (Sarwar 1980).

SUBDURAL EMPYEMA

Subdural empyema is a pyogenic infection of the subdural space. This may occur following meningitis in 2 per cent of infected infants (Dodge and Swartz 1965, Wise and Farmer 1969), or in older children and adults following otorhinologic infections, craniofacial trauma or surgery (Butler and Johnson 1974). This is a neurosurgical emergency requiring prompt drainage.

The empyema may be located over the convexity of one or both cerebral hemispheres, in the parafalcine region, or rarely beneath the tentorium. Delay in diagnosis may lead to irreparable central nervous system damage or death (Farmer and Wise 1973). A markedly improved prognosis has been reported by Jacobson and Farmer (1981) attributed to early diagnosis by CT and subdural paracentesis, combined with adequate surgical drainage and intensive antibiotic therapy.

Subdural empyema may appear as an extracerebral low-density collection with an associated mass effect (Zimmerman et al. 1976). Medial or border enhancement following contrast administration has been noted by Sadhu et al. (1980) and Sarwar (1980). This is presumed to be due to development of granulation tissue. The medially concave border of a subdural empyema is a distinguishing feature from an epidural abscess which usually has convex border medially (Sarwar 1980). The mass effect is mostly due to cerebral edema related to ischemia secondary to inflammatory angiospasm, although venous thrombosis and cerebritis may also be contributory factors (Sadhu et al. 1980) (Fig. 8.5).

THROMBOSIS

Infection and thrombosis of major intracranial venous sinuses may follow meningitis and infection of contiguous sites, and may also result from local infection of areas where veins drain into the sinuses.

Increased density within the involved sinus on the pre-contrast scan coupled with a filling defect in the involved sinus on a subsequent post-contrast scan has been found to be the most consistent CT finding in sinus thrombosis (Ford and Sarwar 1981). These authors stress that the appearance of sinus thrombosis may also be simulated by calcification or ossification of the falx, prominent subarachnoid spaces, or areas of low density which are adjacent to the falx. The filling defect within the sinus has also been noted by Buonanno et al. (1978), who referred to it as the 'empty triangle' sign.

Increased density within the vein of Galen and straight sinus on the

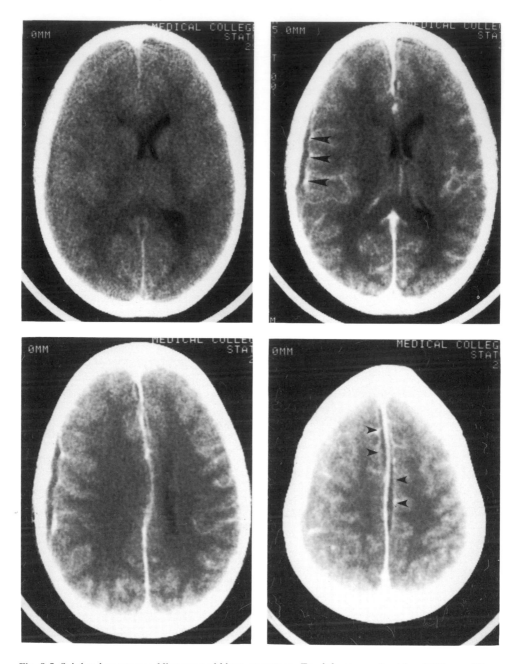

Fig. 8.5. Subdural empyema. Nine-year-old boy, comatose. *Top left:* non-contrast head CT scan. There is mass effect on the frontal horn of the right lateral ventricle, with evidence of a contralateral ventricular shift. *Top right:* contrast-enhanced head CT scan. The ventricular compression is again demonstrated. A right subdural empyema with enhancement of the medial border is demonstrated. *Bottom left and right:* contrast-enhanced head CT scans (higher level sections). In addition to the peripheral subdural empyema there is a parafalcine empyema *(arrowheads)*, and bowing of the falx.

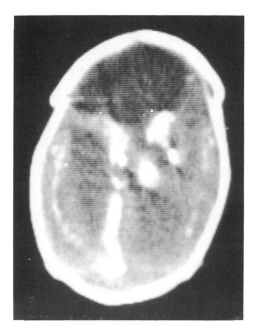

Fig. 8.6. Post-meningitic infarction. Two-year-old girl with previous group B streptococcal meningitis. Non-contrast head CT scan demonstrates low-density areas anteriorly representing infarction, with diffuse areas of calcification.

pre-contrast scan, with subsequent enhancement on the post-contrast scan, was described by Wendling (1978) in a child with bilateral otitis media. The diagnosis of thrombosis within these venous sinuses was confirmed angiographically. This appearance within the course of the vein of Galen and straight sinus on the pre-contrast scan was also noted by Eick *et al.* (1981) in three young patients with proven or strongly suspected cases of meningitis. The diagnosis of deep cerebral thrombosis was subsequently confirmed by angiography or at autopsy.

Other CT appearances of thrombosis include cerebral edema manifested by low-density areas, visualization of medullary veins and diffuse gyral enhancement on post-contrast CT scans (Buonanno *et al.* 1978, Banna and Groves 1979, Zilkha and Daiz 1980).

INFARCTION

Cerebral infarction may occur secondary to vasculitis of intracranial arteries following bacterial meningitis. Contrast enhancement may occur during the acute phase of the illness (Stovring and Snyder 1980).

Focal necrosis and atrophy of the cerebral cortex adjacent to the area of meningeal inflammation are well-described complications of meningitis (Smith and Landing 1960) (Fig. 8.6).

VENTRICULITIS

Ventriculitis refers to the presence of infected purulent exudate within the ventricular system. This is a common occurrence in all types of meningitis, but it is more severe in neonates than older infants and children (Berman and Banker 1966,

149

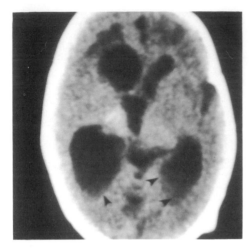

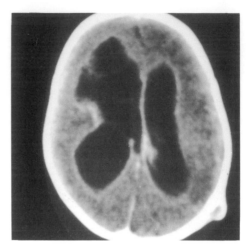

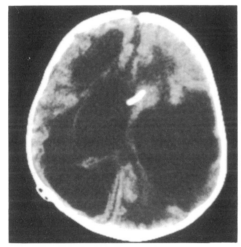

Fig. 8.7. Pyoventriculitis. Five-month-old infant with meningitis. *Top left:* non-contrast head CT scan demonstrates hydrocephalus. Accumulation of pus within the lateral ventricles accounts for the differential densities *(arrowheads)* within the ventricles. *Top right:* contrast-enhanced head CT scan demonstrates contrast enhancement of the ependyma representing ventriculitis. Loculation within the ventricles is noted. *Left:* non-contrast head CT scan (performed one month later). There is evidence of marked hydrocephalus with ventricular loculation. A ventriculoperitoneal shunt has been placed.

Salmon 1972, Bell and McCormick 1981). Ventriculitis and meningitis may occur concomitantly, especially in the neonatal period (Berman and Banker 1966).

The pathogenesis is incompletely understood, but it appears related to decreased host resistance and virulence of the organism (Brown *et al.* 1979). Direct hematogenous spread across the choroid plexi into the ventricular fluid may occur (Gilles *et al.* 1977). When the infected fluid becomes frank pus there is lack of flow through the aqueduct of Sylvius and it is referred to as ventricular empyema or pyoventriculitis (Bell and McCormick 1981). There is a high mortality and direct ventricular drainage is necessary (Izquierdo *et al.* 1978).

The CT appearances of ventriculitis may include focal contrast enhancement within the ventricular system and along the ventricular wall, or subsequent development of polycystic loculation within the ventricles (Brown *et al.* 1979) (Fig. 8.7).

Brain abscesses

Brain abscesses may develop from direct extension from infected sinuses, middle ear or intracranial foci of infection, or as metastatic foci from the bacteremia of pulmonary disease, systemic infection and cyanotic congenital heart disease. There is a 3 to 5 per cent incidence of brain abscesses in children with cyanotic congenital heart disease. This etiology accounts for almost 30 per cent of cerebral abscesses in childhood (Clark 1967). Although the most commonly associated cardiac lesion is Tetralogy of Fallot, any condition with a right-to-left intracardiac shunt, or with a pulmonary arterovenous fistula, may be involved (Stern and Naffziger 1953).

Abscesses may be located in various sites within the cerebrum and cerebellum. Abscesses resulting from sinusitis are more commonly frontal while temporal lobe or cerebellar hemisphere involvement follows chronic suppurative otitis or mastoiditis. The abscesses resulting from staphylococcal sepsis, infected meningomyelocele or secondary ventriculitis are usually multiple. When associated with cardiac lesions the abscesses are often solitary, usually located in the distribution of the middle cerebral artery (Bell and McCormick 1981). Abscesses within the brainstem, basal nuclei and thalamus are rare, usually hematogeneous in origin (Law *et al* 1976).

The organism responsible depends on the source. Staphylococcus aureus, viridans streptococcus, hemolytic streptococcus, and pneumococcus are the most common organisms, with the anaerobic streptococcus being implicated as the most frequent causative organism of metastatic abscesses in patients with respiratory infections or cyanotic heart disease.

The over-all mortality has decreased since the advent of CT which has facilitated early diagnosis, afforded localization of the site of the abscess and aided evaluation of efficacy of therapy (Stevens *et al.* 1978, Holtas *et al.* 1982).

The various stages in the evolution of a brain abscess will be described in conjunction with the CT findings.

Cerebritis

The early stage of cerebral suppuration is an area of cerebritis, which occurs most commonly at the junction of gray and white matter. This area has a relatively poor vascular supply (Kindt and Gosch 1972). The localized area of suppuration is soft and congested and contains petechial hemorrhages.

The initial CT appearances may be normal. Irregular mottled areas of contrast enhancement may subsequently be seen, associated with mass effect (Zimmerman *et al.* 1976).

With progression of the cerebritis the enhancement becomes more prominent, increasing in intensity (Enzmann *et al.* 1979). Subsequently ring configuration develops, and becomes increasingly evident with development of the cerebritis. This appearance correlates with vascular proliferation and a well-defined necrotic center. This appearance on CT can be visualized prior to microscopic evidence of a capsule, and therefore cannot be equated with the formation of a capsule (Enzmann *et al.* 1979). The ring enhancement is often diffuse and thick, but it can also be thin. If the lesion is small it will appear as a solid nodule, but if it is larger a

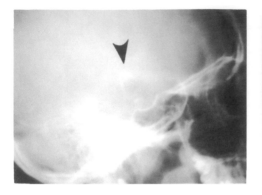

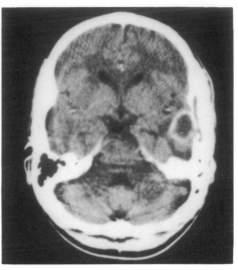

Fig. 8.8. Cerebral abscess. Three-year-old girl who sustained head trauma. *Above:* lateral skull radiograph demonstrates depressed skull fracture *(arrowhead)*. *Right:* contrast-enhanced head CT scan demonstrates temporal lobe abscess.

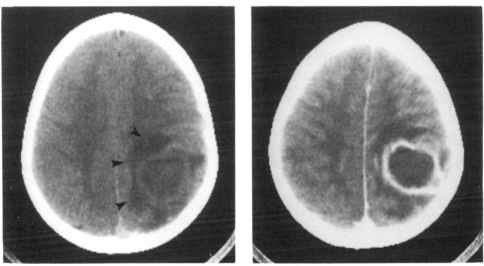

Fig. 8.9. Cerebral abscess. Nine-year-old cyanotic girl with Tetralogy of Fallot presented with right hemiparesis. *Left:* non-contrast head CT scan. Well-defined area of decreased density is noted in left posterior parietal region surrounded by ill-defined areas of low density due to surrounding edema *(arrowheads)*. *Right:* contrast-enhanced scan, showing well-defined area of ring enhancement.

lucent center is noted. There is no significant decrease in contrast enhancement if delayed scans are performed between 30 and 60 minutes after contrast administration (Britt and Enzmann 1983).

Capsule formation
Encapsulation of the localized area of necrosis with a pus-filled center is referred to

152

as an abscess. The capsule is composed of reticulin and collagen fibers within a network of proliferating vessels.

The appearance of an encapsulated abscess on the non-contrast CT scan is that of a low-density lesion with a ring of increased density, relative to the adjacent area of edema. It is this feature which suggests capsule formation (Enzmann 1982). Following contrast administration the ring displays a smooth, round pattern of enhancement. Approximately half of the brain abscesses have a uniform ring thickness after contrast enhancement. The ring enhancement is generally thinner on the medial or ventricular side of the abscess (Britt and Enzmann 1983). The lesions may be multiple, denoting hematogenous spread, or single (Figs. 8.8, 8.9, 8.10).

However, this enhancing ring is not unique to cerebral abscesses, and it must be correlated with the appropriate clinical history, physical examination and laboratory findings. Other causes of this appearance cited by Leeds (1979) are gliostoblastoma multiforme, metastasis, resolving hematoma and infarct, contusion, post-surgery, pituitary adenoma and craniopharyngioma, lymphoma, leukemia and radiation necrosis (Fig. 8.11).

Nodulations projecting from the inner capsular wall into the central low-density area are rarely seen in cerebral abscess (Sarwar 1980). The extent of surrounding edema does not distinguish an abscess from a metastatic lesion (Sarwar 1980).

The management of patients with cerebral abscesses is individualized, varying with the clinical presentation and early response to antibiotics (Whelan and Hilal 1980). CT is the modality of choice in the follow-up of these patients, where either medical or surgical treatment is instituted. Non-operative treatment of brain abscesses requires a CT scan at weekly intervals (Britt and Enzmann 1983). In these patients the abscess usually decreases in size by 2.4 weeks (range one to four weeks), with resolution of mass effect and contrast enhancement occurring after 10 weeks (Rosenblum et al. 1980).

Serial follow-up scans in patients with brain abscesses may demonstrate resolution only after three to four months, or as long as eight months (Whelan and Hilal 1980). This delay in resolution is attributed to an alteration in the blood-brain barrier (possibly due to formation of a different type of small vessel) and is considered to be a non-specific response of the brain parenchyma to various forms of insult (Whelan and Hilal 1980).

Subacute and chronic infections
Tuberculosis
Tuberculosis in its many forms remains a major disease problem, especially with the increasing number of immigrants to Europe and North America from the Far East and South America. The variable clinical presentations of tuberculosis in the pediatric age-groups probably depends on nutritional status, virulence and source of organisms, and correlates with geographic distribution (Udani et al. 1971). Tuberculous meningitis is the most common form of cerebral nervous system infection seen in North America; tuberculomata are seen more frequently in India

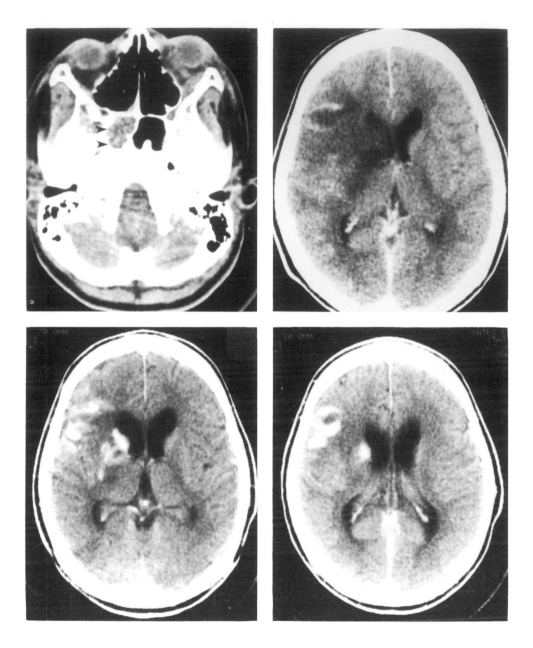

Fig. 8.10. Multiple cerebral abscesses. 13-year-old boy with sinusitis. *Top left:* non-contrast head scan. Sphenoid sinusitis is present. There is partial opacification of the sphenoid sinus *(arrowheads)*. *Top right:* contrast-enhanced head CT scan reveals evidence of mass effect on the frontal horn of the right lateral ventricle, with contralateral shift. There is also evidence of adjacent low-density areas, consistent with a cerebritis. *Bottom left and right:* contrast-enhanced head CT scan obtained 16 days later reveals evidence of contrast enhancement within the area of cerebritis. There is increased ventricular size. *Opposite top:* contrast-enhanced head CT scans reveal multiple cerebral abscesses bilaterally. The surrounding low-density areas represent edema.

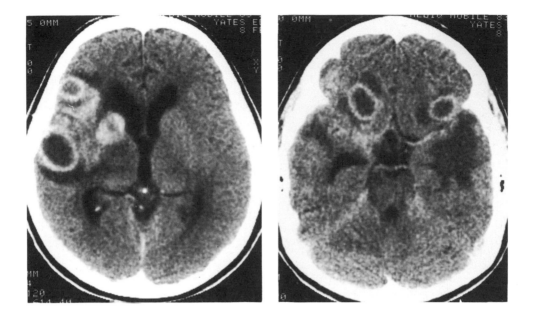

Butler and Johnson 1974).

Tuberculous meningitis is demonstrated on CT by sulcal and meningeal enhancement (Fig. 8.12). Obstructive hydrocephalus is usually present (Price and Danziger 1978). Tuberculoma is most commonly a single lesion (Asenjo *et al.* 1951) with a slight propensity to occur infratentorially in children. Two distinct CT appearances of tuberculoma have been described by Whelan and Stern (1981). Following administration of contrast medium there may be nodular enhancement (Fig. 8.13), or a small contrast-enhancing ring with a central lucent area is demonstrated. The 'micro-ring' appearance represents the caseating granuloma. 'Micro-ring' lesions are smaller than the ring lesions seen in other pyogenic abscesses and are not seen in fungal abscesses.

Small tubercles may coalesce to form larger lesions. The enlarging tuberculoma may adhere to dura simulating a meningioma (Whelan and Stern 1981,

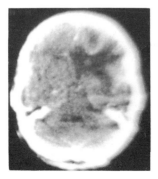

Fig. 8.11. Radiation necrosis. Contrast-enhanced head CT scan demonstrates an enhancing lesion which may simulate an abscess. (Courtesy of Samuel Wolpert MD, Boston.)

155

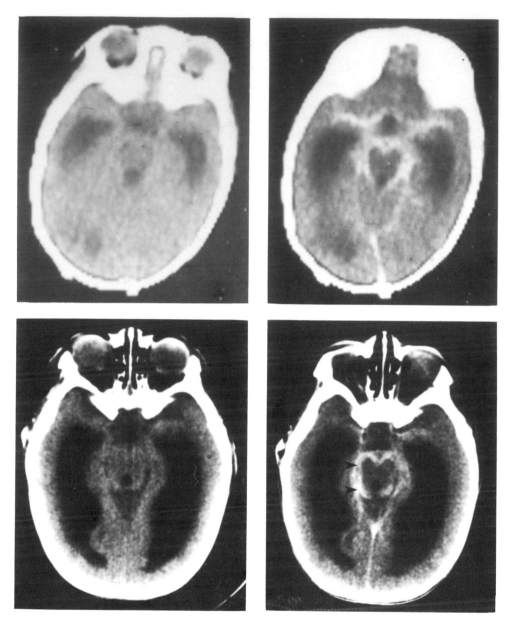

Fig. 8.12. Tuberculous meningitis. *Top:* 10-year-old presenting with confusion and headaches. Non-contrast head CT scan *(left)* and contrast-enhanced head CT scan *(right)*, demonstrating marked enhancement of the basal cisterns with extension into both Sylvian fissures. (Courtesy of Mohammed Naheedy MD, Illinois.) *Bottom:* six-month-old girl with repeated exposure to tuberculosis contacts. Non-contrast head CT scan demonstrates enlarged ventricles *(left)*; contrast-enhanced head CT scans *(right and opposite left)* demonstrate prominent cisternal enhancement *(arrowheads)*. *Opposite right:* calcified tuberculoma. Four-year-old boy with previous history of tuberculous meningitis. Non-contrast head CT scan demonstrates a calcified mass within the suprasellar cistern. Cerebral angiography excluded an aneurysm.

156

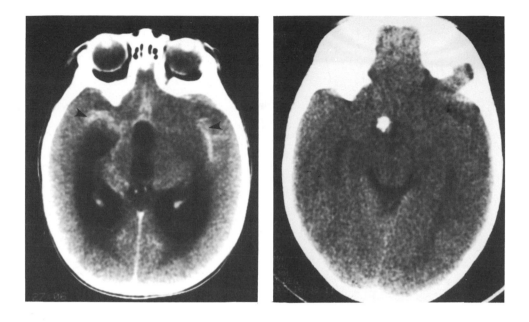

Elisevich and Arpin 1982). Calcification is uncommon in tuberculomas (Fig. 8.13), with a 6 per cent incidence in the series of Ramamurthi and Varadarajan (1961). A higher incidence of calcification within these lesions since the advent of CT has not yet appeared in the literature.

Sarcoidosis
Although not of infectious origin, sarcoidosis is included in this section describing intracranial granulomata. Sarcoidosis in the pediatric age-group is uncommon. The central nervous system disease occurs in 5 per cent of cases, with the cranial nerves, meninges and hypothalamus being the most common sites of involvement (Powers and Miller 1981).

Granulomas infiltrate both the meninges and brain parenchyma. When meningeal involvement is present, the mass may simulate a meningioma (Skillicorn and Garrity 1955, Goodman and Margulies 1959). Subdural involvement may rarely occur (Healton *et al.* 1982). Parenchymal involvement may take the form of multiple small granulomas or, less commonly, a single large granuloma which produces the symptoms and signs of an expanding intracranial mass.

The CT appearance of granulomas is variable but usually shows an increased density, higher than surrounding normal brain on the pre-contrast scan, and will display enhancement on the post-contrast scan (Bahr *et al.* 1978, Powers and Miller 1981). The typical appearance is of a granuloma with well-circumscribed margins, homogeneous enhancement and minimal edema, although both the amount of enhancement and edema may be variable (Powers and Miller 1981). Communicating hydrocephalus is a common finding; obstruction of the aqueduct or fourth ventricle have also been reported (Lawrence *et al.* 1974, Lukin *et al.* 1975).

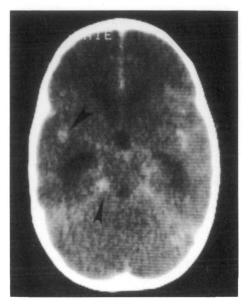

Fig. 8.13. Tuberculoma. Two-year-old boy. Contrast-enhanced scan displays evidence of enhancing nodules *(arrowheads)*.

Intracranial mycosis (fungi)

The incidence of intracranial mycotic lesions has risen with increased use of steroid therapy, antibacterial agents, chemotherapy, and other immunosuppressive agents. Clinically, the most frequent encountered mycoses are candidiasis and aspergillosis (Whelan *et al.* 1981). Cerebral involvement usually occurs in association with disseminated infection of other organs, or may follow direct sinus involvement.

The varied CT appearance has been correlated by Whelan *et al.* (1981) with the three known histopathological patterns of the CNS fungal infection as described by Parker *et al.* (1978). As described by Whelan *et al.* the CT findings will depend on the type of fungus and the dominating infecting form (hyphae or yeast).

Obstruction of intracerebral vessels

This pattern is usually seen with aspergillus and zygomycetes. Infarction, commonly hemorrhagic, ensues as a result of obstruction of vessels. Invasion and erosion of the fungus through the vessel wall into surrounding brain parenchyma produces a mixed inflammatory reaction and necrosis. A mycotic aneurysm may result, more commonly seen with aspergillus. The CT manifestation of this process is that of infarction.

Granulomas and leptomeningitis

Cryptococcus, histoplasma and blastomyces are the fungi usually responsible for this pattern. On the pre-contrast CT scan a fungal granuloma has low density or may appear normal, with subsequent homogeneous opacification of nodules measuring 5 to 15mm in diameter. If the lesion is large, a low-density central area may be noted (Newton *et al.* 1977).

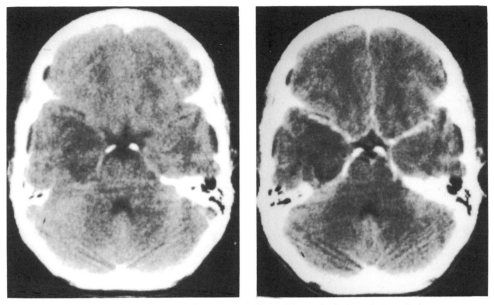

Fig. 8.14. Herpes encephalitis type I. Eight-year-old boy with marked obtundation. *Left:* non-contrast head CT scan demonstrates diffuse low-density area within right temporal lobe. *Right:* contrast-enhanced head CT scan demonstrates minimal contrast enhancement within the lesion.

Prominent enhancement of the basal subarachnoid cisterns has been demonstrated by Enzmann *et al.* (1976) in patients with granulomatous basal arachnoiditis. Neovascularity of granulation tissue or extravasation of contrast medium into the extravascular port through newly formed capillaries are thought to be responsible for this finding (Waggener 1974).

Small abscesses
Multiple small abscesses are a result of hematogenous seeding, and usually occur in the distribution of the middle cerebral artery. This pattern is typical of infection due to Candida.

Viral infections
CNS involvement is common in systemic viral illnesses, and in most cases the sequelae are mild (Butler and Johnson 1974). Changes in level of consciousness, seizures, or focal neurologic deficits are indicative of parenchymal brain involvement, or encephalitis.

Herpes simplex
Herpes simplex virus (type I) is the most common cause of fatal encephalitis in the United States (Olson *et al.* 1977). The clinical modes of presentation are results of non-specific changes of encephalitis, or the effects of focal necrosis especially of the temporal and orbital regions (Davis *et al.* 1978).

159

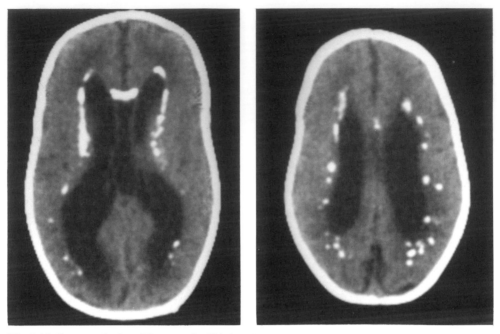

Fig. 8.15. Cytomegalovirus. Three-week-old infant. Non-contrast head CT scans demonstrate extensive periventricular calcification. (Courtesy of Soroosh Mahboubi MD, Philadelphia.)

The rôle of CT in the diagnosis of herpes simplex encephalitis is well established (Davis *et al.* 1978, Enzmann *et al.* 1978, Kaufman *et al.* 1979, Zimmerman *et al.* 1980). Three major CT abnormalities have been described:

1. AREAS OF LOW DENSITY

This was the most common finding in the series of Davis *et al.* (1978), and is a manifestation of tissue necrosis. Predilection for the temporal lobe is typical (Fig. 8.14), sometimes with anterior extension to the frontal lobe. The temporal lobe involvement may be bilateral. The low-density abnormality has been noted six days after the onset of neurological signs and symptoms, and has persisted for 39 days (Davis *et al.* 1978).

2. MASS EFFECT

Mass effect may be the earliest CT abnormality, preceding the low-density abnormality described above. This may occur within one to three days after the onset of neurologic signs (Davis *et al.* 1978). There may be compression of adjacent structures and contralateral shift of midline structures (Kaufman *et al.* 1979).

3. CONTRAST ENHANCEMENT

Enhancement of gyri surrounding the Sylvian fissure and opercular area has been described by Davis *et al.* (1978), who attribute this appearance to abnormal permeability of damaged blood vessels and brain tissue.

Occasionally streaks of high density extending from the cortical margin to the deep gray matter may be seen (Newton *et al.* 1977). This appearance is considered to be non-specific, reflecting damaged brain with increased permeability.

Cytomegalovirus (cytomegalic inclusion disease, salivary gland virus diseases)
Cytomegalic inclusion disease is a generalized infection of infants which follows intra-uterine or early postnatal infection with cytomegalovirus. This disease is responsible for severe congenital infection in approximately 10,000 infants in the USA annually (Jawetz *et al.* 1980).

Fetal death *in utero* may result, or the clinical syndrome of the disease may ensue. This is characterized by CNS involvement including microcephaly, cataracts, optic atrophy, mental or motor retardation, periventricular calcification, thrombocytopenic purpura, pneumonitis and hepatosplenomegaly.

CT may demonstrate calcification within the basal ganglia, choroid plexus and in the periventricular areas (Newton *et al.* 1977) (Fig. 8.15).

Subacute sclerosing panencephalitis (SSPE)
Subacute sclerosing panencephalitis (SSPE) is a rare progressive neurodegenerative disease of the brain affecting children and young adults. It can last for years, and spontaneous remissions are rare. (Zeman and Kolar 1968). SSPE is the result of a slow virus infection of the brain caused by the measles virus (Lancet 1971).

The CT appearances have been found to correlate best with the stage and duration of the disease, rather than with the patient's mental state (Krawiecki *et al.* 1984). In the early stages, or in patients with a short clinical history and rapidly progressive course, the CT appearance may be normal or minimally abnormal (Duda *et al.* 1980). Cerebral edema with small lateral ventricles and obliteration of the sulci and interhemispheric fissure was reported by Pedersen and Wulff (1982) in three patients with SSPE of two to six months' duration.

Between six and 164 months after the onset of SSPE, further abnormalities due to acute demyelination may be detected by CT (Krawiecki *et al.* 1984). Low-density lesions may become evident in the paraventricular regions with subsequent contrast enhancement, and supraventricular areas of white-matter involvement may also exhibit contrast enhancement. This finding is attributed to acute inflammation of the white matter occurring in the earlier stages of the demyelinating process (Loizou and Cole 1982). Contrast enhancement of the abnormal areas was not found, however, in the cases of Duda *et al.* (1980).

The chronic changes which may begin 17 months after onset (Krawiecki *et al.* 1984) include dilatation of the lateral ventricles, cortical atrophy, and atrophy of the cerebellum and brainstem (Duda *et al.* 1980, Krawiecki *et al.* 1984).

Parasites
Toxoplasmosis
Toxoplasmosis is a common parasitic infection produced by the protozoan, *Toxoplasma gondii*. The definitive hosts are the domestic cat and related wild

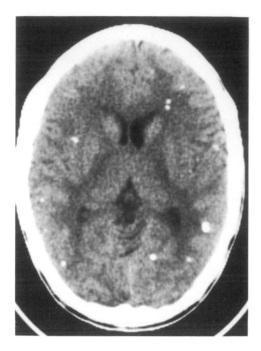

Fig. 8.16. Toxoplasmosis. 14-year-old male with behavioral changes, with previous diagnosis of congenital toxoplasmosis. Non-contrast head CT scan demonstrates diffuse bilateral parenchymal calcific densities.

animals. The infection may be congenital or acquired in origin. Fetal death or severe congenital disease has been observed with maternal infection during the second to sixth months of gestation (Desmonts and Couvreur 1974). Central nervous system manifestations of the congenital form include microcephaly, hydrocephalus, convulsions, encephalitis and chorioretinitis. Cerebral calcification is common, with an incidence of 60 per cent of infected children (Feldman 1958, Harwood-Nash and Fitz 1976). Toxoplasmosis and cytomegalic inclusion disease are the two commonest causes of cerebral calcification in infants under one year of age although congenital rubella, herpes and polioencephalitis are other causative agents (Harwood-Nash and Fitz 1976). Acute infection of the central nervous system has been reported with immuno-suppressed patients with malignancies or acquired immune deficiency syndrome (AIDS).

CT appearance

CONGENITAL FORM

Multiple punctate calcifications are present within the cerebral hemispheres, basal ganglia, choroid plexus and periventricular areas (Fig. 8.16) (Collins and Cromwell 1980, Post and Hoffman 1984). The presence of cortical and basal ganglionic calcifications helps differentiate toxoplasmosis from congenital cytomegalic inclusion disease (Post and Hoffman 1984). The periventricular calcification may be initially focal and punctate with progressive necrosis of brain parenchyma and basal ganglia. Dense broad calcific bands are noted within the basal ganglia, considered to be specific for toxoplasmosis (Dunn and Weisberg 1984).

162

Multiple densely enhancing nodules are noted in the periventricular area and cortico-medullary junction or white matter (Post and Hoffman 1984). The lesions may also be demonstrated in the form of ring lesions with thin or thick walls (McLeod *et al.* 1979).

Cestodes (tapeworms), cysticercosis

Cysticercosis is the most common parasitic infection involving the central nervous system (Grisolia and Wiederholt 1982).

Following ingestion of ova of the pork tapeworm, Taenia solium, the human becomes an intermediate host. Cysticercosis is the subsequent extra-intestinal disease due to dissemination of larvae. Clinical symptoms following infestation may occur a few months or up to 30 years later (Dixon and Lipscomb 1961).

Cysticercosis may be widespread throughout the central nervous system involving the brain parenchyma, ventricles, cisterns and meninges (Lobato *et al.* 1981). When the ventricular system is involved, the order of preference appears to be fourth ventricle, lateral ventricles, foramen of Monro, third ventricle, and aqueduct of Sylvius (Madrazo *et al.* 1981). The flow of CSF may be obstructed with resulting hydrocephalus.

The acute encephalitic phase is more common in children, with a rapid course which may be fatal despite supportive treatment for the convulsive crisis and cerebral edema (Rodriguez-Carbajal *et al.* 1983).

The parenchymal form is most common (Fig. 8.17) and may be classified into four groups (Byrd *et al.* 1982):

1. *Calcified lesions.* These lesions are round or oval, appearing larger, more dense and homogeneous on CT than on skull radiographs (Bentson *et al.* 1977). The typical location is in the gray matter, or near the gray-white matter junction; less common sites are the basal ganglia and deep white matter (Santin and Vargas 1966). The presence of calcification does not exclude the presence of live larvae, as active cysts have been demonstrated concomitantly with calcific lesions on CT (Rodriguez-Carbajal *et al.* 1977). Calcific lesions which have been found by Byrd *et al.* (1982) to be less common in children, usually do not enhance after contrast administration.

2. *Cystic lesions.* These may appear as poorly defined low-density areas or well-defined cysts with subsequent ring enhancement. Mass effect is usually present.

3. *Homogeneously enhancing lesions.* These are found in all age-groups. The unenhanced CT scan may demonstrate a normal appearance or a low-density area, with subsequent uniform enhancement.

The enhancement usually persists throughout the acute encephalitic stage. Cerebral edema is manifested by low-density areas with irregular contours. This may persist for several months, even following disappearance of the lesions on CT scan and lack of clinical symptoms (Rodriguez-Carbajal *et al.* 1983). Small

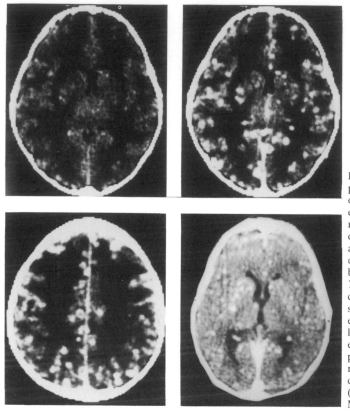

Fig. 8.17. Cysticercosis—parenchymal form. Eight-year-old male presenting with acute encephalitis. *Top left:* non-contrast head CT scan demonstrates diffuse edema, and multiple spherical lesions of increased density within both cerebral hemispheres. *Top right and bottom left:* contrast-enhanced head CT scans demonstrate contrast enhancement within the lesions. *Bottom right:* contrast-enhanced head CT scan performed one year later reveals evidence of multiple calcific lesions bilaterally. (Courtesy of Enrique Palacios MD, Illinois.)

calcifications have been demonstrated on follow-up CT in the majority of patients, some as early as eight months after the acute stage (Rodriguez-Carbajal *et al.* 1983).

4. *Mixed lesions.* A combination of the above lesions may be noted.

MENINGEAL EPENDYMAL INVOLVEMENT

The presence of cysts in the meninges or ependyma produces an inflammatory response leading to obstructive hydrocephalus. This is readily demonstrated by CT.

VENTRICULAR-CISTERNAL INVOLVEMENT

Intraventricular location of cisticerci is common, most frequently within the fourth ventricle. There may be local enlargement of the ventricles. The cysts are commonly not demonstrated by CT, as the absorption values are similar to that of cerebrospinal fluid (Rodriguez-Carbajal *et al.* 1977). There are however reports of enhancement of intraventricular cysts in the third ventricle (Jankowski *et al.* 1979) and fourth ventricle (Zee *et al.* 1980). In the latter case, enhancement has been attributed to attachment of the cyst to adjacent ependyma and parenchyma, evoking inflammatory response.

164

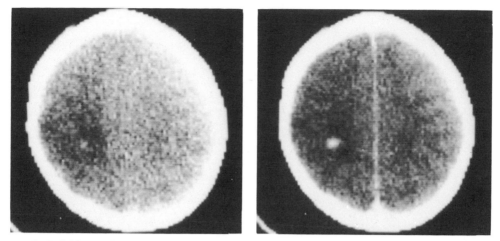

Fig. 8.18. Schistosomiasis. Three-year-old girl with seizures. *Left:* non-contrast head CT scan shows a small calcific area in the right parietal region. Surrounding edema is present. *Right:* contrast-enhanced scan demonstrates minimal contrast enhancement of the lesion. Cerebral angiography confirmed the presence of an avascular parietal mass. A granuloma removed at surgery was found to contain Schistosoma mansoni ova.

Basal meningeal involvement may similarly cause an inflammatory response with subsequent cisternal enhancement in association with deformity of cisterns and surrounding edema (Zee *et al.* 1980).

Hydatid disease (echinococcosis)

Hydatid disease is caused by the larval or hydatid stage of the tapeworm Echinococcus granulosus. The usual hosts for the adult worms are dogs, wolves and foxes. Cattle and sheep are the intermediate hosts, although man may also be involved in this way. Infection in children takes place by accidental contamination with feces of dogs harboring the adult worm.

Involvement of the central nervous system by hydatid disease is rare. Cerebral involvement is however common in childhood with 50 to 75 per cent of cases occurring in this age-group (Dew 1928). Cerebral cysts are most commonly single and are supratentorial, usually occurring in the distribution of the middle cerebral arteries (Kaya *et al.* 1975). Multiple cysts occur following spontaneous rupture of the cyst or by embolization of larvae.

The CT appearance of a cyst is a large, spherical, well-defined lesion. The fluid within the cyst is of low density, comparable to cerebrospinal fluid or slightly higher (Abbassioun *et al.* 1978). Peripheral edema and contrast enhancement are not observed when differentiating this lesion from pyogenic abscesses.

Schistosomiasis (bilharziasis)

Schistosomiasis is a parasitic disease produced in man and animals by three trematodes or blood flukes. These are Schistosoma mansoni, Schistosoma

165

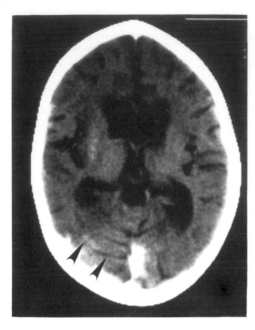

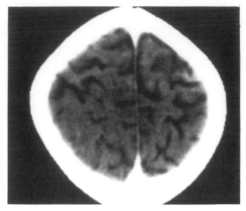

Fig. 8.19. Acquired immune deficiency syndrome (AIDS). Five-year-old boy with AIDS encephalopathy. His mother is a known intravenous drug abuser. Contrast-enhanced head CT scans demonstrate ventricular enlargement and gyral prominence, indicative of an atrophic process. There is evidence of cerebellar atrophy *(arrowheads)*. (Courtesy of Leon Epstein MD, Newark.)

hematobium and Schistosoma japonicum. The most common form of this disease in the Western hemisphere is due to Schistosoma mansoni.

Involvement of the central nervous system is rare. Granulomatous lesions which contain ova have been found within the brain, notably infections due to Schistosoma japonicum (Schochet 1984).

CT appearances

There are at present no documented CT reports of intracranial schistosomiasis in children. A contrast-enhancing parenchymal lesion, proven to be due to Schistosoma mansoni infection, is demonstrated in Figure 8.18.

Immunodeficiency disorders

Acquired immune deficiency syndrome

Acquired immune deficiency syndrome (AIDS) consists of a spectrum of life-threatening disorders which are associated with varying degrees of acquired immune deficiency. These disorders include Kaposi sarcoma and numerous opportunistic infections such as Pneumocystis carinii, herpes virus and atypical mycobacteria.

The syndrome was initially described in male homosexuals, intravenous drug abusers, hemophiliacs and Haitian refugees. Although AIDS has previously appeared to be limited to adults, there is now an increasing incidence in infants and children (Oleske *et al.* 1983, Belman *et al.* 1984, Epstein *et al.* 1984, Scott *et al.* 1984).

Progressive encephalopathy was observed in eight of 12 children with this disorder in the series of Epstein *et al.* (1984). Microcephaly is commonly encountered (Epstein *et al.* 1984, Belman *et al.* 1984). Central nervous system infection was documented in two of six patients involved (Belman *et al.* 1984), one of which was cytomegalovirus.

CT *appearances*

The CT appearances of this disorder have been described by Epstein *et al.* (1984) and Belman *et al.* (1984). Cortical atrophy is frequently demonstrated. This was observed in six of eight patients by Epstein *et al.* (1984), and three of six patients by Belman *et al.* (1984) (Fig. 8.19). Basal ganglia calcifications, periventricular calcifications and hypodense white matter lesions are less common (Belman *et al.* 1984).

REFERENCES

Abbassioun, K., Rahmat, H., Ameli, N. O., Tafazoli, P. (1978) 'Computerized tomography in hydatid cyst of the brain.' *Journal of Neurosurgery,* **49,** 408–411.

Adams, R. D., Kubik, C. S., Bonner, F. J. (1948) 'The clinical and pathological aspects of influenzal meningitis.' *Archives of Pediatrics,* **65,** 354–376, 408–441.

Asenjo, A., Valladares, H., Fierro, J. (1951) 'Tuberculomas of the brain.' *Archives of Neurology and Psychiatry,* **65,** 146–160.

Bahr, A. L., Krumholz, A., Kristt, D., Hodges, F. J. (1978) 'Neurological manifestations of intracranial sarcoidosis.' *Radiology,* **127,** 713–717.

Banna, M., Groves, J. T. (1979) 'Deep vascular congestion in dural venous thrombosis in computed tomography.' *Journal of Computer Assisted Tomography,* **3,** 539–541.

Bell, W. E., McCormick, W. F. (1981) *Neurologic Infections in Children.* Philadelphia: W. B. Saunders. pp. 1–709.

Belman, A. L., Novick, B., Ultmann, M. H., Spiro, A., Rubinstein, A., Horoupian, D. S., Cohen, H. (1984) 'Neurological complications in children with acquired immune deficiency syndrome.' *Annals of Neurology,* **16,** 414. *(Abstract).*

Bentson, J. R., Wilson, G. H., Helmer, E., Winter, J. (1977) 'Computed tomography in intracranial cysticercosis.' *Journal of Computer Assisted Tomography,* **1,** 464–471.

Berman, P. H., Banker, B. Q. (1966) 'Neonatal meningitis: a clinical and pathological study of 29 cases.' *Pediatrics,* **38,** 6–24.

Bilaniuk, L. T., Zimmerman, R. A., Brown, L., Yoo, H. J., Goldberg, H. I. (1978) 'Computed tomography in meningitis.' *Neuroradiology,* **16,** 13–14.

Bonstelle, C. T. (1983) 'Infectious diseases of the brain.' *In:* Haaga, J. R., Alfidi, R. J. (Eds.) *Computed Tomography of the Whole Body.* St. Louis: C. V. Mosby. pp. 110–135.

Britt, R. H., Enzmann, D. R. (1983) 'Clinical stages of human brain abscesses on serial CT scans after contrast infusion.' *Journal of Neurosurgery,* **59,** 972–989.

Brown, L. W., Zimmerman, R. A., Bilaniuk, L. T. (1979) 'Polycystic brain disease complicating neonatal meningitis: documentation of evolution by computed tomography.' *Journal of Pediatrics,* **94,** 757–759.

Buonanno, F. S., Moody, D. M., Ball, M. R., Laster, D. W. (1978) 'Computed cranial tomographic findings in cerebral sinovenous occlusion.' *Journal of Computer Assisted Tomography,* **2,** 281–290.

Butler, I. J., Johnson, R. T. (1974) 'Central nervous system infections.' *Pediatric Clinics of North America,* **21,** 649–668.

Byrd, S. E., Locke, G. E., Biggers, S., Percy, A. K. (1982) 'The computed tomographic appearance of cerebral cysticercosis in adults and children.' *Radiology,* **144,** 819–823.

Clark, D. E. (1967) 'Brain abscess and congenital heart disease.' *Clinical Neurosurgery,* **14,** 274–287.

Collins, A. T., Cromwell, L. D. (1980) 'Computed tomography in the evaluation of congenital cerebral toxoplasmosis.' *Journal of Computer Assisted Tomography,* **4,** 326–329.

Davis, J. M., Davis, K. R., Kleinman, G. M., Kirchner, H. S., Taveras, J. M. (1978) 'Computed tomography of *Herpes simplex* encephalitis, with clinicopathological correlation.' *Radiology,* **129,** 409–417.

Desmonts, G., Couvreur, J. (1974) 'Congenital toxoplasmosis: a prospective study of 378 pregnancies.' *New England Journal of Medicine,* **290,** 1110–1116.

Dew, H. R. (1928) *Hydatid Disease. Its Pathology, Diagnosis and Treatment.* Sydney: Australasian Medical Publishing Co.

Dixon, H. B. F., Lipscomb, F. M. (1961) *Cysticercosis: An Analysis and Followup of 450 Cases. Medical Research Council Special Report, No. 299.* London: H.M.S.O. pp. 1–58.

Dodge, P. R., Swartz, M. N. (1965) 'Bacterial meningitis: a review of selected aspects. Part II.' *New England Journal of Medicine,* **272,** 1003–1010.

Duda, E. E., Huttenlocher, P. R., Patronas, N. J. (1980) 'CT of subacute sclerosing panencephalitis.' *American Journal of Neuroradiology,* **1,** 35–38.

Dunn, D., Weisberg, L. A. (1984) 'Serial changes in a patient with congenital CNS toxoplasmosis as observed with CT.' *Computerized Radiology,* **8,** 133–139.

Eick, J. J., Miller, K. D., Bell, K. A., Tutton, R. H. (1981) 'Computed tomography of deep cerebral venous thrombosis in children.' *Radiology,* **140,** 399–402.

Elisevich, K., Arpin, E. J. (1982) 'Tuberculoma masquerading as a meningioma.' *Journal of Neurosurgery,* **56,** 435–438.

Enzmann, D. R., Britt, R. H., Yeager, A. S. (1979) 'Experimental brain abscess evolution: computed tomographic and neuropathologic correlation.' *Radiology,* **130,** 113–133.

—— Norman, D., Mani, J., Newton, T. H. (1976) 'Computed tomography of granulomatous basal arachnoiditis.' *Radiology,* **120,** 341–344.

—— Ranson, B., Norman, D., Talberth, E. (1978) 'Computed tomography of *Herpes simplex* encephalitis.' *Radiology,* **129,** 419–425.

—— Britt, R. H., Placone, R. C. Jr., Obana, W., Lyons, B., Yeager, A. S. (1982) 'The effect of short-term corticosteroid treatment on the CT appearance of experimental brain abscesses.' *Radiology,* **145,** 79–84.

Epstein, L. G., Sharer, L. R., Joshi, V. V., Fojas, M. M., Koenigsberger, M. R., Oleske, J. M. (1984) 'Progressive encephalopathy in children with acquired immune deficiency syndrome. Clinical and neuropathological findings.' *Annals of Neurology,* **16,** 414. *(Abstract).*

Farmer, T. W., Wise, G. R. (1973) 'Subdural empyema in infants, children and adults.' *Neurology,* **23,** 254–261.

Feldman, H. A. (1958) 'Toxoplasmosis.' *Pediatrics,* **22,** 559–574.

Ford, K., Sarwar, M. (1981) 'Computed tomography of dural sinus thrombosis.' *American Journal of Neuroradiology,* **2,** 539–543.

Gilles, F. H., Jammes, J. L., Berenberg, W. (1977) 'Neonatal meningitis. The ventricle as bacterial reservoir.' *Archives of Neurology,* **34,** 560–562.

Goodman, S. S., Margulies, M. E. (1959) 'Boeck's sarcoid simulating a brain tumor.' *Archives of Neurology and Psychiatry,* **81,** 419–423.

Grisolia, J. S., Wiederholt, W. C. (1982) 'CNS cysticercosis.' *Archives of Neurology,* **39,** 540–544.

Harwood-Nash, D. C., Fitz, C. R. (1976) *Neuroradiology in Infants and Children.* St. Louis: C. V. Mosby. pp. 855–901.

Healton, E. B., Zito, G., Chauhan, P., Brust, J. C. M. (1982) 'Intracranial subdural sarcoid granuloma.' *Journal of Neurosurgery,* **56,** 728–731.

Holtås, S., Tornquist, C., Cronqvist, S. (1982) 'Diagnostic difficulties in computed tomography of brain abscesses.' *Journal of Computer Assisted Tomography,* **6,** 683–688.

Izquierdo, J. M., Sanz, F., Coca, J. M., Vila, F., Dierssen, G. (1978) 'Pyocephalus of the newborn child.' *Child's Brain,* **4,** 161–169.

Jacobson, P. L., Farmer, T. W. (1981) 'Subdural empyema complicating meningitis in infants: improved prognosis.' *Neurology,* **31,** 190–193.

Jankowski, R., Zimmerman, R. D., Leeds, N. E. (1979) 'Cysticercosis presenting as a mass lesion at foramen of Monro.' *Journal of Computer Assisted Tomography,* **3,** 694–696.

Jawetz, E., Melnick, J. L., Adelberg, E. A. (1980) *Review of Medical Microbiology.* Langes: Los Altos.

Kaufman, D. M., Zimmerman, R. D., Leeds, N. E. (1979) 'Computed tomography in *herpes simplex* encephalitis.' *Neurology,* **29,** 1392–1396.

Kaya, U., Ozden, B., Türker, L., Tarcan, B. (1975) 'Intracranial hydatid cysts: study of 17 cases.' *Journal of Neurosurgery,* **42,** 580–584.

Kindt, G. W., Gosch, H. K. (1972) 'Cerebral pyogenic abscess.' *Surgical Clinics of North America,* **52,** 1439–1445.

Krawiecki, N. S., Dyken, P. R., El Gammal, T., Durant, R. H., Swift, A. (1984) 'Computed tomography of the brain in subacute sclerosing panencephalitis.' *Annals of Neurology,* **15,** 489–493.

Lancet, Editorial (1971) 'Measles—quick and slow.' *Lancet,* **2,** 27–28.

Law, J. D., Lehman, R. A. W., Kirsch, W. M., Ehni, F. (1976) 'Diagnosis and treatment of abscess of the central ganglia.' *Journal of Neurosurgery,* **44,** 226–232.

Lawrence, W. P., El Gammal, T., Pool, W. H., Apter, L. (1974) 'Radiological manifestations of neurosarcoidosis: report of three cases and review of the literature.' *Clinical Radiology,* **25,** 343–348.

Leeds, N. E. (1979) 'Masses (tumors, abscess, etc.) excluding sella and cerebellopontine angle.' *In: Computed Syllabus Course 209B,* Chicago: Radiological Society of North America, 1–20.

Lobato, R. D., Lamas, E., Portillo, J. M., Roger, R., Esparza, J., Rivas, J. J., Munoz, M. J. (1981) 'Hydrocephalus in cerebral cysticercosis.' *Journal of Neurosurgery,* **55,** 786–793.

Loizou, L. A., Cole, G. (1982) 'Acute cerebral demyelination: clinical and pathological correlation with computed tomography.' *Journal of Neurology, Neurosurgery and Psychiatry,* **45,** 725–728.

Lorber, J., Pickering, D. (1966) 'Incidence and treatment of post-meningitic hydrocephalus in the newborn.' *Archives of Disease in Childhood,* **41,** 44–50.

Lukin, R. R., Chambers, A. A., Soleimanpour, M. (1975) 'Outlet obstruction of the fourth ventricle in sarcoidosis.' *Neuroradiology,* **10,** 65–68.

Madrazo, I., Renteria, J. A. G., Paredes, G., Olhagaray, B. (1981) 'Diagnosis of intraventricular and cisternal cysticercosis by computed tomography with positive intraventricular contrast medium.' *Journal of Neurosurgery,* **55,** 947–951.

McLeod, R., Berry, P. F., Marshall, W. H., Jr., Hunt, S. A., Ryning, F. W., Remington, J. S. (1979) 'Toxoplasmosis presenting as brain abscesses: diagnosis by computerized tomography and cytology of aspirated purulent material.' *American Journal of Medicine,* **67,** 711–714.

Newton, T. H., Norman, D., Alvord, E. C., Shaw, C. M. (1977) 'The CT scan in infectious diseases of the CNS.' *In: Diagnostic Radiology.* St. Louis: C. V. Mosby. pp. 719–740.

Oleske, J., Minnefor, A., Cooper, R., Jr., Thomas, K., dela Cruz, A., Ahdieh, H., Guerrero, I., Joshi, V. V., Desposito, F. (1983) 'Immune deficiency syndrome in children.' *Journal of the American Medical Association,* **249,** 2345–2349.

Olson, L. C., Buescher, E. L., Artenstein, M. S., Parkman, P. D. (1977) 'Herpes virus infections of the human central nervous system.' *New England Journal of Medicine,* **277,** 1271–1277.

Parker, J. C., McCloskey, J. J., Lee, R. S. (1978) 'The emergence of candidosis: the dominant postmortem cerebral mycosis.' *American Journal of Clinical Pathology,* **70,** 31–36.

Pedersen, H., Wulff, C. H. (1982) 'Computed tomographic findings of early subacute sclerosing panencephalitis.' *Neuroradiology,* **23,** 31–32.

Post, M. J. D., Hoffman, T. A. (1984) 'Cerebral inflammatory disease.' *In:* Rosenberg, R. N. (Ed.) *The Clinical Neurosciences. Volume 4: Neuroradiology.* New York: Chuchill Livingstone. pp. 525–594.

Powers, W. J., Miller, E. M. (1981) 'Sarcoidosis mimicking glioma: case report and review of intracranial sarcoid mass lesions.' *Neurology,* **31,** 907–910.

Price, H. I., Danziger, A. (1978) 'Computed tomography in cranial tuberculosis.' *American Journal of Roentgenology,* **130,** 769–771.

Ramamurthi, B. Varadarajan, M. G. (1961) 'Diagnosis of tuberculomas of the brain.' *Journal of Neurosurgery,* **18,** 1–7.

Rodriguez-Carbajal, J., Palacios, E., Azar-Kia, B., Churchill, R. (1977) 'Radiology of cysticercosis of the central nervous system including computed tomography.' *Radiology,* **125,** 127–131.

—— Salgado, P., Gutierrez-Alvarado, R., Escobar-Izquierdo, A., Aruffo, C., Palacios, E. (1983) 'The acute encephalitic phase of neuro-cysticercosis: computed tomographic manifestations.' *American Journal of Neuroradiology,* **4,** 51–55.

Rosenblum, M. L., Hoff, J. T., Norman, D., Edwards, M. S., Berg, B. O. (1980) 'Nonoperative treatment of brain abscesses in selected high risk patients.' *Journal of Neurosurgery,* **52,** 217–225.

Sadhu, V. K., Handel, S. F., Pinto, R. S., Glass, T. F. (1980) 'Neuroradiologic diagnosis of subdural empyema and CT limitations.' *American Journal of Neuroradiology,* **1,** 39–44.

Salmon, J. A. (1972) 'Ventriculitis complicating meningitis.' *American Journal of Diseases of Children,* **124,** 35–40.

Santin, G., Vargas, J. (1966) 'Roentgen study of cysticercosis of central nervous system.' *Radiology,* **86,** 520–528.

Sarwar, M. (1980) 'Current status of neuroradiologic investigation of CNS inflammatory disease.' *Current Problems in Diagnostic Radiology,* **9,** 1–61.

Schochet, S. S., Jr. (1984) 'Infectious diseases.' *In:* Rosenberg, R. N. (Ed.) *The Clinical Neurosciences.* New York: Churchill Livingstone. pp. 195–240.

Schultz, P., Leeds, N. E. (1973) 'Intraventricular septations complicating neonatal meningitis.' *Journal*

169

of Neurosurgery, **38**, 620–626.

Scott, G. B., Buck, B. E., Letterman, J. G., Bloom, F. L., Parks, W. P. (1984) 'Acquired immunodeficiency syndrome in infants.' *New England Journal of Medicine*, **310**, 76–81.

Skillicorn, S. A., Garrity, R. W. (1955) 'Intraventricular Boeck's sarcoid tumor resembling meningioma.' *Journal of Neurosurgery*, **12**, 407–413.

Smith, J. F., Landing, B. H. (1960) 'Mechanisms of brain damage in *H. influenzae* meningitis.' *Journal of Neuropathology and Experimental Neurology*, **19**, 248–265.

Stern, W. E., Naffziger, H. C. (1953) 'Brain abscess associated with pulmonary angiomatous malformation.' *Annals of Surgery*, **138**, 521–531.

Stevens, E. A., Norman, D., Kramer, R. A., Messina, A. B., Newton, T. H. (1978) 'Computed tomographic brain scanning in intraparenchymal pyogenic abscesses.' *American Journal of Roentgenology*, **130**, 111–114.

Stovring, J., Snyder, R. D. (1980) 'Computed tomography in childhood bacterial meningitis.' *Journal of Pediatrics*, **96**, 820–823.

Udani, P. M., Parekh, U. C., Dastur, D. K. (1971) 'Neurological and related syndromes in central nervous system tuberculosis.' *Journal of the Neurological Sciences*, **14**, 341–357.

Waggener, J. (1974) 'The pathophysiology of bacterial meningitis and cerebral abscesses: an antomical interpretation.' *Advances in Neurology*, **6**, 1–17.

Wendling, L. R. (1978) 'Intracranial venous sinus thrombosis: diagnosis suggested by computed tomography.' *American Journal of Roentgenology*, **130**, 978–980.

Whelan, M. A., Hilal, S. K. (1980) 'Computed tomography as a guide in the diagnosis and follow up of brain abscesses.' *Radiology*, **135**, 663–671.

—— Stern, J. (1981) 'Intracranial tuberculoma.' *Radiology*, **138**, 75–81.

—— —— deNaopli, R. A. (1981) 'The computed tomographic spectrum of intracranial mycosis. Correlation with histopathology.' *Radiology*, **141**, 703–707.

Wise, G. R., Farmer, T. W. (1969) 'Subdural empyema in infants.' *In:* Locke, S. (Ed.) *Modern Neurology: Papers in tribute to D. Denny-Brown*. Boston: Little, Brown. p. 515.

Zee, C., Segall, H. D., Miller, C., Tsai, F. Y., Teal, J. S. Hieshima, G., Ahmadi, J., Halls, J. (1980) 'Unusual neuroradiological features of intracranial cysticercosis.' *Radiology*, **137**, 397–407.

Zeman, W., Kolar, O. (1968) 'Reflections on the etiology and pathogenesis of subacute sclerosing panencephalitis.' *Neurology*, **18**, 1–7.

Zilkha, A., Daiz, A. S. (1980) 'Computed tomography in the diagnosis of superior sagittal sinus thrombosis. *Journal of Computer Assisted Tomography*, **4**, 124–126.

Zimmerman, R. A., Patel, S., Bilaniuk, L. T. (1976) 'Demonstration of purulent bacterial intracranial infection by computed tomography.' *American Journal of Roentgenology*, **127**, 155–165.

Zimmerman, R. D., Russell, E. J., Leeds, N. E., Kaufman, D. (1980) CT in the early diagnosis of *Herpes simplex* encephalitis.' *American Journal of Roentgenology*, **134**, 61–66.

9
BRAIN TUMORS

Brain tumors are the second commonest group of childhood neoplastic diseases, following leukemia. The tumors may occur at any age, with a peak incidence between five and 10 years. There is a slightly higher male preponderance. In childhood, primary brain tumors are collectively more commonly infratentorial in location, in contrast to the supratentorial location found in adults. In the neonatal period, however, Sato *et al.* (1975) found them to be almost entirely supratentorial.

The specific symptoms and signs will vary with the type of tumor. Supratentorial tumors may have a more gradual onset of presentation, especially in young children where expansion of the head is made possible by suture diastasis. Masses within the infratentorial compartment may rapidly produce symptoms due to expansion within a relatively confined space.

Radiologic investigation of brain tumors has been revolutionized by the advent of CT. In the past, skull radiographs were used as the initial screening test, augmented by cerebral angiography and in selected cases pneumo-encephalography or radionuclide scanning. CT has emerged as the prime modality for investigation of suspected brain tumors, as it provides precise anatomic location of the tumor mass with additional information regarding the size, constituent components, mass effect, and relation to surrounding vital structures and vessels. Ventricular size is readily assessed at the time of this examination.

Axial scans form the basis of the examination; coronal scans can delineate the mass in an additional plane, which is invaluable for treatment planning. Sagittally reformatted images add a further dimension in the demonstration of the tumor mass. CT is the modality of choice for subsequent follow-up imaging of tumors.

Following CT demonstration of supratentorial tumors, cerebral angiography is often used to give the neurosurgeon a 'roadmap' of the vasculature involved. This is particularly important in the suprasellar and pineal regions. Angiography is less essential for posterior fossa tumors, unless the CT scan is not adequately diagnostic or unusual appearances are noted on the scan (Bruce 1982).

Pneumo-encephalography, although less commonly used since the advent of CT, is effective in the detection of small tumors in the parasellar and suprasellar regions, the base of the posterior fossa, and third and fourth ventricles. Radionuclide imaging is a non-invasive screening modality which was used before CT was available. The detection rate by this modality will vary with the size and site of the tumor mass.

Infratentorial tumors
Posterior fossa tumors account for 50 to 60 per cent of all intracranial neoplasms in the pediatric age-group (Koos and Miller 1971, Matson 1969, Sayers and Hunt

171

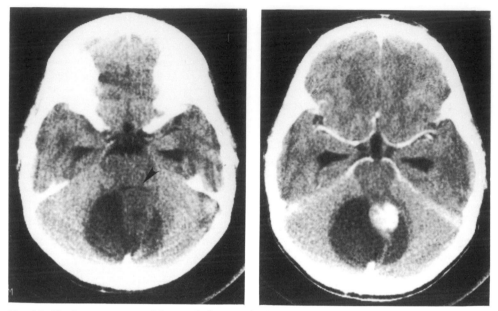

Fig. 9.1. Cystic astrocytoma of the cerebellar vermis. Seven-year-old boy. *Left:* non-contrast head CT scan. There is a sharply defined cyst. The fourth ventricle is compressed posteriorly *(arrowhead)*. *Right:* contrast-enhanced head CT scan displays enhancement of the mural nodule.

1973, Hooper 1975, Heiskanen 1977). The vast majority of histologically verified tumors have been found to arise within the fourth ventricle and cerebellum (Segall *et al.* 1982). The clinical features will depend on the tumor location. Cerebellar astrocytomas, medulloblastomas and ependymomas present with symptoms of increased intracranial pressure and ataxia, unlike brainstem gliomas where cranial nerve nuclei and long tracts are involved early (Bilaniuk 1983). Cerebellar astrocytoma and medulloblastoma are the two most common types encountered.

Cerebellar astrocytoma

These tumors occur predominantly in the first two decades of life. In the series of Harwood-Nash and Fitz (1976), presentation was more common between the ages of four and eight, with decreasing incidence thereafter. The location may be in the vermis or hemispheres with possible extension into the cavity of the fourth ventricle (Rosai 1981). In comparison with other posterior fossa tumors there may be a longer delay before the clinical diagnosis is made.

The lesion may be cystic or solid in nature. 20 per cent of cerebellar astrocytomas are mainly solid (Naidich *et al.* 1977), with 60 to 80 per cent displaying one or more large cysts at surgery (Schott *et al.* 1983). Cystic tumors tend to be large at the time of initial diagnosis. The fluid within the cyst is highly proteinaceous, with a density higher than cerebrospinal fluid, and can thus be differentiated on CT (Segall *et al.* 1982). A direct linear relationship has been

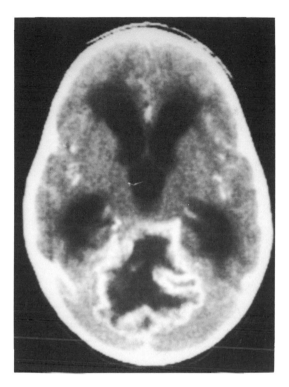

Fig. 9.2. Cystic astrocytoma. Contrast-enhanced head CT scan demonstrates inhomogeneous enhancement of the tumor. Hydrocephalus is present.

demonstrated between the albumin content and attenuation coefficient (Norman *et al.* 1977). Calcification is present in approximately 25 per cent of cases (Hilal 1979).

CT appearances
The cystic type usually is a low-density lesion (less dense than normal brain, but of greater density than cerebrospinal fluid) with well-defined margins. Half of the cystic tumors have a mural nodule, and display variable enhancement on the post-contrast scan (Gol 1963, Harwood-Nash and Fitz 1976, Naidich 1977, Zimmerman *et al.* 1978*a*) (Fig. 9.1).

Solid astrocytomas also appear as low-density lesions on pre-contrast scans, with less well-defined margins, and tend to be more inhomogeneous (Segall *et al.* 1982) (Fig. 9.2). In some cases they are only detected by the surrounding edema (Hilal 1979).

Uniform enhancement occurs after contrast administration (Zimmerman *et al.* 1978*a*). Calcification occurs in 14 per cent of cerebellar astrocytomas (Fitz and Rao 1983). The rôle of CT after therapy is well established (Zimmerman *et al.* 1978*a*). Recurrences may be detected long before the onset of symptoms. CT differentiation between recurrent tumor and fluid within the surgical defect can be made by assessment of the fluid density. The density within a recurrent cystic tumor is twice that of cerebrospinal fluid, compared to the fluid in the area of previous surgery which has a density similar to cerebrospinal fluid.

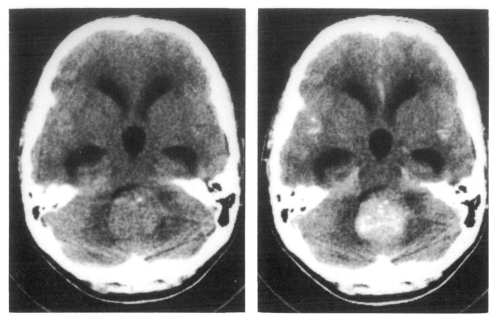

Fig. 9.3. Medulloblastoma. 12-year-old boy. *Left:* non-contrast head CT scan demonstrates a large midline tumor of the vermis, containing calcification. There is compression of the fourth ventricle. A surrounding rim of edema is demonstrated. *Right:* contrast-enhanced head CT scan reveals inhomogeneous contrast enhancement within the tumor.

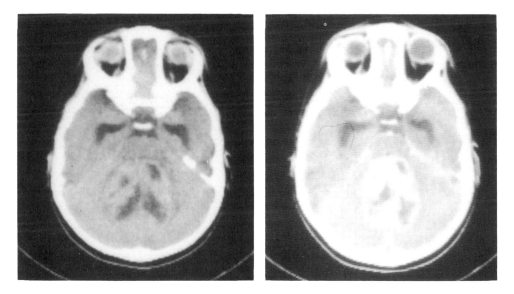

Fig. 9.4. Medulloblastoma. Two-year-old girl. *Left:* non-contrast head CT scan demonstrates a midline soft tissue mass containing low-density areas representing necrosis. *Right:* contrast-enhanced head CT scan demonstrates homogeneous enhancement. The areas of necrosis are again displayed.

174

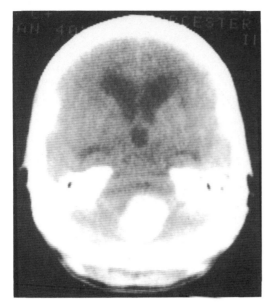

Fig. 9.5. Medulloblastoma. Four-year-old girl. Contrast-enhanced head CT scan reveals dense homogeneous enhancement within the tumor mass. Fourth ventricle compression is demonstrated.

Medulloblastoma

Medulloblastomas are tumors arising from primitive cells which may originate in the fetal granular layer of the cerebellum or the posterior medullary velum (Raaf and Kernohan 1944).

They occur mainly in childhood, with approximately 50 per cent in the first decade. A second peak in adults has been described by Russell and Rubinstein (1971). In childhood the location is in the midline, in contrast to those arising in later life which tend to be situated more laterally within the cerebellar hemisphere (Zimmerman *et al.* 1978*b*). The association of medulloblastoma and the basal cell nevus syndrome of Gorlin is not uncommon (Herzberg and Wiskemann 1963).

The CT appearance is of a smoothly ovoid or spherical mass of slightly greater density than the surrounding cerebellum, with a rim of edema (Fitz and Rao 1983) (Figs. 9.3, 9.4). There is usually uniform enhancement (Fig. 9.5) of the tumor in both the midline and lateral locations (Zimmerman *et al.* 1978*b*), although non-enhancement has also been observed rarely (Woodrow *et al.* 1981). Calcification is usually small, homogeneous and eccentric in location, detected on CT in 10 per cent of medulloblastomas (Fitz and Rao 1983).

Medulloblastomas are disseminated by seeding of the subarachnoid space, retrograde ventricular extension and by extracranial metastases. Distant metastases are usually osseous (Fig. 9.6), followed in frequency by lymph node and soft tissue involvement. Skin, liver, lung and mediastinum are less commonly involved (Brutschin and Culver 1973).

CT is accurate in demonstrating tumor recurrence. Contrast enhancement of the lesion, subarachnoid space, or progressive ventricular enlargement are readily detected (Enzmann *et al.* 1978*a*).

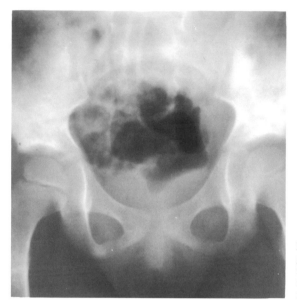

Fig. 9.6. Medulloblastoma. Two-year-old girl. Osteoblastic metastases are present in the pelvis and proximal femora, six months after the initial diagnosis was made.

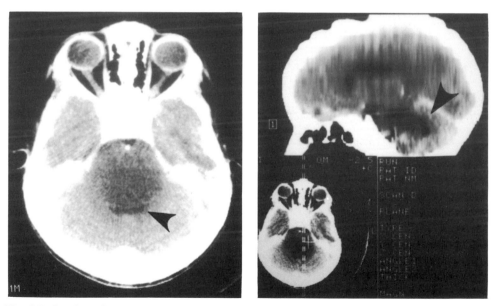

Fig. 9.7. Pontine glioma. Two-year-old girl. *Left:* non-contrast head CT scan. A large low-density pontine tumor displaces the fourth ventricle *(arrowhead)* posteriorly. *Right:* sagittal reformatted contrast-enhanced CT scan shows the tumor with posterior displacement of the fourth ventricle *(arrowhead)*.

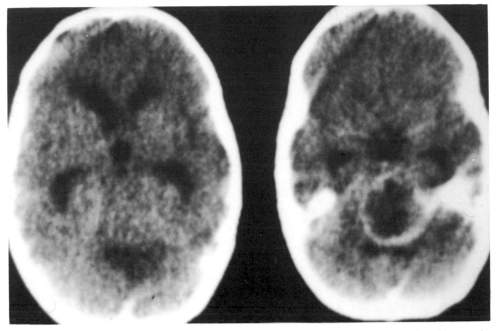

Fig. 9.8. Pontine glioma. Four-year-old boy. *Left:* non-contrast head CT scan reveals evidence of a pontine mass isodense to surrounding parenchyma. *Right:* contrast-enhanced head CT scan shows ring enhancement of the tumor mass.

Brainstem glioma

Brainstem gliomas are relatively common tumors of the posterior fossa. They are mainly tumors of childhood with a peak incidence at four to five years of age. There is a slight male preponderance (Harwood-Nash and Fitz 1976). The tumors may arise in the midbrain pons or medulla. The pons is the most frequent site of origin (Kieffer and Lee 1983).

The duration of onset may be long before the diagnosis is established, because of the location and the tendency to infiltrate cranial nerve nuclei and long tracts without producing obstruction to the flow of CSF until late in the course of the tumor growth (Panitch and Berg 1970). CT has now replaced pneumo-encephalography as the investigation of choice, as it is extremely effective in the demonstration of these lesions. Correct diagnosis is dependent on a scan without patient motion and thorough examination of the posterior fossa with numerous slices as low as foramen magnum (Segall *et al.* 1982). A wide spectrum of CT appearances is encountered. The tumors are usually of low density, either the same or lower than normal tissue (Fig. 9.7). Non-homogeneous contrast enhancement varies from minimum to moderate (Bilaniuk *et al.* 1980) (Fig. 9.8).

Calcification within brainstem gliomas is extremely uncommon. The presence of calcification has been considered by Duffner *et al.* (1978) to correlate with less aggressive tumor pathology. Visualization of the normal configuration of the fourth

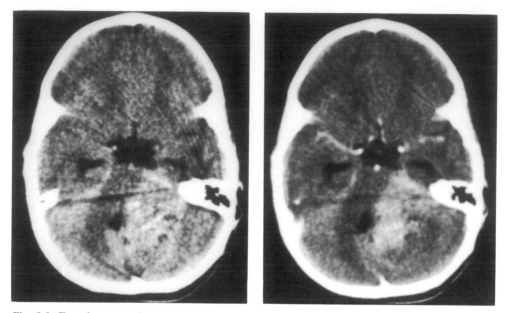

Fig. 9.9. Ependymoma. 13-year-old girl. *Left:* non-contrast head CT scan demonstrates tumor mass involving fourth ventricle, with presence of calcification. *Right:* contrast-enhanced scan demonstrates homogeneous contrast-enhancement.

ventricle, prepontine cistern, pons and basilar artery has been stressed by Segall *et al.* (1982) in order to exclude the presence of a midbrain glioma. The fourth ventricle should always be noted, and if the rounded configuration is replaced by flattening of the anterior portion or an anterior concavity, a lesion must be suspected (Fig. 9.7). The normal prepontine cistern is usually seen in its entirety, but may be encroached upon by exophytic tumors. The sagittal dimension of the pons is less than that of the structures behind the fourth ventricle. Any alteration of this ratio is abnormal (Segall *et al.* 1982).

The basilar artery projects anterior to the ventral surface of the pons. The presence of tissue anterior to the anterior margin of the basilar artery is indicative of tumor (Segall *et al.* 1982). The basilar artery may be encased by the tumor (Rubinstein 1972). Distention and compression of the third ventricle, perimesencephalic and quadrigeminal cisterns may occur as a result of upward tumor extension into the thalamus (Bilaniuk *et al.* 1980).

The tumors may be cystic. CT demonstration of this feature is important in treatment as cyst aspiration usually results in clinical improvement and contributes to longterm survival (Lassiter *et al.* 1971).

Ependymoma
Ependymomas are predominantly tumors of childhood and adolescence. They constitute approximately 6 per cent of all intracranial gliomas (Russell and Rubinstein 1971). They are relatively slow-growing tumors which arise from

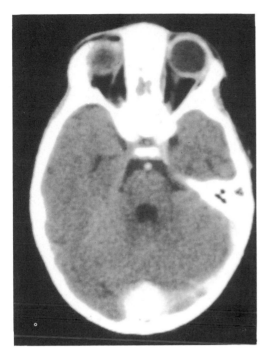

Fig. 9.10. Metastatic neuroblastoma. 11-month-old boy. Contrast-enhanced head CT scan demonstrates a biconvex homogeneously enhancing epidural mass.

ependymal cells. In many instances a large element of the ependymal neoplasm is contributed to by the subependymal glia, leading to the description of a subependymoma by Scheinker (1945).

Intracranial ependymomas are more commonly situated within the posterior fossa (Fokes and Earle 1969, Swartz *et al.* 1982). They arise most commonly from the floor of the fourth ventricle, but may also arise in relation to any part of the ventricular system.

The tumor is usually solitary, except in the subependymoma variant or in patients with von Recklinghausen's disease.

The CT appearance of ependymal tumors is variable. In the series of Swartz *et al.* (1982) they were usually isodense (80 per cent) on the pre-contrast scan, with subsequent enhancement varying from non-homogeneous to homogeneous, and containing calcification in about 50 per cent of the cases, in the form of small round calculi. Calcification within a fourth ventricular mass or adjacent to the fourth ventricle should lead to the diagnosis of an ependymoma (Segall *et al.* 1982) (Fig. 9.9). Calcification within medulloblastomas tends to be less common and is more in the form of clumps. CT is of use in the demonstration of subarachnoid seeding, particularly around the spinal cord (Enzmann *et al.* 1978*a*).

Choroid plexus papilloma
The commonest location of choroid plexus papillomas is in the lateral ventricle; however they may also be found within the fourth ventricle. When arising from

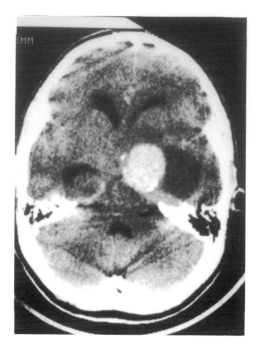

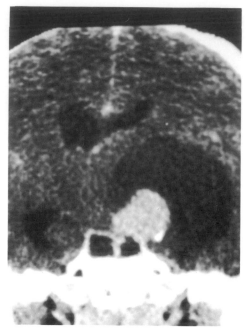

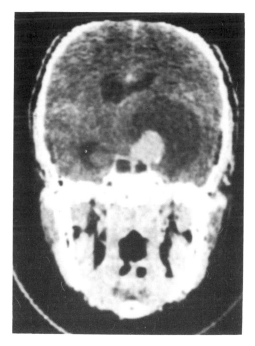

Fig. 9.11. Temporal lobe astrocytoma (grade II). 12-year-old boy. *Above left:* non-contrast head CT scan demonstrates a large low-density lesion in the uncus of the left temporal lobe. *Above right:* axial contrast-enhanced head CT scan displays homogeneous contrast enhancement. *Left:* coronal contrast-enhanced head CT scan displays close proximity of the mass to the Circle of Willis. Tumor adherence to the left internal carotid artery was demonstrated at surgery.

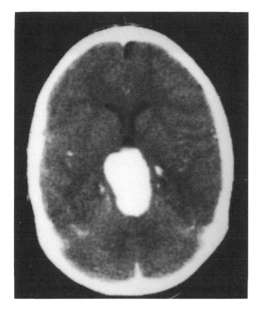

Fig. 9.12. Intraventricular astrocytoma. Nine-year-old girl. Contrast-enhanced head CT scan demonstrates homogeneous enhancement of tumor mass within the third ventricle.

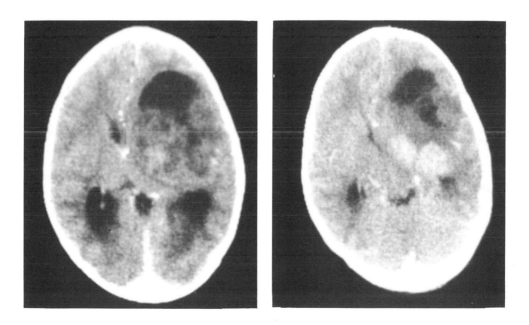

Fig. 9.13. Frontal lobe astrocytoma. Two-year-old boy. *Left:* non-contrast head CT scan demonstrates calcification and necrosis in a large tumor mass. There is a surrounding cap of edema. *Right:* contrast-enhanced head CT scan reveals nodular enhancement within the mass. Ventricular shift due to mass effect is demonstrated on both scans.

181

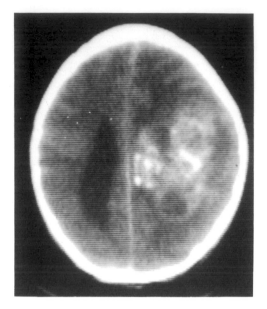

Fig. 9.14. Ependymoma. Two-year-old boy. Contrast-enhanced head CT scan demonstrates a large intraventricular mass which contains calcification and displays inhomogeneous enhancement.

choroid plexus in the foramen of Luschka, a cerebellopontine angle mass is produced which may present as a brainstem glioma (Hammock *et al.* 1976).

Extra-axial tumors

Extra-axial tumors are uncommon within the posterior fossa in the pediatric age-group. Tumors which may be encountered include metastatic neuroblastoma (Fig. 9.10), teratoma, meningioma, dermoid, epidermoid, chordoma, trigeminal neurinoma, acoustic neuroma and inferior extension of supratentorial tumors (Segall *et al.* 1982).

Supratentorial tumors

Astrocytoma

Astrocytomas are the commonest hemispheric tumors of childhood, occurring within the cerebral cortex or deep in the hypothalamus and basal ganglia. Commonest sites include the parietal and frontal lobes, followed in frequency by location in the temporal and occipital lobes and hypothalamus (Harwood-Nash and Fitz 1976). Optic nerve and chiasmatic astrocytomas are less common and will be discussed below.

A wide spectrum of symptoms will result from this form of tumor, varying with patient age and location. Hypothalamic gliomas may produce the 'diencephalic syndrome' which includes progressive emaciation with almost total loss of subcutaneous fat, intermittent vomiting, euphoria, hyperactivity, pallor and optic atrophy (Russell 1951).

Astrocytomas have been graded by Kernohan *et al.* (1949) into types 1 to 4, ranging from benign (grade 1) to malignant glioblastoma multiforme (grade 4). The

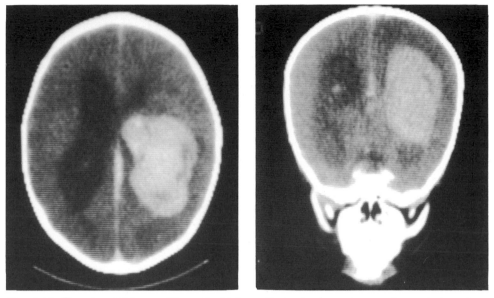

Fig. 9.15. Ependymoblastoma. 18-month-old boy. Contrast-enhanced scans demonstrate a large contrast-enhancing intraventricular mass lesion.

most common appearance is a decreased-density lesion (Tchang *et al.* 1977). The low-density lesion in a low-grade atrocytoma tends to be well defined and regular in shape with absence or paucity of surrounding edema. The area of low density in a glioblastoma is more irregular and less well defined, with a finger-like appearance due to edema in the subcortical white matter. Following contrast administration, homogeneous enhancement of the lesion may occur in all grades and is thus non-specific. The enhanced mural nodule in the wall of a cyst with decreased density tends to suggest a low-grade glioma. Enhancement in a ring-like fashion, with thick irregular margins surrounding a central low-density area, is considered virtually diagnostic of a glioblastoma (Tchang *et al.* 1977). The differential diagnosis of ring-like enhancement is discussed in the chapter on intracranial infection.

Necrotic and cystic change in the malignant type may be readily detected on CT. Calcification within the mass may signify a lower grade of malignancy but may however also be found in the anaplastic types. Figures 9.11, 9.12 and 9.13 display some of the varying CT appearances of astrocytomas.

Ependymoma
Ependymoma is a slow-growing neoplasm arising from ependymal cells. The location of this tumor may be supratentorial, but is more commonly infratentorial. The peak incidence is at two years of age, with most cases occurring under the age of 15 (Kricheff *et al.* 1964). The tumors arise from the ependymal surface of the ventricle and may subsequently fill the ventricle if aggressive, or spread toward the

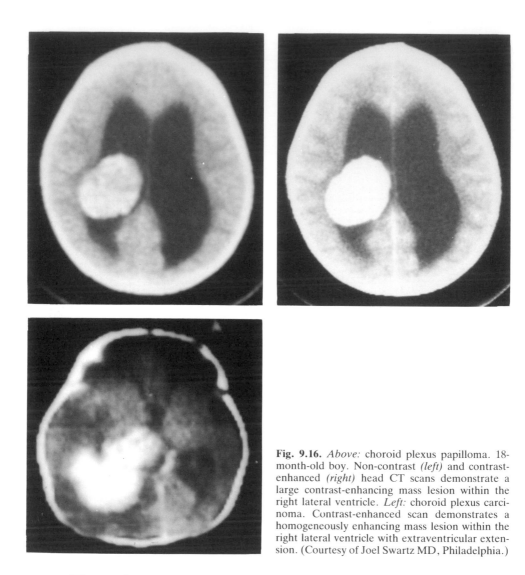

Fig. 9.16. *Above:* choroid plexus papilloma. 18-month-old boy. Non-contrast *(left)* and contrast-enhanced *(right)* head CT scans demonstrate a large contrast-enhancing mass lesion within the right lateral ventricle. *Left:* choroid plexus carcinoma. Contrast-enhanced scan demonstrates a homogeneously enhancing mass lesion within the right lateral ventricle with extraventricular extension. (Courtesy of Joel Swartz MD, Philadelphia.)

cortex (Fig. 9.14).

Ependymoblastomas are uncommon. They occur in a younger age-group and may fill the ventricular system and extend into adjacent brain producing few symptoms (Fig. 9.15).

Choroid plexus papilloma
This tumor arises from the epithelial cells of the choroid plexus and accounts for 3 per cent of all intracranial neoplasms of childhood (Matson 1969). There is a male preponderance, with most reported cases occurring under five years of age. The lateral ventricle is the commonest site, followed by the fourth and third ventricles in order of frequency. Malignant change may occur. Signs and symptoms related to

raised intracranial pressure are the most frequent form of presentation. The association of choroid plexus papilloma and communicating hydrocephalus has been attributed to over-production of cerebrospinal fluid.

The CT appearances are typically of communicating hydrocephalus, with a large mass within the ventricular system. Marked enhancement of the lesion may be noted (Fig. 9.16). Ependymomas and meningiomas may also be located within the ventricular system.

Supratentorial midline tumors
Craniopharyngioma
Craniopharyngiomas constitute a spectrum of solid and cystic tumors originating from epithelial rests following incomplete closure of the hypophyseal or cranio-pharyngeal duct. They are also named hypophyseal duct tumors, craniopharyngeal duct tumors, and Rathke's pouch tumors. The rests may occur at numerous sites along the entire craniopharyngeal duct from the floor of the third ventricle inferiorly to the body of the sphenoid bone and retropharyngeal space (Duffy 1920).

In the pediatric age-group, craniopharyngiomas account for 7 to 13 per cent of all intracranial tumors (Ingraham and Scott 1946, Matson and Crigler 1969, Koos and Miller 1971). They generally occur in childhood, but may occur at all ages from the neonatal period (Majd et al. 1971) to old age. The occurrence in later life has led to speculation that they may represent metaplasia of anterior pituitary cells (Hunter 1955). There is an equal sex incidence (Matson and Crigler 1969, Koos and Miller 1971), although a slightly higher male incidence is reported by Harwood-Nash and Fitz (1976). Most craniopharyngiomas occur in the suprasellar subarachnoid space, with some extending into the sella or third ventricle; they may also present as tumors of the clivus within the posterior fossa. They may be found rarely within the sphenoid bone or sinus, intranasally or within the retropharyngeal space.

Calcification is extremely common within these tumors occurring within 70 to 80 per cent of cases in childhood. CT may reveal calcification not visible on skull radiographs or conventional tomography. The tumor usually presents on CT as a hypodense or isodense lesion with calcification in the suprasellar region (Fig. 9.17). Rarely the tumor may be hyperdense, due to the increased protein content outweighing the low density of the cholesterol within the cyst (Lipper et al. 1981). Contrast enhancement may occur in the more solid tumors or around the rim of the cystic lesion, and has been found to be more commonly demonstrated in children than adults in the pre-operative state (Fitz et al. 1978). These workers consider that the combination of at least two of the three signs of contrast enhancement, calcification or cyst formation in a centrally located suprasellar tumor is considered to be a reliable indication of a craniopharyngioma, especially in children. CT is now routinely used in the pre-operative and post-operative course of these patients.

Pituitary adenoma
Pituitary adenomas have long been considered to be rare in infancy and childhood,

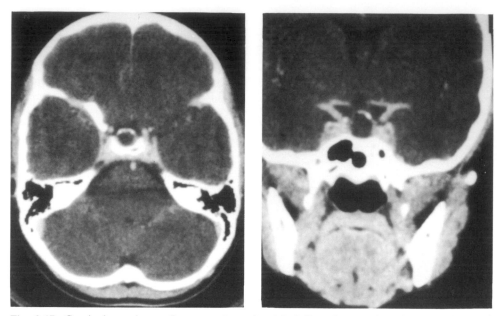

Fig. 9.17. Craniopharyngioma. Contrast-enhanced axial *(left)* and coronal *(right)* head CT scans demonstrate a sellar mass with suprasellar extension. There is calcification within the superior pole of the mass.

accounting for 0.7 per cent of intracranial neoplasms in the series of Harwood-Nash and Fitz (1976) and 1.5 per cent in the Vienna series of Koos and Miller (1971). With earlier detection the frequency has increased. Richmond and Wilson (1978) reported a 33 per cent incidence of pituitary adenomas in 74 parasellar tumors diagnosed in patients under the age of 20. The commonest presentation is failure of sexual maturation.

Pituitary adenomas have been traditionally divided on the basis of normal pituitary cells into chromophile (eosinophilic and basophilic), chromophobe and mixed cell tumors. This classification which correlates poorly with cell types and corresponding hormone secretion is not considered worthy of retention (Rosai 1981). Pituitary tumors may be usefully classified according to their hormone output into secretory (prolactinomas with high prolactin secretion and ACTH secretory tumors) and non-secretory types (Wolpert 1979). The prolactin-secreting adenoma was the commonest type encountered in the 25 pituitary adenomas in patients under 20 years of age described by Richmond and Wilson (1978).

Pituitary adenomas in children have been found to be extrasellar and invasive by Ortiz-Suarez and Erickson (1975), although these characteristics were not found in the more recent series of Richmond and Wilson (1978).

CT appearances

High-resolution computed tomography permits visualization of the tumor mass,

186

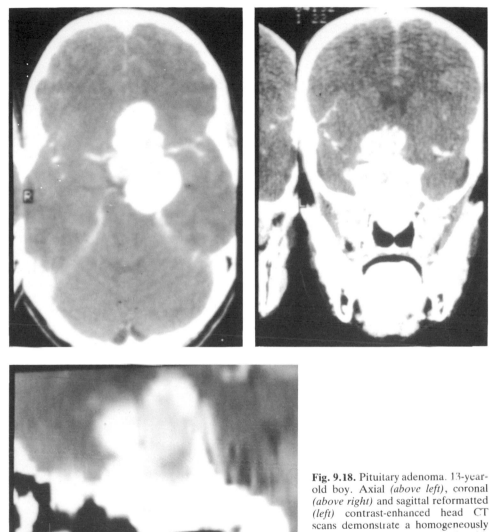

Fig. 9.18. Pituitary adenoma. 13-year-old boy. Axial *(above left)*, coronal *(above right)* and sagittal reformatted *(left)* contrast-enhanced head CT scans demonstrate a homogeneously enhancing mass within the sella with suprasellar extension.

compression or distortion of adjacent structures and bone erosion, if present (Levine *et al.* 1983). The tumors on non-contrast scan may be isodense or hyperdense compared with the surrounding brain, and usually exhibit considerable contrast enhancement (Naidich *et al.* 1976a). Direct coronal CT scanning results in the best detail, with sagittal reconstructed views used to augment the study (Wolpert 1984). The patient may be placed either in the supine position or prone with neck extension in order to obtain a direct coronal scan. The height of the pituitary gland is the best parameter for measuring an increased size of the gland since the border between the cavernous sinus and pituitary gland is not well defined

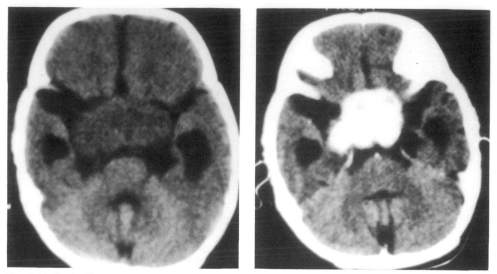

Fig. 9.19. Optic glioma. Two-year-old boy. *Left:* non-contrast head scan demonstrates a large soft tissue mass within the suprasellar cistern. *Right:* dense homogeneous enhancement is shown on the contrast-enhanced head CT scan.

(Wolpert 1984). Gland height varies with age and is larger in adolescents than adults (Peyster *et al.* 1983).

Optic glioma

Optic gliomas occur almost exclusively in childhood. Harwood-Nash (1972) reported an incidence of 7 per cent in all intracranial neoplasms, and 13 per cent of the astrocystomas. There is a frequent association with von Recklinghausen's disease.

Computed tomography has become established as the single most useful method in the diagnosis of optic gliomas, in all locations extending from within the orbit to the intracranial anterior optic pathways (Savoiardo *et al.* 1981). CT demonstrates the anatomic location, tumor extension and presence of calcification, if present. In the series of Savoiardo *et al.* (1981), 17 of 22 gliomas were isodense on the pre-contrast CT scan, with varying degrees of enhancement after contrast administration (Fig. 9.19).

Hypothalamic hamartoma

Hypothalamic hamartomas are rare lesions. A hamartoma is a congenital malformation which consists of a tumor-like collection of normal tissue in an abnormal location. The nerve cells within a hypothalamic hamartoma resemble these of the tuber cinereum together with normal glial cells (Lin *et al.* 1978*b*).

There is an equal incidence in males and females (List *et al.* 1958). The clinical presentation is precocious puberty, seizure disorder and mental changes. Although

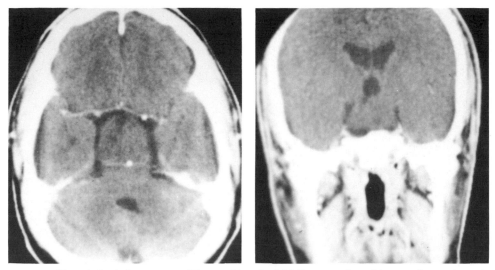

Fig. 9.20. Hypothalamic hamartoma. 25-year-old male, initially presenting with precocious puberty in infancy. *Left:* axial contrast-enhanced head CT scan demonstrates a soft tissue mass expanding the suprasellar cistern. *Right:* coronal contrast-enhanced head CT scan demonstrates expansion of the suprasellar cistern. Areas of low density are present within the mass. There is encroachment on the anterior aspect of the third ventricle.

most mass lesions around the posterior hypothalamus act in a destructive way to diminish the suppressive activity of the hypothalamus or gonadotrophin secretion, the hypothalamic hamartoma is the exception by independently secreting luteinizing hormone releasing hormone (LHRH) which stimulates pituitary gonadotrophin (LH and FSH) secretion (Judge *et al.* 1977). Although most reported cases are single lesions, hamartomas may be multiple (Fitz and Rao 1983).

The CT appearances are non-specific (Lin *et al.* 1978*b*, Fitz and Rao 1983). Obliteration and distortion of the suprasellar cistern, and distortion of anterior portion of the third ventricle may be demonstrated if the mass is large (Fig. 9.20). Contrast enhancement is usually not observed (Lin *et al.* 1978*b*, Mori *et al.* 1981).

Pineal tumors
Tumors of the pineal region are uncommon, accounting for 1 per cent of intracranial tumors in all ages (Zulch and Christensen 1956). They have been classified by Russell and Rubinstein (1971) into four main groups:
  I. Teratomas
     Typical and teratoid
     Germinoma, or atypical teratoma
  II. Pinealomas
     Pineoblastoma
     Pineocytoma

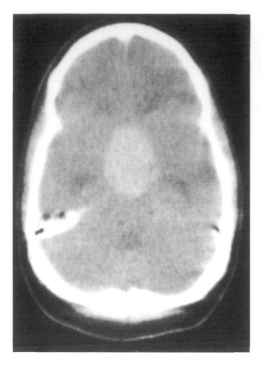

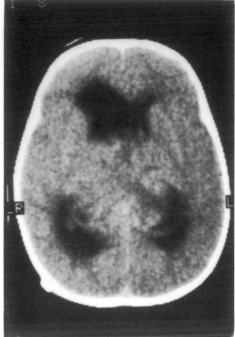

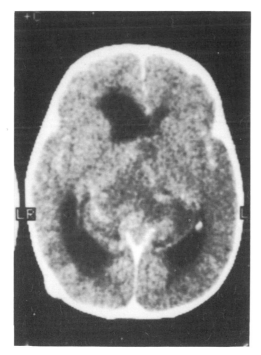

Fig. 9.21. *Above left:* germinoma. Six-year-old boy. Contrast-enhanced head CT scan demonstrates a contrast-enhancing mass related to the third ventricle. *Left and above right:* pinealoblastoma. 18-month-old boy. Non-contrast *(above right)* and contrast-enhancing *(left)* head CT scans reveal evidence of ventricular distortion. A soft tissue mass in the pineal region with inhomogeneous enhancement is present.

III. Glial and the other forms
  Glioma
  Ganglioneuroma
  Chemodectoma
  Meningioma
IV. Cysts
  Epidermoid and dermoid cyst
  Non-neoplastic cyst

Teratomas are almost entirely restricted to males, occurring usually within the first two decades of life. Germinomas have a male predominance, clinically diagnosed between the ages of 15 and 25 years. Germinoma (atypical teratoma) is the commonest tumor in the pineal area. Besides this location it may also be encountered in the floor of the third ventricle and adjacent pituitary infundibulum (Fitz and Rao 1983) (Fig. 9.21). Pinealomas exhibit no sex predilection. Both children and adults may be affected by either the pineoblastoma or pineocytoma (Russell and Rubenstein 1971). A tumor located within the pineal region should always be considered to be a primary pineal tumor (Zimmerman *et al.* 1980).

The CT appearances of the tumors of the pineal region have been shown to display a wide variety of appearances by Futrell *et al.* (1981) (Fig. 9.21). They found no definite correlation between tumor type and appearance on CT. Calcification occurs in teratomas and it may also occur in pineoblastomas (Lin *et al.* 1978*a*). The cells in pinealomas have a greater tendency to calcify than germinal cells (Zimmerman *et al.* 1980). Benign teratomas are diagnosed by the presence of fat, calcification, ossification, or other variable soft-tissue densities (Zimmerman *et al.* 1980). The non-contrast CT appearance of a germinoma is that of a mass which is isodense or slightly hyperdense in comparison with surrounding brain, followed by intense homogeneous enhancement after contrast administration (Naidich *et al.* 1976*b*, Takeuchi *et al.* 1978, Neuwelt *et al.* 1979, Zimmerman *et al.* 1980) (Fig. 9.21). CT has added a new dimension in the anatomic and pathologic delineation of pineal region tumors which because of their deep location were not previously amenable for histologic verification. Advances in microsurgical techniques have led to decreased operative morbidity and mortality (Stein 1982).

Ganglioglioma

Gangliogliomas are benign, slow-growing parenchymal tumors of the brain. They are composed of neurons and supporting neuroglial cells which are predominantly astrocytic (Russell and Rubinstein 1962). There is a variable neoplastic spectrum extending from the ganglioneuroma to astrocytoma. Malignant change 23 years after the initial diagnosis of ganglioma has been described (Russell and Rubinstein 1962). Most cases occur under the age of 30 years (Russell and Rubinstein 1977). Although this tumor may be found in any location, the commonest site is in the region of the anterior third ventricle (Russell and Rubinstein 1962).

The CT appearance is non-specific. The appearances described by Zimmerman and Bilaniuk (1979) are of isodense masses with some enhancement. The tumors are usually solid, although a single large cyst or multiple cysts may be present.

191

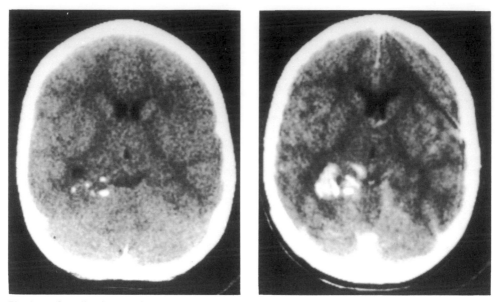

Fig. 9.22. Ganglioglioma. Nine-year-old boy. *Left:* non-contrast head CT scan shows numerous calcific densities within a mass adjacent to the atrium of the right lateral ventricle. *Right:* contrast-enhancement is demonstrated within the mass on the contrast-enhanced head CT scan.

Punctate calcifications within the tumor are common (Fitz and Rao 1983) (Fig. 9.22). Although the CT appearances are non-specific, the diagnosis of ganglioglioma should always be considered in a young patient with a prolonged clinical history and the CT features as described above (Zimmerman and Bilaniuk 1979).

Neuroblastoma
Primary cerebral neuroblastomas are rare in infancy and childhood. These tumors arising in the cerebral hemispheres are termed central neuroblastomas, compared with the more common peripheral neuroblastomas which arise from the adrenal medulla and sympathetic ganglia (Koos and Miller 1971).

Primary cerebral neuroblastoma has been classified as a distinct clinicopathological entity which differs from other similar neuro-ectodermal tumors (Horten and Rubenstein 1976). There are three histologic variants, consisting of the classic type with little connective tissue, the desmoplastic type with a more prominent stroma, and a transitional type. This tumor may occur at any site within the cerebral hemispheres growing into the meninges, compared with the secondary form which involves the skull base, orbit and calvarium (Koos and Miller 1971).

The age of onset in more than half the patients with primary cerebral neuroblastoma, and more than 70 per cent with the primary extracerebral form reported by Zimmerman and Bilaniuk (1980), was five years or younger. In their series all three cases of primary cerebral neuroblastoma were boys.

The CT appearances of primary cerebral neuroblastoma described by Zimmer-

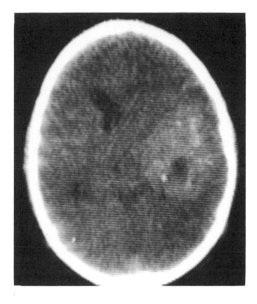

Fig. 9.23. Cerebral neuroblastoma. Four-year-old boy. Non-contrast head CT scan demonstrates an ill-defined left parietal mass, containing coarse calcification.

man and Bilaniuk (1980) and Chambers *et al.* (1981) are of hypodense or isodense tumor masses which display contrast enhancement. Coarse calcification may be present (Fig. 9.23). Cystic, hemorrhagic and necrotic foci may also be noted within the lesions. Intratumoral hemorrhage has been found to be relatively frequent (Bilaniuk and Zimmerman 1980).

Primitive neuro-ectodermal tumors
The primitive neuro-ectodermal tumors are a rare group of tumors located within the central hemispheres. They are composed of undifferentiated cells which resemble the germinal matrix cells found embryologically in the neural tube (Hart and Earle 1973). These tumors bear a histologic resemblance to medulloblastoma, pineoblastoma and peripheral neuroblastoma sharing histological malignancy, primitive nature and variable differentiation into both glial and neuronal elements (Kosnik *et al.* 1978).

The tumor presents in infancy or early childhood. The average age of occurrence is about three years, with no sex predilection (Kosnik *et al.* 1978). It is clinically highly malignant with a rapid fatal course (Duffner *et al.* 1981). Subarachnoid and ventricular invasion may occur, and distant metastases beyond the central nervous system to spinal cord, lungs and bronchi, pulmonary hilar lymph nodes, pericardium, diaphragm and liver have been recorded (Kosnik *et al.* 1978, Duffner *et al.* 1981).

The CT appearances are of bulky tumors which are sharply marginated, have cystic and necrotic areas and exhibit variable degrees of contrast enhancement (Ganti *et al.* 1982, Hinshaw *et al.* 1983). Severe displacement of the ventricular system with hydrocephalus is usually noted. Multiple small irregular calcifications

193

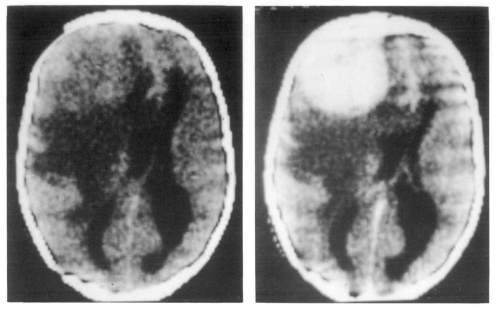

Fig. 9.24. Meningioma. Eight-year-old girl. Non-contrast *(left)* and contrast-enhanced *(right)* CT scans demonstrate right frontal soft tissue mass, and marked homogeneous contrast enhancement. There is surrounding edema and evidence of mass effect.

may be present within the tumor. Extensive invasion of the adjacent meningeal surface has also been noted (Hinshaw *et al.* 1983).

Meningioma

Meningiomas are rare tumors of childhood, arising from dural arachnoid villi. The series of Jefferson and Jackson (1939) and Harwood-Nash and Fitz (1976) reported an incidence of 1.4 and 1.5 per cent of all brain tumors in children.

A collaborative study of 48 meningiomas in childhood by Merten *et al.* (1974) has shown these tumors to be more commonly located within the posterior fossa or ventricular system than in adulthood. Extracranial meningiomas and multiple discrete tumors, especially when associated with neurofibromatosis, were also encountered in the pediatric age-group. Calcification within the meningiomas was also noted with increased frequency.

The CT appearance on non-contrast scan is usually that of a hyperdense or isodense mass which displays dense homogeneous enhancement following contrast administration. The shape may be variable, appearing as a 'carpet-like' mass along the dura (*en plaque*) or globular (*en masse*); the broad dural attachment is typical of meningioma (Rosenbaum and Rosenbloom 1984) (Fig. 9.24).

Leukemia

Leukemic involvement of the central nervous system (CNS) is common, usually in the form of diffuse leptomeningeal disease. Parenchymal involvement of the brain is uncommon. Evans *et al.* (1970) noted a high incidence in children with acute lymphocytic leukemia who did not receive CNS prophylaxis. They attributed the increased incidence to prolonged survival rates in children with leukemia. The subsequent use of prophylactic CNS radiation and intrathecal methotrexate has considerably decreased this incidence (Aur *et al.* 1972, Hustu *et al.* 1973). CT detection of meningeal disease has been found to be very low by Enzmann *et al.* (1978*b*) and Pagani *et al.* (1981). The parenchymal masses have been found on CT to be isodense or slightly higher in density than normal brain on the pre-contrast scan. Following contrast administration, homogeneous enhancement has been found with varying amounts of edema (Wendling *et al.* 1979). The masses are contiguous with cortical or subependymal surfaces, following extension from the meninges or seeding of the ependyma with resultant infiltration of brain parenchyma (Pagani *et al.* 1981) (Fig. 9.24).

Chloroma (granulocytic sarcoma) represents a subtype of myelogenous leukemia in which extramedullary foci of malignant granulopoiesis are formed (Liu *et al.* 1973). Chloromas occur most commonly in children and young adults, with a peak incidence between four and five years of age (Atkinson 1939, Liu *et al.* 1973). The nodules may occur at any site of the body. They may occur together with, following, or more rarely before the onset of acute, subacute or chronic myelogenous leukemia.

The CT appearance is that of a hyperdense focal mass with surrounding edema on the pre-contrast CT scan. Well-circumscribed homogeneous enhancement is noted on the post-contrast scan (Sowers *et al.* 1979). However, the appearances are non-specific and may appear similar to those of primary lymphoma of the central nervous system or meningioma in older patients (Figs. 9.25, 9.26).

Methotrexate leuko-encephalopathy may result as the complication of the combined effect of radiation and methotrexate toxicity. Peylan-Ramu *et al.* (1977) have demonstrated areas of low density in the periventricular region and centrum semiovale which did not enhance after contrast injection. Calcification may be noted within the deep and cortical gray matter (Fig. 9.27).

Lymphoma

Lymphomas in childhood are classified into Hodgkin and non-Hodgkin types by the same histologic criteria for adults (Weinstein and Link 1979). In children under the age of 15, non-Hodgkin lymphoma is the more common form, occurring 1.4 times as frequently as Hodgkin disease (Kushner *et al.* 1980).

Hodgkin disease

Hodgkin disease occurs in childhood but is uncommon under the age of five years. There is a male preponderance. Extranodal primary sites are unusual in childhood. An increased incidence of cerebral involvement in adults with Hodgkin disease has been reported by Cuttner *et al.* (1979); this is attributed to longer survival rates in these patients receiving total nodal radiotherapy and MOPP (nitrogen mustard, vincristine, prednisone and procarbazine). The CT scans in these cases revealed evidence of contrast-enhancing mass lesions within cerebral parenchyma.

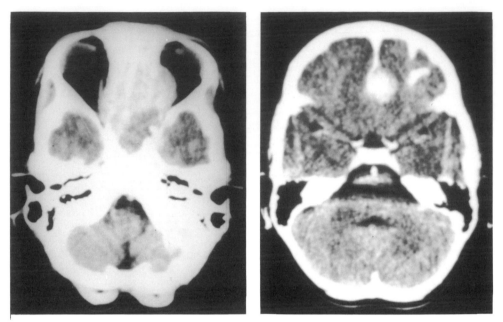

Fig. 9.25. Chloroma. Four-year-old boy with myelocytic leukemia. Contrast-enhanced head CT scans demonstrate a homogeneously enhancing frontal mass lesion.

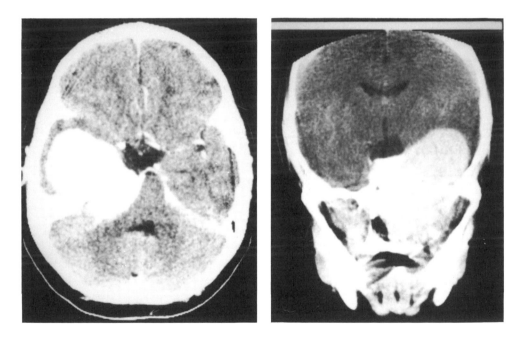

Fig. 9.26. Chloroma. 10-year-old girl with myelocytic leukemia. Axial *(left)* and coronal *(right)* contrast-enhanced head CT scans demonstrate a temporal lobe mass lesion with infratemporal extension.

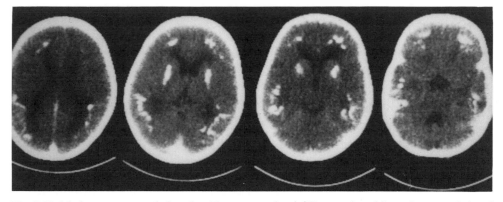

Fig. 9.27. Methotrexate encephalopathy. Non-contrast head CT scans show bilateral symmetric basal ganglia and parenchymal calcification following intrathecal methotrexate therapy for leukemia. (Courtesy of Samuel Wolpert MD, Boston.)

Non-Hodgkin lymphoma

The origin of primary neoplastic proliferation of lymphoreticular tissue within the brain is uncertain (Tadmor *et al.* 1978). The term 'malignant lymphoma' encompasses many subtypes including lymphosarcoma, reticulum cell sarcoma, histiocytic lymphoma, microglioma and adventitial sarcoma (Kazner *et al.* 1978).

Primary malignant lymphoma of the brain in childhood is rare. The lesions in both children and adults are more commonly primary in origin, rather than from secondary involvement of systemic lymphoma (Henry *et al.* 1974). Secondary involvement of the brain and meninges occurs more frequently with some subtypes *e.g.* diffuse histiocystic lymphoma, diffuse underdifferentiated lymphoma, diffuse lymphoma poorly differentiated, and Hodgkin disease (Brant-Zawadzki and Enzmann 1978).

The commonest form of intracranial spread is leptomeningeal infiltration; dural and parenchymal involvement are less common. Parenchymal involvement is most frequently caused by diffuse histiocytic lymphoma (Brant-Zawadzki and Enzmann 1978). Immunosuppressed allograft recipients are at increased risk (Barnett and Schwartz 1974, Cho *et al.* 1974), and there is an increased incidence in children with the Wiskott-Aldrich syndrome (Heidelberger and LcGolvan 1974). The lesions may be single or multiple. The basal ganglia, thalamus, corpus callosum and periventricular white matter are the commonest sites; but the brainstem, cerebellar hemispheres, vermis and meninges may also be involved (Lee and Rao 1983).

The CT appearances of malignant lymphoma have been described in the series of Brant-Zawadzki and Enzmann (1978), Kazner *et al.* (1978), Tadmor *et al.* (1978) and Pagani *et al.* (1981). On the non-contrast scans the masses are isodense to brain, or slightly denser. A varying amount of edema and mass effect is present, depending on the size of the tumor. There is homogeneous enhancement after contrast administration (Fig. 9.28).

Diffusely growing malignant lymphomas appear as low-density lesions with

197

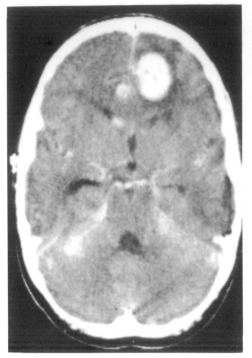 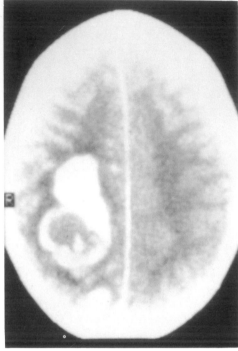

Fig. 9.28. Histiocytic lymphoma. 14-year-old boy. Contrast-enhanced head CT scan shows a large contrast-enhancing mass lesion within the left frontal region. There is surrounding edema.

Fig. 9.29. Cerebral metastases from rhabdomyosarcoma. Contrast-enhanced head CT scan demonstrates contrast-enhancing metastases within the right cerebral hemisphere.

ill-defined margins and a lack of enhancement following contrast administration (Ebhardt and Meese 1977, Kazner *et al.* 1978).

Leptomeningeal involvement of lymphoma is not visualized on CT, in contrast to the enhancement within the subarachnoid space due to carcinomatous meningitis and subarachnoid extension of brain tumors (Brant-Zawadzki and Enzmann 1978).

Lipoma
Lipomas are rare tumors of maldevelopmental origin. These are described in Chapter 4.

Teratoma, epidermoid, dermoid
These are rare congenital disorders, similar in development and clinical course. These are also described in Chapter 4.

Metastases
Metastatic involvement of the brain is rare in childhood, accounting for 0.5 to 1.8 per cent of all pediatric intracranial tumors (Han *et al.* 1983). Tumors which

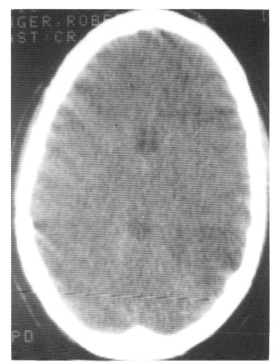

Fig. 9.30. Pseudotumor cerebri. 15-year-old male. Non-contrast head CT scan reveals evidence of decreased lateral ventricular size.

metastasize to brain include Wilms tumor, sarcomas of soft tissue (Fig. 9.29) and bone, non-Hodgkin lymphoma, and neuroblastoma.

The cerebral involvement of Wilms tumor is related to the propensity of this tumor to metastasize to the lung (Klapproth 1959, Westra *et al.* 1967). The few CT examples of metastatic Wilms disease in the literature (Hammock and Milhorat 1981, Han *et al.* 1983) demonstrate either single or multiple lesions which may often be cystic in nature. Primary metastases to the brain or spinal cord parenchyma from extracranial neuroblastoma are extremely rare with parenchymal involvement generally resulting from primary skull metastases which extend to the dura and then involve brain (Koizumi and Dal Canto 1980).

Benign intracranial hypertension (pseudotumor cerebri)
Benign intracranial hypertension or pseudotumor cerebri is a clinical syndrome characterized by raised intracranial pressure, normal cerebrospinal fluid findings and a ventricular system of normal or smaller than normal size demonstrated radiologically (Rose and Matson 1967).

Although more frequent in young obese women this disorder may also occur not uncommonly in childhood (Rose and Matson 1967, Grant 1971). In Grant's series most cases were between four and 10 years of age with no significant difference in sex incidence.

A variety of disorders have been associated with benign intracranial hypertension. Lateral venous sinus thrombosis is the commonest disorder, often with preceding otitis media or viral infection (Symonds 1931, DeVivo 1982).

Associated hormonal disorders include decreased or withdrawn corticosteroid therapy (Greer 1963, Neville and Wilson 1970) Addison disease (Walsh 1952) and congenital adrenal hyperplasia (DeVivo 1982). Drug-induced causes which have been incriminated are tetracycline (Fields 1961) chlortetracycline (Gellis 1956), vitamin A excess (Marie and See 1954) and deficiency (Keating and Feigin 1970).

Pernicious anemia (Murphy and Costanzi 1969), iron deficiency anemia (Lubeck 1959) and hypocalcemia (Sugar 1953) are other causes.

The CT scan should be performed with contrast enhancement to exclude the presence of mass lesions. The ventricular system is normal or may be decreased in size (Fig. 9.30). Cerebral angiography may also be required in some instances to demonstrate patency of the venous system.

REFERENCES

Atkinson, F. R. B. (1939) 'Chloroma in children.' *British Journal of Children's Diseases*, **36**, 18–34.
Aur, R. J. A., Simone, J. V., Hustu, H. O., Verzosa, M. S. (1972) 'A comparative study of central nervous system irradiation and intensive chemotherapy early in remission of childhood acute lymphocytic leukemia.' *Cancer*, **29**, 381–391.
Barnett, L. B., Schwartz, E. (1974) 'Cerebral reticulum cell sarcoma after multiple renal transplants.' *Journal of Neurology, Neurosurgery and Psychiatry*, **37**, 966–970.
Bilaniuk, L. T. (1983) 'Computed tomography of pediatric brain tumors.' *Paper presented at the Neuroradiology Conference, Vail, Colorado. March 21–25.*
—— Zimmerman, R. A., Littman, P., Gallo, E., Rorke, L. B., Bruce, D. A., Schut, L. (1980) 'Computed tomography of brainstem gliomas in children.' *Radiology*, **134**, 89–95.
Brant-Zawadzki, M., Enzmann, D. R. (1978) 'Computed tomographic brain scanning in patients with lymphoma.' *Radiology*, **129**, 67–71.
Bruce, D. A. (1982) 'Pediatric brain tumors.' *Surgical Rounds*, **5**, 22–31.
Brutschin, P., Culver, G. J. (1973) 'Extracranial metastases from medulloblastomas.' *Radiology*, **107**, 359–362.
Chambers, E. F., Turski, P. A., Sobel, D., Wara, W., Newton, T. H. (1981) 'Radiologic characteristics of primary cerebral neuroblastomas.' *Radiology*, **139**, 101–104.
Cho, E. S., Connolly, E., Porro, R. S. (1974) 'Primary reticulum cell sarcoma of the brain in a renal transplant recipient.' *Journal of Neurosurgery*, **41**, 235–239.
Cuttner, J., Meyer, M., Huang, Y. P. (1979) 'Intracerebral involvement in Hodgkin's disease.' *Cancer*, **43**, 1497–1506.
DeVivo, D. C. (1982) 'Benign intracranial hypertension.' *In:* Rudolph, A. M. (Ed.) *Pediatrics 17th edn.* Norwalk, Conn.: Appleton–Century–Crofts. pp. 1635-1637.
Duffner, P. K., Klein, D. M., Cohen, M. E. (1978) 'Calcification in brainstem gliomas.' *Neurology*, **28**, 832–834.
—— Cohen, M. E., Heffner, R. R., Freeman, A. I. (1981) 'Primitive neuroectodermal tumors of childhood.' *Journal of Neurosurgery*, **55**, 376–381.
Duffy, W. C. (1920) 'Hypophyseal duct tumors; a report of three cases and a fourth case of cyst of Rathkes pouch.' *Annals of Surgery*, **72**, 537–555.
Ebhardt, G., Meese, W. (1977) 'Malignant lymphomas of the brain.' *Advances in Neurosurgery*, **4**, 303–308.
Enzmann, D. R., Norman, D., Levin, V., Wilson, C., Newton, T. H. (1978a) 'Computed tomography in the follow-up of medulloblastoma and ependymomas.' *Radiology*, **128**, 57–63.
—— Krikorian, J., Yorke, C., Hayward, R. (1978b) 'Computed tomography in leptomeningeal spread of tumor.' *Journal of Computer Assisted Tomography*, **2**, 448–455.
Evans, A. E., Gilbert, E. S., Zandstra, R. (1970) 'The increasing incidence of central nervous system leukemia in children.' *Cancer*, **26**, 404–409.
Fields, J. P. (1961) 'Bulging fontanelle: a complication of tetracycline therapy in infancy.' *Journal of*

Pediatrics, **58**, 74–76.

Fitz, C. R., Wortzman, G., Harwood-Nash, D. C., Holgate, R. C. Barry, J. F., Boldt, D. W. (1978) 'Computed tomography in craniopharyngiomas.' *Radiology*, **127**, 687–691.

—— Rao, K. C. V. G. (1983) 'Primary tumors in children.' *In:* Lee, H., Rao, K. C. V. G. (Eds.) *Cranial Tomography.* New York: McGraw-Hill. pp. 295–343.

Fokes, E. C., Earle, K. M. (1969) 'Ependymomas: clinical and pathological aspects. *Journal of Neurosurgery*, **30**, 585–594.

Futrell, N. N., Osborn, A. G., Cheson, B. D. (1981) 'Pineal region tumors: computed tomographic–pathologic spectrum.' *American Journal of Roentgenology*, **137**, 951–956.

Ganti, S. R., Diefenbach, P., Mawad, M. E., Silver, A. J., Sane, P., Hilal, S. K. (1982) 'Computed tomography of primitive neuroectodermal tumors.' *Paper presented at: XII Symposium Neuroradiologicum, October 10–16, Washington, D.C.*

Gellis, G. S. (1956) *The Yearbook of Pediatrics 1956–1957.* Chicago: Yearbook Medical Publishers. p. 40.

Gol, A. (1963) 'Cerebellar astrocystomas in children.' *American Journal of Diseases of Children*, **106**, 21–24.

Grant, D. N. (1971) 'Benign intracranial hypertension. A review of 79 cases in infancy and childhood.' *Archives of Disease in Childhood*, **46**, 651–655.

Greer, M. (1963) 'Benign intracranial hypertension. II: Following corticosteroid therapy.' *Neurology*, **13**, 439–441.

Hammock, M. K., Milhorat, T. H. (1981) *Cranial Computed Tomography in Infancy and Childhood.* Baltimore: Williams & Wilkins. p. 229.

—— —— Breckbill, D. L. (1976) 'Primary choroid plexus papilloma of the cerebellopontine angle presenting as a brainstem tumor in a child.' *Child's Brain*, **2**, 132–142.

Han, J. S., Zee, C., Ahmadi, J., Ro, H. I., Segall, A. D., Stowe, S. (1983) 'Intracranial metastatic Wilm's tumor in children: a report of two cases.' *Surgical Neurology*, **20**, 157–159.

Hart, M. N., Earle, K. M. (1973) 'Primitive neuroectodermal tumors of the brain in children.' *Cancer*, **32**, 890–897.

Harwood-Nash, D. C. (1972) 'Optic gliomas and pediatric neuroradiology.' *Radiologic Clinics of North America*, **10**, 83–100.

—— Fitz, C. R. (1976) *Neuroradiology in Infants.* St. Louis: C. V. Mosby. pp. 699–700.

Heidelberger, K. P., LeGolvan, D. P. (1974) 'Wiskott–Aldrich syndrome and cerebral neoplasia: report of a case with localized reticulum cell sarcoma.' *Cancer*, **33**, 280–284.

Heiskanen, O. (1977) 'Intracranial tumors of children.' *Child's Brain*, **3**, 69–78.

Henry, J. M., Heffner, R. R., Dillard, S. H., Earle, K. M., Davis, R. L. (1974) 'Primary malignant lymphomas of the cerebral nervous system.' *Cancer*, **34**, 1293–1302.

Herzberg, J. J., Wiskemann, A. (1963) 'Die fünfte Phakomatose, Basalzellnaevus mit familiarer Belastung und Medulloblastom.' *Dermatologica*, **126**, 106–123.

Hilal, S. K. (1979) 'The diagnosis of posterior fossa masses by computed tomography.' *Categorical Course in Neuroradiology.* Toronto: American Roentgen Ray Society Meeting.

Hinshaw, D. B., Ashwal, S., Thompson, J. R., Hasso, A. M. (1983) 'Neuroradiology of primitive neuroectodermal tumors.' *Neuroradiology*, **24**, 87–92.

Hooper, R. (1975) 'Intracranial tumors in childhood.' *Child's Brain*, **1**, 136–140.

Horten, B. C., Rubenstein, L. J. (1976) 'Primary cerebral neuroblastomas. A clinicopathological study of 35 cases.' *Brain*, **9**, 735–736.

Hunter, I. J. (1955) 'Squamous metaplasia of cells of the anterior pituitary gland.' *Journal of Pathology and Bacteriology*, **69**, 141–145.

Hustu, H. O., Aur, R. J. A., Verzosa, M. S., Simone, J. V., Pinkel, D. (1973) 'Prevention of central nervous system leukemia by irradiation.' *Cancer*, **32**, 585–597.

Ingraham, P. D., Scott, H. W. (1946) 'Craniopharyngiomas in children.' *Journal of Pediatrics*, **29**, 95–116.

Jefferson, G., Jackson, H. (1939) 'Tumors of the lateral and of the third ventricles.' *Proceedings of the Royal Society of Medicine*, **32**, 1105–1137.

Judge, D. M., Kulin, H. E., Page, R., Santeu, R., Suriyonta, T. (1977) 'Hypothalamic hamartoma: a source of luteinizing-hormone-releasing factor in precocious puberty.' *New England Journal of Medicine*, **296**, 7–10.

Kazner, E., Wilske, J., Steinhoff, H., Stochdorph, O. (1978) 'Computer assisted tomography in primary malignant lymphomas of the brain.' *Journal of Computer Assisted Tomography*, **2**, 125–134.

Keating, J. P., Feigin, R. D. (1970) 'Increased intracranial pressure associated with probable vitamin A deficiency in cystic fibrosis.' *Pediatrics*, **46**, 41–46.

201

Kernohan, J. W., Mabon, R. F., Svien, H. J., Adson, A. W. (1949) 'Symposium on a new and simplified concept of gliomas; simplified classification of gliomas.' *Proceedings of the Staff Meetings of the Mayo Clinic,* **24,** 71–75.

Kieffer, S. A., Lee, S. H. (1983) 'Intracranial neoplasms.' *In:* Haaga, J. R., Alfidi, R. J. (Eds.) *Computed Tomography of the Whole Body.* St. Louis: C. V. Mosby. pp. 64–109.

Klapproth, H. J. (1959) 'Wilm's tumor: a report of 45 cases and an analysis of 1351 cases reported in the world literature from 1940–1958.' *Journal of Urology,* **81,** 633–648.

Koizumi, J. H., Dal Canto, M. (1980) 'Retroperitoneal neuroblastoma metastatic to brain.' *Child's Brain,* **7,** 267–279.

Koos, W. T., Miller, M. H. (1971) *Intracranial Tumors of Infants and Children.* St. Louis: C. V. Mosby. pp. 1–415.

Kosnik, E. J., Boesel, C. P., Bay, J., Sayers, M. P. (1978) 'Primitive neuroectodermal tumors of the central nervous system in children.' *Journal of Neurosurgery,* **48,** 741–746.

Kricheff, I. I., Becker, M., Schneck, S. A., Taveras, J. M. (1964) 'Intracranial ependymomas: factors influencing prognosis.' *Journal of Neurosurgery,* **21,** 7–14.

Kushner, D. C., Weinstein, H. J., Kirkpatrick, J. A. (1980) 'The radiologic diagnosis of leukemia and lymphoma in children.' *Seminars in Roentgenology,* **15,** 316–334.

Lassiter, K. R. L., Alexander, E., Davis, C. H., Kelly, D. L. (1971) 'Surgical treatment of brainstem gliomas.' *Journal of Neurosurgery,* **34,** 719–725.

Lee, S. H., Rao, K. C. V. G. (1983) 'Primary tumors in adults.' *In:* Lee, S. H., Rao, K. C. V. G. (Eds.) *Cranial Computed Tomography.* New York: McGraw-Hill. pp. 241–293.

Levine, H. L., Kleefield, J., Rao, K. C. V. G. (1983) 'The base of the skull.' *In:* Lee, S. H., Rao, K. C. V. G. (Eds.) *Cranial Computed Tomography.* New York: McGraw-Hill. pp. 371–459.

Lin, S. R., Bryson, M. M., Gobien, R. P., Fitz, C. R., Lee, Y. Y. (1978*b*) 'Radiologic findings of hamartomas of the tuber cinereum and hypothalamus.' *Radiology,* **127,** 697–703.

—— Crane, M. D., Lin, Z. S., Bilaniuk, L. T., Plassche, W. M., Marshall, L., Spataro, R. F. (1978*a*) 'Characteristics of calcification in tumors of the pineal gland.' *Radiology,* **126,** 721–726.

Lipper, M. H., Kishore, P. R., Ward, J. D. (1981) 'Craniopharyngioma: unusual computed tomographic presentation.' *Neurosurgery,* **9,** 76–78.

List, C. F., Dowman, C. E., Bagchi, B. K., Bebin, J. (1958) 'Posterior hypothalamic hamartomas and gangliomas causing precocious puberty.' *Neurology,* **8,** 164–174.

Liu, P. I., Ishimaru, T., McGregor, D. H., Okada, H., Steer, A. (1973) 'Autopsy study of granulocytic sarcoma (chloroma) in patients with myelogenous leukemia. Hiroshima–Nagasaki 1949–1969.' *Cancer,* **31,** 948–955.

Lubeck, M. J. (1959) 'Papilledema caused by iron-deficiency anemia.' *Transactions of the American Academy of Ophthalmology,* **63,** 306–310.

Majd, M., Farkas, J., Lopresti, J. M., Chandra, R., Hung, W., Lussenhop, A. J. (1971) 'A large calcified craniopharyngioma in the newborn.' *Radiology,* **99,** 399–400.

Marie, J., See, G. (1954) 'Acute hypervitaminosis of the infant.' *American Journal of Diseases of Children,* **87,** 731–736.

Matson, D. D. (1969) *Neurosurgery of Infancy and Childhood, 2nd edn.* Springfield, Ill.: C. C. Thomas.

—— Crigler, J. F. (1969) 'Management of craniopharyngioma in childhood.' *Journal of Neurosurgery,* **30,** 377–390.

Merten, D. F., Gooding, C. A., Newton, T. H. (1974) 'The radiographic features of meningiomas in childhood and adolescence.' *Pediatric Radiology,* **2,** 89–96.

Mori, K., Handa, H., Takeuchi, J., Hanakita, J., Nakano, Y. (1981) 'Hypothalamic hamartoma.' *Journal of Computer Assisted Tomography,* **5,** 519–521.

Murphy, T. E., Costanzi, J. J. (1969) 'Pseudotumor cerebri associated with pernicious anemia.' *Annals of Internal Medicine,* **70,** 777–782.

Naidich, T. P. (1977) 'Infratentorial masses.' *In:* Norman, D., Korobkin, M., Newton, T. H. (Eds.) *Computed Tomography.* St. Louis: C. V. Mosby. pp.231–242.

—— Pinto, R. S., Kushner, M. J. (1976*a*) 'Evaluation of sellar and parasellar masses by computed tomography.' *Radiology,* **120,** 91–99.

—— —— —— Lin, J. P., Kricheff, I. I., Leeds, N. E., Chase, N. E. (1976*b*) 'Computed tomography in the diagnosis of extra-axial posterior fossa masses.' *Radiology,* **120,** 333–339.

—— Lin, J. P., Leeds, N. E., Pudlowski, R. M., Naidich, J. B. (1977) 'Primary tumors and other masses of the cerebellum and fourth ventricle: differential diagnosis by computed tomography.' *Neuroradiology,* **14,** 153–174.

Neuwelt, E. A., Glasberg, M., Frenkel, E., Barnett, P., Hill, S., Moore, R. J. (1979) 'Malignant pineal region tumors.' *Journal of Neurosurgery,* **51,** 597–607.

Neville, B. G. R., Wilson, J. (1970) 'Benign intracranial hypertension following corticosteroid withdrawal in childhood.' *British Medical Journal*, **3**, 554–556.

Norman, D., Price, D., Boyd, D., Fishman, R., Newton, T. H. (1977) 'Quantitative aspects of computed tomography of the blood and cerebrospinal fluid.' *Radiology*, **123**, 335–338.

Ortiz-Suarez, H., Erickson, D. L. (1975) 'Pituitary adenomas of adolescents.' *Journal of Neurosurgery*, **43**, 437–439.

Pagani, J. J., Libshitz, H. I., Wallace, S., Hayman, L. A. (1981) 'Central nervous system leukemia and lymphoma: computed tomographic manifestations.' *American Journal of Neuroradiology*, **2**, 397–403.

Panitch, H. S., Berg, B. O. (1970) 'Brainstem tumors in childhood and adolescence.' *American Journal of Diseases of Children*, **119**, 465–477.

Peylan-Ramu, N., Poplack, D. G., Blei, C. L., Herdt, J. R., Vermess, M., Di Chiro, G. (1977) 'Computed assisted tomography in methotrexate encephalography.' *Journal of Computer Assisted Tomography*, **1**, 216–221.

Peyster, R. G., Hoover, E. D., Viscarello, R. R. (1983) 'CT appearance of the adolescent and preadolescent pituitary gland.' *American Journal of Neuroradiology*, **4**, 411–414.

Raaf, J., Kernohan, J. W. (1944) 'Relation of abnormal collections of cells in posterior medullary velum of the cerebellum to origin of medulloblastoma.' *Archives of Neurology and Psychiatry*, **52**, 163–169.

Richmond, I. L., Wilson, C. B. (1978) 'Pituitary adenomas in childhood and adolescence.' *Journal of Neurosurgery*, **49**, 163–168.

Rosai, J. (1981) 'Central nervous system and peripheral nerves.' *In: Ackerman's Surgical Pathology, Voulme 2, 6th edn.* St. Louis: C. V. Mosby. pp. 1555–1628.

Rose, A. Matson, D. D. (1967) 'Benign intracranial hypertension in children.' *Pediatrics*, **39**, 227–237.

Rosenbaum, A. E., Rosenbloom, S. B. (1984) 'Meningiomas revisited.' *Seminars in Roentgenology*, **19**, 8–26.

Rubinstein, L. J. (1972) 'Tumors of the central nervous system.' *Atlas of Tumor Pathology, Series 2, Fasc 6*, Washington D.C.: AFIP. pp. 24–25.

Russell, A. (1951) 'A diencephalic syndrome of emaciation in infancy and childhood.' *Archives of Disease in Childhood*, **26**, 274.

Russell, D. S., Rubinstein, L. J. (1962) 'Ganglioglioma: a case with long history and malignant evolution.' *Journal of Neuropathology, and Experimental Neurology*, **21**, 185–193.

—— —— (1971) 'Tumors of the nervous system.' *In: Pathology of Tumors of the Nervous System. 3rd edn.* Baltimore: Williams & Wilkins. pp. 182–188.

—— —— (1977) 'Ganglioneuroma and ganglioma.' *In: Pathology of tumors of the Nervous System. 4th edn.* Baltimore: Williams & Wilkins. pp. 262–268.

Sato, O., Tamura, A., Sano, K. (1975) 'Brain tumors of the early infants.' *Child's Brain*, **1**, 121–125.

Savoiardo, M., Harwood-Nash, D. C., Tadmore, R., Scotti, G., Musgrave, M. A. (1981) 'Gliomas of the intracranial anterior optic pathways in children.' *Radiology*, **138**, 601–610.

Sayers, M. P., Hunt, W. E. (1973) 'Posterior fossa tumors.' *In: Youmans, J. R. (Ed.) Neurological Surgery.* Philadelphia: W. B. Saunders. pp. 1466–1489.

Scheinker, I. M. (1945) 'Subependymoma (A newly recognized tumor of subependymal derivation).' *Journal of Neurosurgery*, **2**, 232–240.

Schott, L. H., Naidich, T. P., Gan, J. (1983) 'Common pediatric brain tumors: typical computed tomographic appearances.' *Journal of Computed Tomography*, **7**, 3–15.

Segall, H. D., Zee, C.-S., Naidich, T. P., Ahmadi, J., Becker, T. S. (1982) 'Computed tomography in neoplasms of the posterior fossa in children.' *Radiologic Clinics of North America*, **20**, 237–253.

Sowers, J. J., Moody, D. M., Naidich, T. P., Ball, M. R., Laster, D. W., Leeds, N. E. (1979) 'Radiographic features of granulocystic sarcoma (chloroma)'. *Journal of Computer Assisted Tomography*, **3**, 226–233.

Stein, B. M. (1982) 'Tumors of the pineal region.' *In: Youmans, J. R. (Ed.) Neurological Surgery, Volume 5.* Philadelphia: W. B. Saunders. pp. 2863–2871.

Sugar, O. (1953) 'Central neurological complications of hypoparathyroidism.' *Archives of Neurology and Psychiatry*, **70**, 86–107.

Swartz, J. D., Zimmerman, R. A., Bilaniuk, L. T. (1982) 'Computed tomography of intracranial ependymomas.' *Radiology*, **143**, 97–101.

Symonds, C. P. (1931) 'Otitic hydrocephalus.' *Brain*, **54**, 55–71.

Tadmor, R., Davis, K. R., Roberson, G. H., Kleinman, G. M. (1978) 'Computed tomography in primary malignant lymphoma of the brain.' *Journal of Computer Assisted Tomography*, **2**, 135–140.

203

Takeuchi, J., Handa, H., Nagata, I. (1978) 'Suprasellar germinoma.' *Journal of Neurosurgery*, **49**, 41–48.

Tchang, S., Scotti, G., Terbrugge, K., Melancon, D., Belanger, G., Milner, C., Ethier, R. (1977) 'Computerized tomography as a possible aid to the histological grading of supratentorial gliomas.' *Journal of Neurosurgery*, **46**, 735–739.

Walsh, F. B. (1952) 'Papilledema associated with increased intracranial pressure in Addison's disease.' *Archives of Ophthalmology*, **47**, 86.

Weinstein, A. J., Link, U. P. (1979) 'Non-Hodgkins lymphoma in childhood.' *Clinical Hematology*, **8**, 699–719.

Wendling, L. R., Cromwell, L. D., Latchaw, R. E. (1979) 'Computed tomography of intracerebral leukemic masses.' *American Journal of Roentgenology*, **132**, 217–220.

Westra, P., Kieffer, S. A., Mosser, D. G. (1967) 'Wilm's tumor: a summary of 25 years of experience before actinomycin D.' *American Journal of Roentgenology*, **100**, 214–221.

Wolpert, S. M. (1979) 'The sella turcica and parasellar lesions.' *Categorical Course on Neuroradiology. American Roentgen Ray Society Annual Meeting. Toronto. March 24–30.*

—— (1984) 'The radiology of pituitary adenomas.' *Seminars in Roentgenology*, **19**, 53–69.

Woodrow, P. K., Gajarawala, J., Pinck, R. L. (1981) 'Computed tomographic documentation of a non-enhancing posterior fossa medulloblastoma: an uncommon presentation.' *CT: Journal of Computed Tomography*, **5**, 41–43.

Zimmerman, R. A., Bilaniuk, L. T., Bruno, L., Rosenstock, J. (1978*a*) 'Computed tomography of cerebellar astrocytoma.' *American Journal of Roentgenology*, **130**, 929–933.

—— —— Pahlajanih, H. (1978*b*) 'Spectrum of medulloblastomas demonstrated by computed tomography.' *Radiology*, **126**, 137–141.

—— (1979) 'Computed tomography of intracerebral gangliogliomas.' *CT: Journal of Computed Tomography*, **3**, 24–29.

—— —— Wood, J. H., Bruce, D. A., Schut, L. (1980) 'Computed tomography of pineal, parapineal and histologically related tumors.' *Radiology*, **137**, 669–677.

—— —— (1980) 'CT of primary and secondary craniocerebral neuroblastoma.' *American Journal of Neuroradiology*, **1**, 431–434.

Zulch, K. J., Christensen, E. (1956) 'Biologie und pathologie der hirngeschwulste.' *In:* Ferner, H. (Ed.) *Pathologische Anatomie der raumbeengenden intracraniellen Prozesse. In:* Olivecrona, H., Tönnis, W., (Ed.) *Handbuch der Neurochirurgie, Bd. 4.* Berlin: Springer. pp. 1–702.

10
DEGENERATIVE AND METABOLIC DISORDERS

Disorders of the central nervous system

The degenerative disorders of the central nervous system encompass a wide spectrum of diseases, in many of which a specific etiology or biochemical basis has not yet been established. The rôle of CT is twofold: (i) in some disorders the appearance may be diagnostic, precluding the necessity for brain biopsy; and (ii) traumatic, infective, vascular and neoplastic etiologies which may initially produce similar clinical symptoms can be excluded.

The range of degenerative disorders is extensive, thus the discussion will be limited mainly to diseases where CT is of help in establishing the diagnosis.

Disorders of white matter

Demyelinating diseases

ADRENOLEUKODYSTROPHY

Adrenoleukodystrophy (melanodermic leukodystrophy, Addison-Schilder disease) is a sex-linked recessive neurodegenerative disorder associated with adrenocortical atrophy. Males are affected, with involvement commencing in the first decade of life, and fatal within several years (Powers and Schaumburg 1981). An infantile type has also been described, with neurological abnormalities and adrenal hypoplasia, and without clinical adrenal cortical insufficiency. The infantile form has also been recently described in both males and females, suggestive of an autosomal pattern of inheritance (Haas et al. 1982).

Adrenoleukodystrophy is considered a systemic metabolic disorder following the demonstration of cytoplasmic inclusions in the central nervous system and other organs (Schaumburg et al. 1974). The presence of abnormal long-chain fatty acids in cerebral tissues in patients with the infantile form supports the concept that infantile onset adrenoleukodystrophy is a clinically and pathologically distinctive entity (Haas et al. 1982).

Neurologic manifestations are progressive, and precede adrenal symptoms (Johnson 1982). The development of abnormal behavior and disturbance of gait or vision in a young patient are highly suggestive of the diagnosis (Schaumburg et al. 1975). The clinical features, progressive neurologic deterioration, adrenal hypofunction and CT appearances all contribute to the diagnosis (Johnson 1982).

Three histopathologic zones of white matter destruction were described by Schaumburg et al. (1975). The first and second zones were most prominent in the frontal edges of the lesion, while the third zone was located in the center of the occipitoparietal portion of the white matter lesion. Cerebral lesions are most severe in the posterior temporal parietal and occipital lobes. There is usually extension across the splenium of the corpus callosum to a lesion within the opposite hemisphere. Posterior cerebral lesions are usually symmetric, whereas the frontal lesions are often asymmetric.

cr appearances

Characteristic CT appearances are noted in approximately two-thirds of cases (Auborg and Diebler 1982). Low-density lesions are noted in the posterior cerebral white matter extending asymmetrically into the frontal areas (Greenberg *et al.* 1977). These areas correlate with Schaumburg's third zone, as described above, the zone of gliosis with little inflammatory reaction. Disintegration of myelin, reactive edema, and degeneration of protein structures may be responsible for the areas of decreased density observed on CT (Auborg and Diebler 1982).

Enhancement anterior and adjacent to the low-density areas following contrast administration corresponds to Schaumburg's first and second zones, where there is an active demyelinating process with perivascular mononuclear response (Greenberg *et al.* 1977). Decreased enhancement has been described following steroid therapy (Eiben and DiChiro 1977).

Atypical CT findings have been described by Dubois *et al.* (1981). These include calcification and low density in the periatrial white matter in addition to pathologic enhancement in the centrum semiovale, internal capsules, posterior corpus callosum and pyramidal tracts extending caudally to the pons. The authors speculate that these features may represent a link between the classic (type I) form of the disease and type II described by ·DiChiro *et al.* (1980) in which there is marked contrast enhancement of the white matter of the internal capsule, anterior corpus callosum and cingulate gyrus. The three different CT appearances described may possibly also represent stages of the same disease process (Dubois *et al.* 1981).

Calcification in the involved white matter especially around the trigones of the lateral ventricles has been described by Inoue *et al.* (1983). Periventricular calcification around the trigone was initially the sole abnormality, without evidence of low-density lesions in white matter.

Mass effect is an unusual feature which may very rarely be encountered in the active period of the disease (Inoue *et al.* 1983). The authors speculate that accumulation of water during this period may be an important factor in pathogenesis of the mass effect.

With progression of the disease, the demyelination process includes the frontal lobes and cerebellum. The rim enhancement fades, and central and cortical atrophy ensues, indistinguishable from many other degenerative processes (Quisling and Andriola 1979).

Schilder's disease

Schilder in 1912 described a non-familial condition as 'encephalitis periaxialis diffusa'. Most patients originally diagnosed as having Schilder's disease are now considered to be examples of adrenoleukodystrophy, multiple sclerosis, or demyelination process following viral encephalitis (Schaumburg *et al.* 1975, Rubinstein 1978).

Dysmyelination (leukodystrophies)

GLOBOID CELL LEUKODYSTROPHY (KRABBE DISEASE)

Globoid body leukodystrophy is an autosomal recessive hereditary disorder described by Krabbe in 1916. The etiology is considered to be a deficiency in galactocerebroside-B-galactosidase (Suzuki and Suzuki 1970). Most patients manifest symptoms and signs of this disease between three and six months of age.

Clinical features include tonic spasms and general rigidity with peripheral nerve involvement and a high CSF protein level (Adams and Lyon 1982). Frequent episodes of pyrexia are common.

There is widespread demyelinization of the central nervous system, with associated peripheral nerve involvement. Characteristic globoid cells are PAS-positive mononucleated or multinucleated histiocytes, present in demyelinated areas.

The CT findings described previously in this disorder included a normal scan initially in the early stage followed by low density in the periventricular white matter in the intermediate state, progressing to atrophy (Kendall and Kingsley 1978, Lane *et al.* 1978, Heinz *et al.* 1979, Barnes and Enzmann 1981, Kingsley and Kendall 1981).

Specific appearances for the acute phase of the disease have been described by Kwan *et al.* (1984). These include symmetric increased density in the thalami, caudate nuclei, corona radiata, brainstem and cerebellum, detected preceding or associated with decreased density in the white matter, with ensuing atrophy at a later stage. The areas of increased density were noted in the series of Kwan *et al.* (1984) as early as five months of age.

Multiple sclerosis

Multiple sclerosis is a disease of unknown etiology which occurs less commonly in children than in adults. The onset is infrequent in the first 10 years of life, usually commencing between 10 and 16 years of age (Chaves and Frank 1983).

Many theories of etiology have been postulated. These include viruses, allergic autosensitization, and a defect in polyunsaturated fatty acid metabolism (Belin *et al.* 1971, Allen 1982). HLA-A3 and HLA-A7 antigens occur more frequently in patients with this disorder than in healthy individuals in North America and Europe (Terasaki and Mickey 1976). Ethnic and geographic predisposition has also been postulated by Kurtzke *et al.* (1979).

The clinical course is characterized by widespread symptoms and signs with numerous relapses and remissions. Myelin destruction is followed by astrocytic proliferation and gliosis resulting in plaque formation. Multiple plaques are found in the white matter of cerebrum, cerebellum, brainstem, and spinal cord. The optic nerves may also be involved.

CT appearances

Prior to the advent of CT, angiography, myelography and pneumo-encephalography were utilized in establishing the diagnosis of multiple sclerosis and in excluding many other disease entities with similar symptoms and signs.

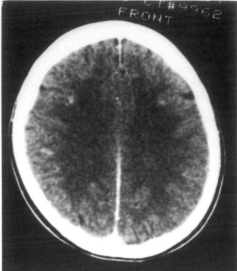

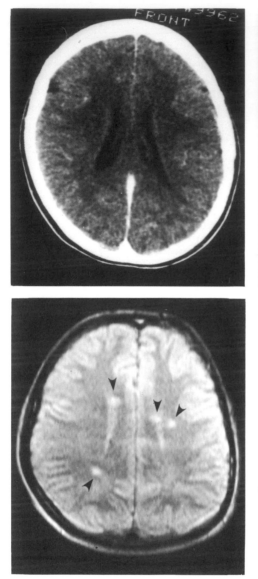

Fig. 10.1. Multiple sclerosis. 30-year-old female. *Above:* non-contrast head CT scans reveal no parenchymal abnormalities. *Left:* cerebral magnetic resonance imaging (MRI) scan (axial plane, spin echo sequence) demonstrates numerous high signal intensity areas *(arrowheads)*, indicative of multiple sclerosis plaques. (Courtesy of Gary DeFilipp MD and Eugene Roos DO, Philadelphia.)

Angiography and myelography are normal in this disorder. Pneumoencephalography is usually also normal, but may demonstrate atrophy with progression of the disease. Until recently CT was the prime modality used, but there are now many reports of increased detection of plaques with magnetic resonance imaging (Fig. 10.1).

The appearances on CT are variable and include a normal scan, low-density lesions of deep white matter, optic nerves and periventricular areas without associated mass effect, ventricular enlargement and cerebral atrophy (Cala and

Mastagua 1976, Huckman *et al.* 1977, Robertson *et al.* 1977, Aita *et al.* 1978). Contrast enhancement of varying size and shape and homogeneity is noted in the acute phase, correlating with early demyelinating lesions. Enhancement is thought to be due to breakdown of the blood-brain barrier, which is important in the pathogenesis of demyelination (Lebow *et al.* 1978). Corticosteroid therapy has been shown to reduce the amount of contrast enhancement, presumably by re-establishing the integrity of the blood-brain barrier (Sears *et al.* 1978). Contrast enhancement may only be detected with delayed scans in some patients (Morariu 1980). Following contrast enhancement of the lesions during the acute phase, there is usually subsequent isodensity and non-enhancement in the subacute and chronic phases of the disease (Aita *et al.* 1978, Weinstein *et al.* 1978), although there has also been a report of enhancement in a patient with clinical regression (Marano *et al.* 1980).

Metachromatic leukodystrophy
Metachromatic leukodystrophy (MLD) is an autosomal hereditary disorder due to deficiency of the enzyme arylsulfatase-A. Metachromatic lipid material, galactosyl sulfatide, accumulates in the peripheral and central nervous system, mainly in the white matter, and other organs notably the liver and kidney.

Since the original description by Alzheimer in 1910, the disease has been classified into late infantile, juvenile, adult, and multiple sulfatase deficiency forms. The commonest type is late infantile MLD, which is four times commoner than the juvenile form and usually occurs toward the end of the second year (Dulaney and Moser 1978). The juvenile form commences between four and 21 years of age, with the onset of adult form following after 21 years of age.

The clinical features of late infantile MLD are the onset of spastic ataxia, with lower motor neuron signs and elevated cerebrospinal fluid protein. Diagnostic tests include enzyme assay in urine and leukocytes, urinary sulfatide estimation, and peripheral nerve biopsy in some cases.

CT appearances
All reported CT scans in MLD have been abnormal (Dubal and Wiggli 1977, Robertson *et al.* 1977, Buonanno *et al.* 1978).

The CT appearances are of moderate ventricular enlargement and low-density lesions within white matter (Fig. 10.2). Robertson *et al.* (1977) attributed these low-density lesions to demyelinization.

Sudanophilic leukodystrophy
PELIZAEUS-MERZBACHER DISEASE
Pelizaeus-Merzbacher disease is a rare sex-linked recessive demyelinating disorder, first described by Pelizaeus (1885) and Merzbacher (1910). Heterozygous females are affected rarely. Six types have been recognized by Seitelberger (1970).

The onset may begin in the neonatal period. Nystagmus and cerebellar signs are early signs. The disease is usually fatal between five to seven years.

The pathologic findings are of cerebral and cerebellar atrophy with patchy

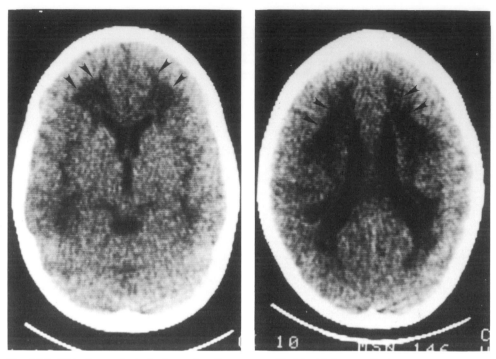

Fig. 10.2. Metachromatic leukodystrophy. Seven-year-old girl with hyperreflexia. Non-contrast head CT scans demonstrate hypodense areas within the white matter bilaterally *(arrowheads)*. Contrast enhancement was not demonstrated within these areas subsequently. (Courtesy of Ehsan Afshani MD, Buffalo.)

demyelination, containing sudanophilic degradation products.

The CT appearance of a case described by Heinz *et al.* (1979) was originally described as normal. This same case has recently been described as showing periventricular hypodense areas (normal and abnormal white matter) (Heinz 1984).

COCKAYNE'S SYNDROME

Cockayne (1936) described a syndrome of unknown cause consisting of microcephaly, cachexia, dwarfism, retinitis pigmentosa, sensorineural deafness, photosensitivity, premature ageing, and progressive encephalopathy associated with calcification in the basal ganglia and cerebellum.

Neuropathological studies reveal patchy demyelinization of the nervous system, and perivascular calcification mostly in the dentate and lenticular nuclei. Segmental demyelinization of peripheral nerves has also been described (Adams and Lyon 1982).

The CT appearances include cerebral atrophy and basal ganglia calcification (Fig. 10.3). Communicating hydrocephalus may also be present (Vermess 1976, Kendall 1981).

210

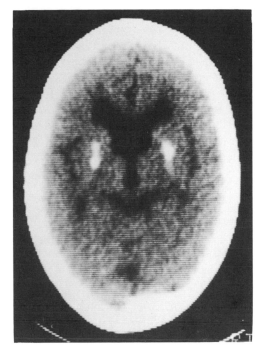

Fig. 10.3. Cockayne's syndrome. 12-year-old boy with dwarfism, ataxia and intention tremors Non-contrast head CT scan shows evidence of hydrocephalus. Calcification is present within the basal ganglia bilaterally. (Courtesy of Ehsan Afshani MD, Buffalo.)

Atypical forms

ALEXANDER'S DISEASE

Alexander's disease (megalencephalic infantile leukodystrophy) is a rare disorder of unknown pathogenesis, inherited on an autosomal recessive basis (Alexander 1949).

Three clinical subgroups are recognized according to the age of onset of clinical symptoms (Russo *et al.* 1976):

1. *Infantile.* Onset occurs at birth or in early childhood. The average age of onset is six months, with a duration of illness of two years and four months. Clinical features are megalencephaly, and/or hydrocephalus, spasticity, psychomotor retardation and seizures.

2. *Juvenile.* The range of onset is seven to 14 years. Progressive paresis with bulbar signs and hyperreflexia occur within this subgroup.

3. *Adult.* The range of onset is 19 to 43 years.

The histologic features of this disorder are a demyelinating process of varying severity, usually marked and diffuse in infancy, and the presence of hyaline eosinophilic Rosenthal fibers in the footplate of astrocytes located mainly in the subpial, subependymal and perivascular regions (Russo *et al.* 1976).

CT appearances

INFANTILE TYPE

The CT appearances in the early stages of the disorder described by Holland and

211

Kendall (1980) and Trommer *et al.* (1983) include: (i) mild to moderate enlargement of the lateral and third ventricles, and (ii) areas of increased density in the white matter of the frontal and temporal lobes, external and extreme capsules. The abnormal lucency within white matter extends peripherally to include subcortical arcuate fibers. Well-defined areas of increased density may be noted in the subependymal regions, corpus striatum, proximal portions of the forceps minor, columns of the fornices and subpial layers. Following contrast administration, marked enhancement of these more dense areas has been noted in some cases. In the later stages of the infantile form the areas of low density appear more well defined, and the areas of increased density appear less prominent on the non-contrast scan. Abnormal contrast enhancement is not observed (Boltshauser *et al.* 1978, Holland and Kendall 1980).

JUVENILE TYPE

Diffuse symmetric low density within white matter predominantly in the frontal lobes, and marked dilatation of the lateral and third ventricles have been described in a nine-year-old patient by Cole *et al.* (1979).

Spongy degeneration of the nervous system

Spongy degeneration of the nervous system (Canavan disease, van Bogaert-Bertrand disease) is an autosomal recessive disorder which affects mostly infants of Jewish extraction. This is a progressive encephalopathy of infancy, characterized by megalencephaly, absence of neurologic development or a rapid regression, hypotonia with tonic spasms and blindness with optic atrophy (Adams and Lyon 1982). The cerebrospinal fluid findings are usually normal, although rarely the protein may be slightly elevated (Banker *et al.* 1964). The outstanding pathological features of this disorder are an increase in brain weight, and spongy changes predominantly in the white matter. There is an absence of myelin, and an increased water-content in the affected areas (Boltshauser and Isler 1976, Adams and Lyon 1982).

CT appearances

The CT appearance, documented by several authors (Boltshauser and Isler 1976, Lane *et al.* 1978, Rushton *et al.* 1981), is that of symmetrical low-density white matter within the cerebral hemispheres. Hydrocephalus is not demonstrated.

The decreased density within white matter in Alexander's disease is especially frontal in distribution and occipital in location in adrenoleukodystrophy.

Localized disorders

Subacute necrotizing encephalomyelopathy

Subacute necrotizing encephalomyelopathy (Leigh's disease) is a rare autosomal recessive condition first described by Leigh in 1951. The disease is commoner in males. The disorder is an inborn error of thiamine due to inhibition of the enzyme ATP-TPP phosphoryl transferase, necessary for the production of coenzyme thiamine triphosphate.

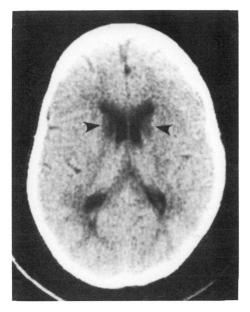

Fig. 10.4. Subacute necrotizing encephalomyel-opathy (Leigh's disease). Seven-year-old boy. Non-contrast head CT scan reveals symmetric low-density areas within the basal ganglia *(arrowheads)*.

The age of presentation is within the first two years of life, with 60 per cent presenting in the first year (Adams and Lyon 1982). In the early infantile period, hypotonia and vomiting may initially be encountered. Psychomotor retardation may occur abruptly or insidiously. Ataxia, dysarthria or intellectual regression are features of later onset.

There is variable duration of the disease, with an 80 per cent mortality in the infantile onset group. Survival beyond five years, and in some cases 10 years, has been reported (Namiki 1965).

The lesions in the nervous system consist of necrotic foci with associated vascular proliferation, and spongiform loosening of the neuropil. The foci are usually symmetric, mainly located in the dorsal part of the brainstem, and also lenticular nuclei, optic nerves, substantia nigra, dentate nuclei of the cerebellum and spinal cord (Adams and Lyon 1982). The mammillary bodies are spared in Leigh's disease, unlike in Wernicke's encephalopathy, which is also due to dietary deficiency of thiamine and which has similar microscopic features to Leigh's disease (Leigh 1951).

CT appearances

Symmetric low-density areas in the basal ganglia, especially with putaminal involvement, have been demonstrated by Hall and Gardner-Medwin (1978) (Fig 10.4). This finding was observed in both the infantile and juvenile forms. Low-density lesions in the basal ganglia may also be due to in-farction, carbon monoxide poisoning, Wilson's disease, and Parkinsonism. The appearance of a low-density lesion should thus assist in the diagnosis of Leigh's disease, after excluding the other clinical entities discussed

213

above. Prominent cerebellar sulci and a large fourth ventricle have been noted on CT in the juvenile form (Hall and Gardner-Medwin 1978).

Disorders of gray matter and its constituents
Neuronal ceroid lipofuscinoses
Neuronal ceroid lipofuscinoses are a group of inherited lysosomal storage disorders. There is excessive accumulation of lipopigments, ceroid and lipofuscin within the body. The defective enzyme has not yet been identified, although peroxidase deficiency in granulocytes has been suggested to be the probable cause of pigment deficiency in Batten disease (Armstrong *et al.* 1974).

The group of diseases includes:

1. INFANTILE TYPE
Hagberg-Santavuori disease (polyunsaturated fatty acid lipidosis). The onset is under two years of age, beginning with psychomotor degeneration and ending with blindness and tetraparesis.

2. LATE INFANTILE TYPE
Batten-Bielschowsky-Jansky disease. Polymyoclonia, cerebellar ataxia and hypotonia usually are detected by two to four years of age, followed by blindness and intellectual deterioration.

3. JUVENILE TYPE
Spielmeyer-Vogt-Sjogren disease. The onset is at five to 12 years of age. There is macular degeneration followed by polymyoclonia, ataxia, and extrapyramidal rigidity.

4. ADULT TYPE
Kuf's disease. Dementia and extrapyramidal signs develop (Adams and Lyon 1982). Neuronal destruction and reactive gliosis accompany the deposition of lipofuscin. The outer retinal layer, upper layers of cerebral cortex, and small granule cells in the olfactory bulb are mainly affected (Friede 1975, Valavanis *et al.* 1980).

CT appearances
The CT appearances of this disease in a 4½-year-old male child were described by Valvanis *et al.* (1980). Diffuse enlargement of cortical sulci, basal, interhemispheric and Sylvian fissures, and ventricular dilatation were demonstrated. These changes are attributed to widespread neuronal destruction, characteristic of the disease. Cerebellar atrophy was also demonstrated, although this is a frequent but inconstant feature of the disorder (Friede 1975). No abnormalities of cerebral white matter were demonstrated. In this disorder the white matter is usually preserved, without evidence of changes of leukodystrophy (Friede 1975).

Phakomatoses
The phakomatoses are described in Chapter 4.

214

TABLE 10.1

Degenerative and metabolic diseases in children: low-density areas on CT

A. *Extensive well-demarcated symmetric low density of supratentorial white matter with microcephaly*
Canavan's spongiform encephalopathy
Gangliosidoses (Gm_1 and Gm_2)
Metachromatic leukodystrophy

B. *Fairly well-defined low density within deep hemispheric white matter (with less peripheral extension)*
Juvenile metachromatic leukodystrophy
Maple syrup urine disease
Phenylketonuria
Transcobalamin II deficiency
Lowe's syndrome
Hurler's syndrome
Alpha ketoglutaric acidemia
Sjogren-Larsson syndrome

C. *Diffuse symmetric ill-defined low density in deep white matter*
Reye's disease—acute phase
Pyridoxine dependent epilepsy
Propionic acidemia
Methylmalonic acidemia

D. *Diffuse asymmetric low density in deep white matter*
Subacute sclerosing panencephalitis

E. *Periventricular low density*
Neonate (physiological)
Anoxia-hypoxia

F. *Low density due to incomplete myelination*
Arrest in cerebral development
Lissencephaly
Congenital microcephaly

G. *Well-defined symmetric low density in parietal and occipital white matter*
Adrenoleukodystrophy
Multiple sclerosis

H. *Symmetric small well-defined paratrigonal low densities*
Krabbe's disease

I. *Low-density lesions mainly in frontal regions with involvement of lentiform nuclei*
Alexander's leukodystrophy
African trypanosomiasis

J. Well-defined low densities in basal ganglia
Subacute necrotizing encephalomyelopathy
Wilson's disease
Mitochondrial cytopathy
Pyruvate decarboxylase deficiency

From: Kendall (1982)

Oculocraniosomatic neuromuscular disease with ragged-red fibers
This is a disease of childhood onset characterized by a wide spectrum of abnormalities which includes ataxia, mild mental impairment, raised CSF protein levels, ophthalmoplegia and ptosis, pigment changes in the retina, cardiac conduction defects, and a tendency for a development of diabetes mellitus.

215

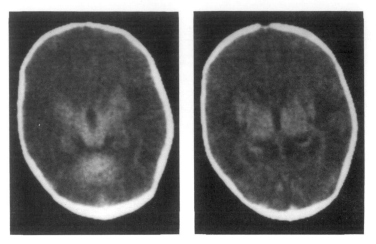

Fig. 10.5. Hyperammonemia. Three-week-old male neonate. Non-contrast head CT scans demonstrate diffuse low density of the white matter.

Mitochondrial abnormalities are present and numerous ragged-red fibers are found (Bertorini *et al.* 1978).

The CT findings confirm the histopathologic lesion of diffuse leuco-encephalopathy. Diffuse leuco-encephalopathy was described by Bertorini *et al.* (1978) in young patients, aged 20 years or younger. Enhancement did not occur after administration of contrast medium. Marked sulcal dilatation may be observed in some cases. Cavitation due to spongiform degeneration may occur frequently in cases of childhood onset. Calcification of the basal ganglia may also occur (Kendall 1982).

Metabolic disorders
Hyperammonemia
The many diverse disorders associated with hyperammonemia have been divided into three main categories by Greenwood *et al.* (1983). These are the urea cycle defects, metabolic defects (*e.g.* methylmalonic acidemia, propionic acidemia), and miscellaneous disorders (including stress, Reye's syndrome, hypoxia, infections and toxins, prematurity, and excessive protein intake).

Urea cycle defects
The disorders in this category include ornithine transcarbamylase deficiency, carbomoyl phosphate synthetase deficiency, citrullinemia, argininosuccinic aciduria, and arginase deficiency.

Ornithine transcarbamylase deficiency
This is the commonest inborn error involving the urea cycle (Kendall *et al.* 1983). This disorder is transmitted as an x-linked recessive trait (Short *et al.* 1973). The enzyme is partially deficient in females, but absent in males (Campbell *et al.* 1973). The clinical picture is devastating in males, and many die within the neonatal period.

The CT appearances, as described by Kendall *et al.* (1983) are variable, depending on the duration and severity of the hyperammonemia and age of the patient. A normal scan may be obtained prior to the development of edema. Thereafter diffuse low density of the white matter with small ventricles is noted as a consequence of brain swelling (Fig. 10.5). The low-density white matter changes were partly reversible following a low-protein diet in one patient. Cerebral atrophy may occur as a result of hyperammonemia in cases of prolonged survival.

Carbomoyl phosphate synthetase deficiency
Cortical atrophy or ventricular dilatation are the CT findings described by Walser (1983).

Methylmalonic and propionic acidemias
Methylmalonic acidemia and propionic acidemia are inborn errors of metabolism due to specific enzyme deficiencies. Keto-acidosis, which is an early feature of both disorders, is the cause of neurologic abnormalities. The diagnosis of both conditions is made biochemically, with normal neurologic development after appropriate therapy.

The CT findings common to both types of acidemia have been described by Gabarski *et al.* (1983). The appearances on CT are directly related to the severity of illness. With mild clinical impairment, small areas of decreased density may be detected in white matter; whereas severely affected patients may exhibit leuco-encephalopathy, with diffuse loss of cerebral substance.

Reye's syndrome
A rapidly progressive encephalopathy following varicella or upper respiratory infection was described by Reye *et al.* (1963). It may occur at any age, but is commonest in white children between six and 12 years of age, especially in rural communities (DeVivo 1982).

The underlying etiology isolated has been influenza A and B in the 10- to 14-year age-group, and varicella has been the cause in the five- to nine-year age-group (LaMontagne 1980). Impairment of immune responses to viral infection following toxic chemical exposure has been postulated by Mullen (1978).

The typical clinical presentation is that of an initial upper respiratory infection or varicella, followed by a short period of clinical improvement. Profuse vomiting is the first symptom of encephalopathy, associated with anorexia, nausea and listlessness . Some patients recover at this stage, whereas others develop neurologic symptoms and signs. In the milder form there are cognitive and behavioral disturbances. Usually these patients become delirious, irritable and disoriented, followed by light coma with accompanying decorticate posturing. Deterioration leads to deepening coma with decerebrate posturing. A few patients will progress beyond this phase and lose brainstem function. They are flaccid, areflexic and apneic with systemic hypotension.

The laboratory findings are of initial hyperammonemia which usually returns to

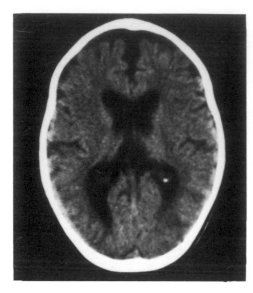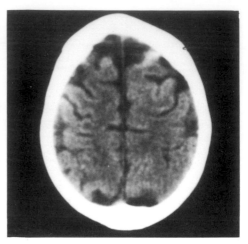

Fig. 10.6. Hurler syndrome. Three-year-old boy. Non-contrast head CT scans show hydrocephalus and prominent sulci.

normal within 48 to 72 hours. The elevated serum transaminases and prolonged prothrombin time are other important biochemical abnormalities.

The pathologic findings are characteristic. The liver is swollen with lipid, mitochondria are abnormal in appearance, and there is glycogen depletion. The brain is edematous with accumulation of intacellular fluid, and abnormal neuronal mitochondria (DeVivo 1978).

CT appearances
Two cases described by Giannotta *et al.* (1978) exhibited evidence of cerebral edema. Marked dilatation of the cerebral vasculature over both hemispheres was demonstrated, especially prominent in the region of large cortical vessels. The vasodilatation is attributed to the high serum ammonia levels (Altenau *et al.* 1976, Giannotta *et al.* 1978).

Nonketotic hyperglycinemia
Nonketotic hyperglycinemia is an inborn error of metabolism due to a block of glycine cleavage. Large amounts of glycine accumulate in body fluids. This disorder is a relatively frequent metabolic cause of overwhelming illness in the first year of life (Nyhan 1983). Abnormal muscle tone and reflexes, pronounced developmental delay and seizures commence in early infancy, with early death in most cases (Langan and Pueschel 1983).

The CT appearances are of hypodensity of the corpus callosum, which may be a specific finding, and white matter (Valavanis *et al.* 1981).

Maple syrup urine disease
Maple syrup urine disease (branched chain ketonuria) is an inborn error of

218

metabolism due to a defect in oxidative decarboxylation. Plasma levels of leucine, isoleucine, valine and keto-acids are elevated. Convulsant stupor, coma with opisthotonus and respiratory difficulty is the presentation of the classic form (Adams and Lyon 1982).

The CT appearances are of well-defined symmetric low-density areas throughout the deep cerebral white matter. Extension almost to the subcortical regions in the anterior half of the frontal lobe have been described (Kendall 1981).

Mucopolysaccharidoses

The mucopolysaccharidoses are a hereditary group of lysosomal storage disorders in which there is accumulation of mucopolysaccharides in various tissues. The original classification of five types has been extended to eight types (McKusick *et al.* 1965, 1978; McKusick and Pyeritz 1980).

Type	Syndrome
IH	Hurler syndrome
IS	Scheie syndrome
I H/S	Hurler-Scheie syndrome
II	Hunter syndrome
III (A,B,C)	Sanfilippo syndrome (A,B,C)
IV (A,B)	Morquio syndrome (A,B)
V	No longer used
VI	Maroteaux-Lamy syndrome
VII	Sly syndrome
VIII	DiFerrante syndrome

There is a deficiency of a specific lysosomal enzyme which is required to break down the two mucopolysaccharides, heparan sulfate and dermatan sulfate in all of the disorders except type IV which involves keratan sulfate (McKusick *et al.* 1965).

The disorders are progressive, with varying severity. Skeletal involvement (dysostosis multiplex) is present in all cases, accompanied with joint changes and limitation of movement in most. Multiple organ systems are involved with each disorder. Hepatosplenomegaly and cardiovascular involvement is frequent (McKusick *et al.* 1965). Clouding of the cornea is present in several disorders.

CT appearances

The CT appearances of mucopolysaccharidoses have been described by Watts *et al.* (1981).

WHITE MATTER LOW DENSITY

There is symmetric low density in the white matter, indicative of increased water content. This was demonstrated in patients with types IH, IH/S, II, IIIB, IV but not in type IS. The low density is more marked around dilated frontal horns, but may extend laterally. Parietal white matter was also involved.

HYDROCEPHALUS

Moderately severe communicating hydrocephalus was demonstrated in some patients with type IH, IS, II and IIIB disorders (Fig. 10.6). Hydrocephalus is commonly found at autopsy in these patients. The observations of Watts *et al.* (1981) show that hydrocephalus can occur at an early stage of the disease; if diagnosed, it may be ameliorated by ventricular shunting which, although palliative, may improve the quality of life.

ATROPHIC CHANGES

Widening of the Sylvian, and occasionally of the interhemispheric fissures or cortical sulci, was observed.

ENLARGEMENT OF THE SKULL

The bones of the skull vault may be thickened due to the deposition of the mucopolysaccharides or due to bone deposition of the inner skull table following relief of hydrocephalus.

ATLANTO-AXIAL SUBLUXATION

Spinal-cord compression may result from atlanto-axial subluxation in type IV (Morquio) and type VI (Maroteaux-Lamy disease). The subluxation is usually associated with laxity of the transverse odontoid ligament, but may also be due to hypoplasia or absence of the odontoid (Blaw and Langer 1969). CT of the upper cervical spine and skull base is thus suggested when the head CT study is performed.

Gangliosidoses

The gangliosidoses are disorders of lipid metabolism, characterized by the excessive accumulation of ganglioside in various soft tissue sites. There are two major groups, Gm_1 and Gm_2, each transmitted as an autosomal recessive trait.

Gm_1 gangliosidoses are due to deficiency of B-galactosidase. More than five subgroups are recognized. There is a wide range of presentation, from the acute infant onset with rapid neurologic decline and marked bony abnormalities, to those with survival into adulthood with normal intelligence (O'Brien 1983).

Excessive accumulation of Gm_2 gangliosidoses occurs in four disorders: Tay-Sachs disease (type 1) due to deficiency of hexosaminidase A, Sandhoff's disease (type 2) due to severe deficiency of hexosaminidase A and B, juvenile Gm_2 gangliosidoses (type 3), and adult Gm_2 gangliosidoses caused by deficiency of hexosaminidase A.

CT appearances

At present there is a paucity of CT descriptions of these disorders in the literature. A few cases of Gm_1 and Gm_2 gangliosidoses with appearances similar to Canavan's spongiform encephalopathy have been described (Kendall 1982).

Wilson's disease

Wilson's disease (hepatolenticular degeneration) is an autosomal recessive disorder due to an abnormality of copper metabolism, which results in the heavy deposition of copper in tissues especially the nervous system, corneas, liver and the kidneys. Since the original description by Wilson in 1912 numerous etiologies have been

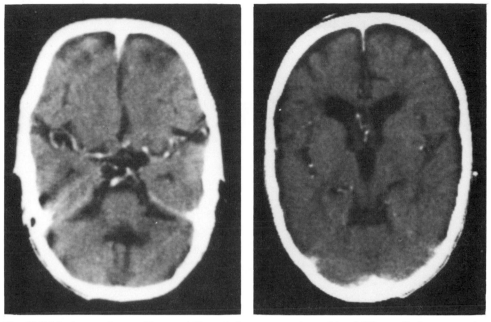

Fig. 10.7. Menkes syndrome. 11-year-old boy. *Left:* contrast-enhanced head CT scan displays tortuosity of the middle cerebral arteries bilaterally. *Right:* ventricular enlargement and atrophic changes are demonstrated.

postulated, including abnormalities of ceruloplasmin synthesis and copper binding, and copper transport across the lysosomal membrane (Sass-Kortsak and Bearn 1978).

The disease is characterized by cerebral degenerative change, especially in the basal ganglia, and hepatic cirrhosis. Greenish-brown Kayser-Fleischer rings at the limbus of the cornea are pathognomonic. The CT appearance is of low-density areas within the basal ganglia without contrast enhancement (Nelson *et al.* 1979).

Menkes disease

Menkes disease (Menkes kinky hair syndrome, or trichopoliodystrophy) is a rare sex-linked progressive neurodegenerative disorder, first described by Menkes *et al.* in 1962. This disease can begin *in utero* and may be recognized at birth (Grover *et al.* 1979). Only males are affected, with an incidence of one in 40,000 livebirths in some areas (Danks *et al.* 1971).

Most patients expire before two years of age; the longest known surviving patient, currently being treated at St. Christopher's Hospital for Children in Philadelphia is 11 years old.

There is abnormality of copper metabolism. Intestinal absorption of copper is defective, possibly due to the transport mechanism within the cells or across the membrane on the serosal aspect (Danks *et al.* 1973). Clinical features include psychomotor retardation, growth failure, seizures, hypothermia and abnormalities

TABLE 10.2

Basal ganglia calcification

Congenital	Idiopathic cerebrovascular ferrocalcinosis (Fahr's disease)
	Tuberous sclerosis
	Cockayne syndrome
	Oculocraniosomatic disease (Kearns-Sayre syndrome)
	Amaurotic idiocy
Infective	Cytomegalic inclusion disease
	Toxoplasmosis
	Post-viral encephalitis
	Congenital rubella
	Cysticercosis
Metabolic	Hypoparathyroidism
	Pseudohypoparathyroidism
	Pseudopseudohypoparathyroidism
	Secondary hyperparathyroidism
	Acquired immune deficiency syndrome
Vascular	Angioma
	Aneurysm
Neoplastic	Glioma
Toxins	Methotrexate
	Carbon monoxide
	Lead
	Radiation

of hair. Scalp hair is sparse, coarse, stubbly and devoid of pigment (Menkes *et al.* 1962). The microscopic appearance is of twisting of the hair shaft (pili torti). A wide variety of developmental abnormalities have been described in this disorder, including high arched palate, pectus excavatum, inguinal and hiatal hernias, undescended testes and club feet (Greenwood *et al.* 1983). Multiple bladder diverticula, considered to be acquired, have been described by Harcke *et al.* (1977).

Osseous changes consisting of flared ribs, bilateral metaphyseal spurring, and parietal wormian bones in the skull have been described by Wesenberg *et al.* (1969). These authors have also described tortuosity of the intracranial arterial vasculature, with supernumerary branches of the anterior and middle cerebral arteries.

CT appearances (Fig. 10.7)

The CT appearances were first described by Seay *et al.* (1979). Initially the CT scan may appear normal. With progressive decrease in head size or even with normal head growth, ventricular enlargement, cerebral atrophy and extra-axial low-density fluid collections may be demonstrated. The fluid collection is considered to be due to subdural effusion secondary to the marked cerebral atrophy, and also to tearing of cortical veins as the brain is separated from the dura. Diffuse multifocal low-density areas have also been noted, attributed to infarction and edema. Arterial tortuosity has been noted on CT in one patient in our series (Fig. 10.7).

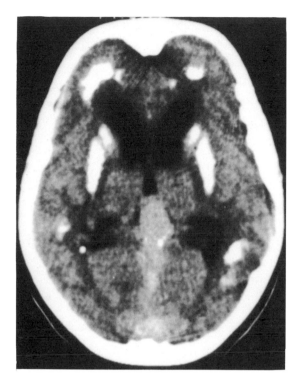

Fig. 10.8. Fahr's syndrome. 14-year-old girl with mental deterioration, seizures and headaches. Non-contrast head CT scan demonstrates calcification in the basal ganglia and cerebral cortex bilaterally.

Basal ganglia calcification
Calcification of the basal ganglia is readily detected by CT, which has greater sensitivity than skull radiographs for the detection of calcium. Numerous disorders may have associated basal ganglia calcification. In many instances there are distinguishing features, and the calcification will also be distributed through the cerebral parenchyma. Table 10.2 incorporates the varied causes, including those described by Reeder and Felson (1975), Harwood-Nash and Fitz (1976), and Weisberg *et al.* (1984).

Idiopathic familial cerebrovascular ferrocalcinosis (Fahr's disease)
Intracranial calcification, associated with progressive mental deterioration, severe growth disorder and familial occurrence, was originally described by Bamberger (1856). This entity is now more commonly known as Fahr's disease, although Fahr (1930) actually described an adult case rather than familial cases occurring in infancy and childhood (Babbitt *et al.* 1969).

   This is a disorder of unknown origin, with normal serum calcium and phosphorous levels, and an absence of somatic or endocrine abnormalities. The symmetric calcification within the basal ganglia and cerebral cortex is readily apparent on non-contrast CT (Fig. 10.8). Calcification may also be noted in the vermis, dentate nucleus, and surrounding cerebellar white matter (Kuroiwa *et al.* 1982).

223

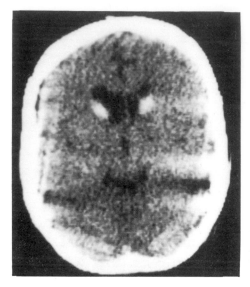

Fig. 10.9. Oculocraniosomatic disease (Kearns-Sayre syndrome). Non-contrast head CT scan demonstrates bilateral symmetric calcification within the basal ganglia. (Courtesy of Samuel Wolpert MD, Boston.)

Oculocraniosomatic disease (Kearns-Sayre syndrome)

The triad of external ophthalmoplegia, retinitis pigmentosa and complete heart block was first described by Kearns and Sayre in 1958. The etiology and pathogenesis of this syndrome are unknown.

Neurosensory hearing loss, decreased intelligence and cerebellar ataxia may be additional features to the classic triad. An abnormal electro-encephalogram and elevated cerebrospinal fluid protein are frequently encountered (Seigel *et al.* 1979). The onset is usually under 20 years of age.

CT appearances

The CT findings, as described by Seigel *et al.* (1979), include calcification of the basal ganglia and white matter of the cerebral hemispheres, low-density areas within the parietocentral white matter, thalamus, midbrain and cerebellar hemispheres in some patients (Fig. 10.9). Cerebellar hypoplasia was noted in one patient in this series.

Renal failure

Neurologic abnormalities contribute largely to the morbidity associated with renal failure (Cooper *et al.* 1978). Central nervous system abnormalities have been correlated with renal failure (secondary hyperparathyroidism) in the presence of elevated parathormone levels and elevated brain calcium content (Cogan *et al.* 1978). The mechanism of action of parathormone on brain tissue remains unknown.

CT findings

Cerebral subcortical calcification has been described in patients with severe chronic

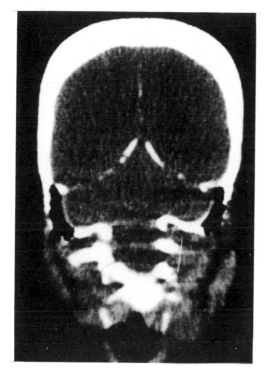

Fig. 10.10. Renal failure. 18-year-old male with chronic renal disease. Coronal non-contrast head CT scan demonstrates calcification within the falx cerebri and tentorium cerebelli. (Courtesy of Ehsan Afshani MD, Buffalo.)

renal failure (Swartz *et al.* 1983). Calcification was also noted in the basal ganglia (Fig. 10.10). Cortical atrophy has also been reported in children with end-stage renal disease (Schnaper and Robson 1964).

Methotrexate encephalopathy

The central nervous system is involved in 50 to 75 per cent of cases of childhood leukemia, and is also the most frequent site of relapse in acute leukemia treated with combination therapy (Evans *et al.* 1970, Aur *et al.* 1972, Price and Johnson 1973). As a consequence, therapy consisting of craniospinal radiation and intrathecal chemotherapeutic agents such as cytosine arabinoside and methotrexate have been used before involvement of the central nervous system is clinically detected.

The administration of intrathecal methotrexate may however result in methotrexate encephalopathy (Kay *et al.* 1972, Price and Jamieson 1975, Rubinstein *et al.* 1975). Multiple foci of necrosis involving the white matter are demonstrated in the brain tissue of these patients examined histopathologically (Rubinstein *et al.* 1975). The demyelination process has been attributed to the antifolic acid process of methotrexate (Kay *et al.* 1972, Norrell *et al.* 1974). Intracranial calcification may also be present within the cerebral and cerebellar hemispheres (Flament-Durand *et al.* 1975). The appearances may simulate the Sturge-Weber syndrome on plain skull radiographs (Borns and Rancier 1974).

225

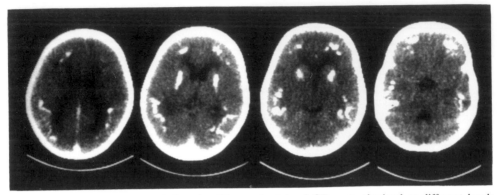

Fig. 10.11. Methotrexate encephalopathy. Non-contrast head CT scans obtained at different levels demonstrate symmetric bilateral basal ganglia and parenchymal calcification. (Courtesy of Smauel Wolpert MD, Boston.)

CT appearances

The CT appearances of methotrexate encephalopathy as described by Mueller *et al.* (1976) and Peylan-Ramu *et al.* (1977) include: (i) symmetric areas of low density, related to demyelinization and edema, in the centrum semiovale of each hemisphere and the periventricular regions of the lateral ventricles. This process commences anteriorly with posterior extension later, in contrast to adrenoleukodystrophy where the initial changes are noted posterior to the lateral ventricles. Contrast enhancement has not been demonstrated; (ii) ventricular dilatation is frequently observed; (iii) calcification may be present in the basal ganglia and gray matter (Fig. 10.11).

Carbon monoxide poisoning

Carbon monoxide poisoning impedes the release of oxygen from hemoglobin in tissues, resulting in hypoxia (Lilienthal 1950). The brain is the organ most affected.

CT appearances

Symmetric low-density lesions of the basal ganglia are the commonest abnormalities (Kim *et al.* 1980). This region is susceptible to hypoxic change, as it is an end arterial zone subject to hypoperfusion following systemic hypotension. Contrast enhancement in the basal ganglia has been described by Nardizzi (1979), demonstrated eight days after the acute carbon monoxide poisoning.

Diffuse white matter low-density lesions have also been noted by Kim *et al.* (1980). The low density is considered to represent incomplete necrosis resulting in demyelination and gliosis. Dilatation of the lateral ventricles and widening of the cortical sulci have been noted at a later stage.

Drowning

The arrest of alveolar oxygen exchange and development of cerebral hypoxia following drowning lead to decreased cerebral bloodflow. The CT appearances in two young patients who had drowned have been described by Murray *et al.* (1984). Low-density areas in the medial temporal lobes and midbrain were noted in one patient aged three years, and similar appearances in the posterior portions of the globus pallidus were demonstrated bilaterally in a 19-month-old patient. The bilateral lucencies of the globus pallidus suggest serious hypoxic cerebral insult.

The putamen and globus pallidus are especially vulnerable to critical reduction in bloodflow (Ames *et al.* 1968) and thus the bilateral low-density areas in the globus pallidus on CT suggest a major hypoxic cerebral insult (Murray *et al.* 1984).

REFERENCES

Adams, R. D., Lyon, G. (1982) *Neurology of Hereditary Metabolic Diseases of Children.* Washington: Hemisphere. pp. 1–442.

Aita, J. F., Bennett, D. F., Anderson, R. E., Ziter, F. (1978) 'Cranial CT appearance of acute multiple sclerosis.' *Neurology,* **28,** 251–255.

Alexander, W. S. (1949) 'Progressive fibrinoid degeneration of fibrillary atrocytes associated with mental retardation in a hydrocephalic infant.' *Brain,* **72,** 373–381.

Allen, R. J. (1982) 'Disorders primarily of white matter.' *In:* Swaiman, K. F., Wright, F. S. (Eds.) *The Practice of Pediatric Neurology.* St. Louis: C. V. Mosby. pp. 885–900.

Altenau, L. L., Kindt, G. W., Chandler, W. F. (1976) 'Effect of elevated serum ammonia on intracranial pressure.' *Surgical Forum,* **27,** 490–491.

Alzheimer, A. (1910) 'Beiträge zur Kenntnis der pathologische Neuroglia und ihrer Beziehungen zu den Abbausorgangen im Nervengewebe.' *In:* Nissl, F., Alzheimer, A. *Histologische und histopathologische Arbeiten über die Grosshirnrinde, Vol. 3.* Jena: Gustav Fischer Verlag. p. 401.

Ames, A., Wright, L., Kowada, M., Thurston, J. M., Majno, G. (1968) 'Cerebral ischemia: the no-reflow phenomenon.' *American Journal of Pathology,* **52,** 437–447.

Armstrong, D., Dimmitts, S., Van Wormer, D. E. (1974) 'Studies in Batten's disease. I: Peroxidase deficiency in granulocytes.' *Archives of Neurology,* **30,** 144–152.

Auborg, P., Diebler, C. (1982) 'Adrenoleukodystrophy—its diverse CT appcarances and an evolutive or phenotypic variant.' *Neuroradiology,* **24,** 33–42.

Aur, R. J. A., Simone, J. V., Hutsu, H. O., Verzosa, M. S. (1972) 'A comparative study of central nervous irradiation and intensive chemotherapy early in remission of childhood acute lymphocytic leukemia.' *Cancer,* **29,** 381–391.

Babbitt, D. P., Tang, T., Dobbs, J., Berk, R. (1969) 'Idiopathic familial cerebrovascular ferrocalcinosis (Fahr's disease) and review of differential diagnosis of intracranial calcification in children.' *American Journal of Roentgenology,* **105,** 352–358.

Bamberger, H. (1856) 'Beobachtungen und bemerkungen über Hirnkrankheiten.' *Verhandlung der physikalische Medizin Gesellschaft Wurzburg,* **6,** 325–328.

Banker, B. Q., Robertson, J. T., Victor, M. (1964) 'Spongy degeneration of the central nervous system in infancy.' *Neurology,* **14,** 981–1001.

Barnes, D. R., Enzmann, D. (1981) 'The evolution of white matter disease as seen on computed tomography.' *Radiology,* **138,** 379–383.

Belin, J., Pettet, N., Smith, A. D., Thompson, R. H. S., Zilkha, K. J. (1971) 'Linoleate metabolism in multiple sclerosis.' *Journal of Neurology, Neurosurgery and Psychiatry,* **34,** 25–29.

Bertorini, E., Engel, W. K., DiChiro, G., Dalakas, M. (1978) 'Leukoencephalopathy in oculocraniosomatic neuromuscular disease with ragged-red fibers.' *Archives of Neurology,* **35,** 643–647.

Blaw, M. E., Langer, L. O. (1969) 'Spinal cord compression in Morquio-Brailsford's disease.' *Journal of Pediatrics,* **74,** 593–600.

Boltshauser, E., Isler, W. (1976) 'Computerized axial tomography in spongy degeneration.' *Lancet,* **1,** 1123.

—— Speiss, H., Isler, W. (1978) 'CT in neurodegenerative disorders in childhood.' *Neuroradiology,* **16,** 41–43.

Borns, P. F., Rancier, L. F. (1974) 'Cerebral calcifications in childhood leukemia mimicking Sturge–Weber syndrome.' *American Journal of Roentgenology,* **122,** 52–55.

Buonanno, F. S., Ball, M. R., Laster, W., Moody, D. M., McLean, W. T. (1978) 'Computed tomography in late infantile metachromatic leukodystrophy.' *Annals of Neurology,* **4,** 43–46.

Cala, L. A., Mastaglia, F. L. (1976) 'Computerized axial tomography in multiple sclerosis.' *Lancet,* **1,** 689.

Campbell, A. G. M. Rosenberg, L. E., Snodgrass, P. J., Nuzum, C. T. (1973) 'Ornithine transcarbamoylase deficiency.' *New England Journal of Medicine,* **288,** 1–6.

Chaves, E., Frank, L. M. (1983) 'Disorders of basal ganglia, cerebellum, brainstem and cranial nerves.' *In:* Farmer, T. (Ed.) *Pediatric Neurology.* Philadelphia: Harper & Row. pp. 605–648.

Cockayne, E. A. (1936) 'Dwarfism with retinal atrophy and deafness.' *Archives of Diseases in Childhood,* **11,** 1–8.

Cogan, M. G., Covey, C. M., Arieff, A. I., Wisniewski, A., Clark, O. H. (1978) 'Central nervous system manifestations of hyperparathyroidism.' *American Journal of Medicine,* **65,** 963–970.

Cole, G., DeVilliers, F., Proctor, N. S. F., Freiman, I., Bill, P. (1979) 'Alexander's disease: case report including histopathological and electron microscopic features.' *Journal of Neurology, Neurosurgery and Psychiatry,* **42,** 619–624.

Cooper, J. D., Lazarowitz, V. C., Arieff, A. I. (1978) 'Neurodiagnostic abnormalities in patients with acute renal failure.' *Journal of Clinical Investigation,* **61,** 1448–1455.

Danks, D. M., Cartwright, E., Campbell, P. E., Mayne, V. (1971) 'Is Menkes' syndrome a heritable disorder of connective tissue?' *Lancet,* **2,** 1089.

—— —— Stevens, B. J., Townley, R. R. W. (1973) 'Menkes' kinky hair disease: further definition of the defect in copper transport.' *Science,* **179,** 1140–1142.

DeVivo, D. (1978) 'Reye syndrome: a metabolic response to an acute mitochondrial insult?' *Neurology,* **28,** 105–108.

—— (1982) 'Acute encephalopathies of childhood.' *In:* Rudolph, A. M., Hoffman, J. I. E. (Eds.) *Pediatrics. 17th edn.* Norwalk, Connecticut: Appleton–Century–Crofts. pp. 1605–1613.

DiChiro, G., Eiben, R. M., Manz, H. J., Jacobs, I. B., Schellinger, D. (1980) 'A new CT pattern in adrenoleukodystrophy.' *Radiology,* **137,** 687–692.

Dubal, L., Wiggli, U. (1977) 'Tomochemistry of the brain.' *Journal of Computer Assisted Tomography,* **1,** 300–307.

Dubois, P. J., Freemark, M., Lewis, D., Drayer, B. P., Heinz, E. R., Osborne, D. (1981) 'Atypical findings in adrenoleukodystrophy.' *Journal of Computer Assisted Tomography,* **5,** 888–891.

Dulaney, J. T., Moser, H. W. (1978) 'Sulfatide lipidosis: metachromatic leukodystrophy.' *In:* Stanbury, J. B., Wyngarden, J. B., Frederickson, O. S. (Eds.) *The Metabolic Basis of Inherited Disease. 4th edn.* New York: McGraw–Hill. pp. 770–809.

Eiben, R. M., DiChiro, G. (1977) 'Computer assisted tomography in adrenoleukodystrophy.' *Journal of Computer Assisted Tomography,* **1,** 308–314.

Evans, A. E., Gilbert, E. S., Zandstra, R. (1970) 'The increasing incidence of central nervous system leukemia in children.' *Cancer,* **26,** 404–409.

Fahr, T. (1930) 'Idiopathische verkalkung der Hirngefasse.' *Zentralblatt für allgemeine Pathologie und pathologische Anatomie,* **50,** 129–133.

Flament-Durand, J., Ketelbant-Balasse, P., Maurus, R., Regnier, R., Spehl, M. (1975) 'Intracerebral calcifications appearing during the course of acute lymphacytic leukemia treated with methotrexate and x-rays.' *Cancer,* **35,** 319–325.

Friede, R. L. (1975) *Developmental Neuropathology.* Berlin: Springer-Verlag. pp. 408–423.

Gabarski, S. S., Gabrielson, T. O., Knake, J. E., Latack, J. T. (1983) 'Cerebral CT findings in methylmalonic and propionic acidemias.' *American Journal of Neuroradiology,* **4,** 955–957.

Giannotta, S. L., Hopkins, J., Kindt, G. W. (1978) 'Computerized tomography in Reye's syndrome: evidence for pathological cerebral vasodilatation.' *Neurosurgery,* **2,** 201–204.

Greenberg, H. S., Halverson, D., Lane, B. (1977) 'CT scanning and diagnosis of adrenoleuko-dystrophy.' *Neurology,* **27,** 884–886.

Greenwood, R. S., Kahler, S. G., Aylsworth, A. S. (1983) 'Inherited metabolic diseases.' *In:* Farmer, T. W. (Ed.) *Pediatric Neurology.* Philadelphia: Harper & Row. pp. 281–401.

Grover, W. D., Johnson, W. C., Henkin, R. I. (1979) 'Clinical and biochemical aspects of trichopoliodystrophy.' *Annals of Neurology,* **5,** 65–71.

Haas, J. E., Johnson, E. S., Farrell, D. L. (1982) 'Neonatal-onset adrenoleukodystrophy in a girl.' *Annals of Neurology,* **12,** 449–457.

Hall, K., Gardner-Medwin, D. (1978) 'CT scan appearances in Leigh's disease (subacute necrotizing encephalopathy).' *Neuroradiology,* **16,** 48–50.

Harcke, H. T., Jr., Capitanio, M. A., Grover, W. D., Valdez-Dapena, M. (1977) 'Bladder diverticula and Menkes' syndrome.' *Radiology,* **124,** 459–461.

Harwood-Nash, D. C., Fitz, C. R. (1976) *Neuroradiology in Infants and Children.* St. Louis: C. V.

Mosby.

Heinz, E. R. (1984) 'Normal and abnormal white matter.' *In:* Rosenberg, R. N. (Ed.) *The Clinical Neurosciences. Volume 4: Neuroradiology.* New York: Churchill Livingstone. pp. 595–623.

——— Drayer, B. P., Haengelli, C. A., Painter, M. J., Crumrine, P. (1979) 'Computed tomography in white matter disease.' *Radiology*, **130**, 371–378.

Holland, I. M., Kendall, B. E. (1980) 'Computed tomography in Alexander's disease.' *Neuroradiology*, **20**, 103-106.

Huckman, M. S., Fox, J. H., Ramsey, R. G. (1977) 'Computed tomography in the diagnosis of degenerative diseases of the brain.' *Seminars in Roentgenology*, **12**, 63–75.

Inoue, Y., Fukuda, T., Takashima, S., Ochi, H., Onoyama, Y., Kusuda, S., Matsuoka, O., Murata, R. (1983) 'Adrenoleukodystrophy: new CT findings.' *American Journal of Neuroradiology*, **4**, 951–954.

Johnson, W. G. (1982) 'Leukodystrophies.' *In:* Rudolph, A., Hoffman, J. I. E. (Eds.) *Pediatrics. 17th edn.* Norwalk, Connecticut: Appleton–Century–Crofts. pp. 1750–1752.

Kay, H. E. M., Knapton, P. J., O'Sullivan, J. P., Wells, D. G., Harris, R. F., Innes, E. M., Stuart, J., Schwartz, F. C. M., Thompson, E. N. (1972) 'Encephalopathy in acute leukemia associated with methotrexate therapy.' *Archives of Disease in Childhood*, **47**, 344–354.

Kearns, T. P., Sayre, G. P. (1958) 'Retinitis pigmentosa, external ophthalmoplegia and complete heart block.' *Archives of Ophthalmology*, **60**, 280–289.

Kendall, B. (1981) 'Computed tomography in diagnosing metabolic disorders in children.' *In:* Margulis, A. R., Gooding, C. A. (Eds.) *Diagnostic Radiology.* San Francisco: University of California Press. pp. 313–318.

——— (1982) 'Cranial CT scans in metabolic diseases involving the CNS of children.' *Resident and Staff Physician*, **32**, 33–42.

——— Kingsley, D. (1978) 'The value of computerized axial tomography in craniocerebral malformations.' *British Journal of Radiology*, **51**, 171–190.

——— ——— Leonard, J. V., Lingam, S., Oberholzer, V. G. (1983) 'Neurological features and computed tomography of the brain in children with ornithine carbamoyl transferase deficiency.' *Journal of Neurology, Neurosurgery and Psychiatry*, **46**, 28–34.

Kim, K. S., Weinberg, P. E., Suh, J. H., Ho, S. U. (1980) 'Acute carbon monoxide poisoning: computed tomography of the brain.' *American Journal of Neuroradiology*, **1**, 339–402.

Kingsley, D. P. E., Kendall, B. E. (1981) 'Demyelinating and neurodegenerative disease in childhood: CT appearances and their differential diagnoses.' *Journal of Neuroradiology*, **8**, 243–255.

Krabbe, K. (1916) 'A new familial infantile form of diffuse brain sclerosis.' *Brain*, **39**, 73-114.

Kwan, E., Drace, J., Enzmann, D. (1984) 'Specific CT findings in Krabbe disease.' *American Journal of Neuroradiology*, **5**, 453–458.

Kuroiwa, Y., Mayron, M. S., Boller, F., Boller, M. (1982) 'Computed tomographic visualization of extensive calcinosis in a patient with idiopathic familial basal ganglia calcification.' *Archives of Neurology*, **39**, 603.

Kurtzke, J. F., Bebbe, G. W., Norman, J. E., Jr. (1979) 'Migration and multiple sclerosis in the United States.' *Neurology*, **29**, 579. *(Abstract.)*

LaMontagne, J. R. (1980) 'Summary of a workshop on influenza B viruses and Reye's syndrome.' *Journal of Infectious Diseases*, **142**, 452–465.

Lane, B., Carroll, B. A., Pedley, T. A. (1978) 'Computerized cranial tomography in cerebral diseases of white matter.' *Neurology*, **28**, 534–544.

Langan, T., Peuschel, S. M. (1983) 'Nonketotic hyperglycemia: clinical, biochemical and therapeutic considerations.' *Current Problems in Pediatrics*, **13**, 1–30.

Lebow, S., Anderson, D. C., Mastri, A., Larson, D. (1978) 'Acute multiple sclerosis with contrast-enhancing plaques.' *Archives of Neurology*, **35**, 435–439.

Leigh, D. (1951) 'Subacute necrotizing encephalomyelopathy in an infant.' *Journal of Neurology, Neurosurgery and Psychiatry*, **14**, 216–221.

Lilienthal, J. L. (1950) 'Carbon monoxide.' *Pharmacological Reviews*, **2**, 324–354.

Marano, G. D., Goodwin, C. A., Ko, J. P. (1980) 'Atypical contrast enhancement in computerized tomography of demyelinating disease.' *Archives of Neurology*, **37**, 523–524.

McKusick, V. A., Kaplan, D., Wise, D., Hanley, W. D., Suddarth, S. D., Sevick, M. E., Maumenee, A. W. (1965) 'The genetic mucopolysaccharidoses.' *Medicine*, **44**, 445–483.

——— Neufeld, E. F., Kelly, T. E. (1978) 'The mucopolysaccharide storage diseases.' *In:* Stanbury, J. B., Wyngaarden, J. B., Fredrickson, D. S. (Eds.) *The Metabolic Basis of Inherited Disease, 4th edn.* New York: McGraw-Hill. pp. 1282–1307.

——— Pyeritz, R. E. (1980) 'Genetic heterogeneity and allelic variation in the mucopolysaccharidoses.'

229

Johns Hopkins Medical Journal, **146,** 71–79.

Menkes, J. H., Alter, M., Steigleder, G. K., Weakley, D. R., Sung, J. H. (1962) 'A sex-linked recessive disorder with retardation of growth, peculiar hair, and focal cerebral and cerebellar degeneration.' *Pediatrics,* **29,** 764–779.

Merzbacher, L. (1910) 'Eine eigenartige familiär-hereditäre Erkrankungsform. (Aplasia axialis extracorticalis congenita).' *Zeitschrift für der gesamte Neurologie und Psychiatrie,* **3,** 1–138.

Morariu, M. A., Wilkins, D. E., Patel, S. (1980) 'Multiple sclerosis and serial computerized tomography.' *Archives of Neurology,* **37,** 189–190.

Mueller, S., Bell, W., Seibert, J. (1976) 'Cerebral calcifications associated with intrathecal methotrexate therapy in acute lymphocytic leukemia.' *Journal of Pediatrics,* **88,** 650–653.

Mullen, P. W. (1978) 'Immunopharmacological considerations in Reye's syndrome: a possible xenobiotic initiated disorder?' *Biochemical Pharmacology,* **27,** 145–149.

Murray, R. R., Kapila, A., Blanco, E., Kagan-Hallet, K. S. (1984) 'Cerebral computed tomography in drowning victims.' *American Journal of Neuroradiology,* **5,** 177–179.

Namiki, H. (1965) 'Subacute necrotizing encephalomyelopathy. Case report with special emphasis on associated pathology of peripheral nervous system.' *Archives of Neurology,* **12,** 98–107.

Nardizzi, L. R. (1979) 'Computed tomographic correlate of carbon monoxide poisoning.' *Archives of Neurology,* **36,** 38–39.

Nelson, R. F., Guzman, D. A., Grahovac, Z., Howse, D. C. N. (1979) 'Computerized cranial tomography in Wilson disease.' *Neurology,* **29,** 866–868.

Norrell, H., Wilson, C. B., Slagel, D. E., Clark, D. B. (1974) 'Leukoencephalopathy following the administration of methotrexate into the cerebrospinal fluid in the treatment of primary brain tumors.' *Cancer,* **33,** 923–932.

Nyhan, W. L. (1983) 'Nonketotic hyperglycinemia.' *In:* Stanbury, J. B., Wyngaarden, J. B., Fredrickson, D. S., Goldstein, J. L., Brown, M. S. (Eds.) *The Metabolic Basis of Inherited Disease. 5th edn.* New York: McGraw-Hill. pp. 561–569.

O'Brien, J. S. (1983) 'The gangliosidoses.' *In:* Stanbury, J. B., Wyngaarden, J. B., Fredrickson, D. S., Goldstein, J. L., Brown, M. S. (Eds.) *The Metabolic Basis of Inherited Disease. 5th edn.* New York: McGraw-Hill. pp. 949–969.

Pelizaeus, F. (1885) Ueber eine eigentümliche Form spasticher Lähmung mit Cerebraler—scheinungen auf hereditärer Grundlage. (Multiple Sklerose). *Archiv für Psychiatrie und Nervenkrankheiten,* **16,** 698–710.

Peylan-Ramu, N., Poplack, D. G., Blei, G. L., Herdt, J. R. Vermess, M., DiChiro, G. (1977) 'Computer assisted tomography in methotrexate encephalopathy.' *Journal of Computer Assisted Tomography,* **1,** 216–221.

Powers, J. M., Schaumburg, H. H. (1981) 'The testis in adrenoleukodystrophy.' *American Journal of Pathology,* **102,** 90–98.

Price, R. A., Johnson, W. W. (1973) 'The central nervous system in childhood leukemia—1. The arachnoid.' *Cancer,* **1,** 520–533.

—— Jamieson, P. A. (1975) 'The central nervous system in childhood leukemia—II. Subacute leukoencephalopathy.' *Cancer,* **35,** 306–318.

Quisling, R. G., Andriola, M. R. (1979) 'Computed tomographic evaluation of the early phase of adrenoleukodystrophy.' *Neuroradiology,* **17,** 285–288.

Reeder, M. M., Felson, B. (1975) *Gamuts in Radiology.* Audiovisual Radiology of Cincinnati, Inc.

Reye, R. D. K., Morgan, G., Baral, J. (1963) 'Encephalopathy and fatty degeneration of the viscera: a disease entity in childhood.' *Lancet,* **2,** 749–752.

Robertson, W. C., Gomez, M. R., Reese, D. F., Okazaki, H. (1977) 'Computerized tomography in demyelinating disease of the young.' *Neurology,* **27,** 838–842.

Rubinstein, L. J. (1978) 'Pathology of white matter disease of the brain.' *Keynote lecture, 16th Annual Meeting American Society of Neuroradiology, New Orleans, Louisiana, 1978.*

—— Herman, M. M., Long, T. F., Wilbur, J. R. (1975) 'Disseminated necrotizing leukoencephalopathy: a complication of treated central nervous system leukemia and lymphoma.' *Cancer,* **35,** 291–305.

Rushton, A. R., Shaywitz, B. A., Duncan, C. C., Geehr, R. B., Manuelidis, E. E. (1981) 'Computed tomography in the diagnosis of Canavan's disease.' *Annals of Neurology,* **10,** 57–60.

Russo, L. S., Jr., Aron, A., Anderson, P. J. (1976) 'Alexander's disease: a report and reappraisal.' *Neurology,* **26,** 607–614.

Sass-Kortsak, A., Bearn, A. G. (1978) 'Hereditary disorders of copper metabolism.' *In:* Stanbury, J. B., Wyngaarden, J. B., Fredrickson, D. S. (Eds.) *The Metabolic Basis of Inherited Disease. 4th edn.* New York: McGraw-Hill. pp. 1098-1126.

230

Schaumburg, H. H., Powers, J. M., Suzuki, K., Raine, C. S. (1974) 'Adrenoleukodystrophy (sex-linked Schilder disease).' *Archives of Neurology*, **31**, 210–213.
—— Raine, C. S., Suzuki, K., Richardson, E. P. (1975) 'Adrenoleukodystrophy. A clinical and pathological study of 17 cases.' *Archives of Neurology*, **32**, 577–591.
Schilder, P. (1912) 'Zur Kenntnis der so-genannten diffusen Sklerose (über Encephalitis periaxialis diffuse).' *Zeitschrift für der gesamte Neurologie und Psychiatrie*, **10**, 1–60.
Schnaper, H. W., Robson, A. M. (1964) 'Cerebral cortical atrophy in children receiving treatment for end stage renal disease.' *Pediatric Research*, **16**, 327A. *(Abstract.)*
Sears, E. S., Tindall, R. S. A., Zarnow, H. (1978) 'Active multiple sclerosis.' *Archives of Neurology*, **35**, 426–434.
Seay, A. R., Bray, P. F., Wing, S. D., Thompson, J. A., Bale, J. F., Williams, D. M. (1979) 'CT scans in Menkes disease.' *Neurology*, **29**, 304–312.
Seigel, R. S., Seeger, J. F., Gabrielsen, T. O., Allen, R. J. (1979) 'Computed tomography in oculocraniosomatic disease (Kearns–Sayre Syndrome).' *Radiology*, **130**, 159–164.
Seitelberger, F. (1970) 'Pelizaeus–Merzbacher disease.' *In:* Vinken, P. J., Bruyn, G. W. (Eds.) *Handbook of Clinical Neurology, Volume 10. Leucodystrophies and Poliodystrophies.* Amsterdam: North Holland. p. 150.
Short, E. M., Conn, H. O., Snodgrass, P. J., Campbell, A. G. M., Rosenberg, L. E. (1973) 'Evidence for X linked dominant inheritance of ornithine transcarbamylase deficiency.' *New England Journal of Medicine*, **288**, 7–12.
Suzuki, K., Suzuki, Y. (1970) 'Globoid cell leukodystrophy: deficiency of galactocerebroside-β-galactosidase.' *Proceedings of the National Academy of Sciences of the United States of America*, **66**, 302–309.
Swartz, J. D., Faerber, E. N., Singh, N., Polinsky, M. (1983) 'CT demonstration of cerebral subcortical calcifications.' *Journal of Computer Assisted Tomography*, **7**, 476–478.
Terasaki, P. I., Mickey, M. R. (1976) 'A single mutation hypothesis for multiple sclerosis based on HL-A system.' *Neurology*, **26**, (6, ii), 56–58.
Trommer, B. L., Naidich, T. P., DalCanto, M. C., McLone, D. G., Larsen, M. B. (1983) 'Noninvasive CT diagnosis of infantile Alexander disease: pathologic correlation.' *Journal of Computer Assisted Tomography*, **7**, 509–516.
Valavanis, A., Friede, R. L., Schubiger, O., Hayek, J. (1980) 'Computed tomography in neuronal ceroid lipofuscinosis.' *Neuroradiology*, **19**, 35–38.
—— Schubiger, O., Hayek, J. (1981) 'Computed tomography in nonketotic hyperglycinemia.' *Computed Tomography*, **5**, 265–270.
Vermess, M. (1976) 'Computer assisted tomography in Cockayne's syndrome.' *Paper presented at the International Symposium on Computer Assisted Tomography in Non-Tumoral Diseases of the Brain, Spinal Cord and Eye, Washington, D.C.*
Walser, M. (1983) 'Urea cycle disorders and other hereditary hyperammonemic syndromes.' *In:* Stanbury, J. B., Wyngaarden, J. B., Fredrickson, D. S., Goldstein, J. L., Brown, M. S. (Eds.) *The Metabolic Basis of Inherited Disease, 5th edn.* New York: McGraw-Hill. pp. 402–438.
Watts, R. W. E., Spellacy, E., Kendall, B. E., DuBoulay, G., Gibbs, D. A. (1981) 'Computed tomography studies on patients with mucopolysaccharidoses.' *Neuroradiology*, **21**, 9–23.
Weinstein, M. A., Lederman, R. J., Rothner, A. D., Duchesneau, P. M., Norman, D. (1978) 'Interval computed tomography in multiple sclerosis.' *Radiology*, **129**, 689–694.
Weisberg, L., Nice, C., Katz, M. (1984) 'Intracranial calcification and bone abnormalities.' *In: Cerebral Computed Tomography. A Text Atlas.* Philadelphia: W. B. Saunders. pp. 294–302.
Wesenberg, R. L., Gwinn, J. L., Barnes, G. R. (1969) 'Radiological findings in the kinky-hair syndrome.' *Radiology*, **92**, 500–506.
Wilson, S. A. K. (1912) 'Progressive lenticular degeneration: a familial nervous disease associated with cirrhosis of the liver.' *Brain*, **34**, 295–509.

INDEX

234